Would you like to...

- Protect your assets against *any* financial threat?

- Achieve a lifetime of financial security for you and your family?

- Avoid lawsuits and hassles from those who want *your* wealth in *their* pocket?

If you answer "yes", read...

Asset Protection Secrets

Here's What They Say About...
ASSET PROTECTION SECRETS

"Just finished reading *Asset Protection Secrets* This book should be required reading for every attorney and financial planner."

A. Cook, Worcester, MA

"I was lucky enough to come across *Asset Protection Secrets* before it was too late to save my home from foreclosure. I can't thank you enough."

M. H., Dennisport, MA

"*Asset Protection Secrets* is simply the best book ever written on this most important subject."

C. Levinson, Scottsdale, AZ

"One reason this book is great is because you make such complex legal and financial matters so very easy to understand."

S. Dantuma, Chicago, IL

"I find real value in the information you offer in *Asset Protection Secrets* . In fact, I recommend it to people I meet - anyone with the common sense to know they could unexpectedly lose their assets in so many different ways."

A. Hann, Ft. Myers, FL

"*Asset Protection Secrets* is a complete encyclopedia of techniques and tactics to safeguard your assets under all circumstances."

P. Order, Hartsdale, NY

"I'm going to recommend your *Asset Protection Secrets* to our town librarian. It belongs in every library because every American deserves access to such vital information."

J. Kosberg, Cambridge, MA

"*Asset Protection Secrets* is bulging with precisely the real-world information that should be taught in law schools."

Attorney D. Mandel, Ft. Lauderdale, FL

"I'm not in the habit of writing letters but I had to make an exception for *Asset Protection Secrets* . It's superb."

H. Ellis, Camden, NJ

"Amidst all the useless books on the market, I finally found a gem."

A. Loughlin, Los Angeles, CA

"Your strategies in *Asset Protection Secrets* helped save me from bankruptcy. Thanks."

M. Trocki, Miami, FL

"The most practical book ever on financial planning. It really gives a no-nonsense look at how things are!"

T. Fricks, Dallas, TX

"With such clever tricks it's a wonder frustrated creditors don't shoot you."

[Anonymous]

"The small investment for this book saved me nearly one million dollars! That's what I call a spectacular investment!"

B. Firestone, Philadelphia, PA

"Send me 30 copies of *Asset Protection Secrets*. I'm making it required reading for my business students."

B. Bleidf, New Orleans, LA

Asset Protection Secrets

Arnold S. Goldstein, Ph.D., J.D.

Published by
GARRETT PUBLISHING, INC.

Asset Protection Secrets
By Arnold S. Goldstein, Ph.D., J.D.
Copyright © 1993 by Garrett Publishing, Inc.

Published by
Garrett Publishing, Inc.
312 South Military Trail
Deerfield Beach, FL 33442
Tel. 305-480-8543
Fax 305-698-0057

This publication is designed to provide accurate and authoritative information in regard to the subject matter covered. It is sold with the understanding that neither the publisher nor author is engaged in rendering legal, accounting, or other professional service. If legal advice or other expert assistance is required, the services of a competent professional should be sought. *From a Declaration of Principles jointly adopted by a Committee of the American Bar Association and a Committee of Publishers.*

Library of Congress Cataloging-in-Publication Data

Goldstein, Arnold S.
    Asset protection secrets/Arnold S. Goldstein, Ph.D.
        p. cm.
    Includes bibliographical references.
    ISBN 1-880539-00-4
         1. Execution (law)–United States–Popular works. 2. Property–United States–Popular works. 3. D
creditor–United States–Popular works. 4. Liability (Law)–United States–Popular works. I. Title.
KF9025.Z9G65   1992
346.73'077–dc20
[347.30677]

91-76105
CIP

Printed in the United States of America
10 9 8 7 6 5 4 3 2 1

About The Author

Dr. Arnold S. Goldstein is one of America's leading experts on asset protection, judgment-proofing and debt restructuring.

He first gained interest in asset protection over twenty-five years ago when he began his legal career specializing in insolvency law and debtors' rights. As a senior partner in the Boston law firm of Meyers, Goldstein & Kosberg he has represented thousands of individuals and businesses with severe financial problems. It was this experience as a lawyer for clients with financially-endangered assets that encouraged Dr. Goldstein to develop many of the asset protection strategies found in this book.

More recently Dr. Goldstein organized the Garrett Group to provide consulting services to financially-troubled companies and organizations throughout America. He personally provides asset protection consulting to both individuals and business organizations. His practice is distinguished by his own imaginative approaches to asset protection and debt management and also by his successful track-record in these fields.

He has written over 50 books on law, business and finance. His titles include: *The Basic Book of Business Agreements; Managing Turnarounds and Troubled Companies; How to Save Your Business From Bankruptcy; Commercial Transactions Deskbook* and *The Small Business Legal Advisor.* Major media sources nationwide regularly cite these and other of his publications as complete, practical and enjoyable.

His work and innovative asset protection ideas have also been featured in over 350 magazines, journal articles and newspapers. Dr. Goldstein has also appeared on many radio and TV talk shows. A popular speaker on asset protection planning and related subjects, he travels across the country presenting workshops and guest lectures on these topics. In addition, he enjoys a distinguished academic career as a full professor at Boston's Northeastern University and has taught law, finance and management at several other colleges and universities.

Dr. Goldstein is a graduate of Northeastern University (B.S., 1961) and Suffolk University (MBA, 1966 and LL.M., 1975). He also holds a law degree from the New England School of Law (J.D., 1964) and a doctorate from Northeastern University (Ph.D. in business and economic policy, 1990). He is a member of the Massachusetts Bar and Federal Bar and numerous professional, academic and civic organizations.

Contents

LITTLE-KNOWN LAWS THAT AUTOMATICALLY SHIELD KEY ASSETS (41)

CHAPTER 4

WEALTH-SAVING STRATEGIES WITH CO-OWNERSHIPS (55)

CHAPTER 5

HOW TO TURN ANY CORPORATION INTO A POWERFUL WEALTH PROTECTOR (67)

CHAPTER 6

BANKRUPTCY: HOW TO LEGALLY KEEP YOUR ASSETS AND LOSE YOUR DEBTS (127)

CHAPTER 10

POWERFUL WAYS TO STOP THE IRS FROM PLUNDERING YOUR ASSETS (143)

CHAPTER 11

MORE SECRETS TO SAFEGUARD YOUR WEALTH (237)

CHAPTER 16

APPENDIX (255)

INDEX (323)

1 TEN SECRETS FOR PERFECT ASSET PROTECTION PLANNING

In today's lawsuit-crazy world you can easily and unexpectedly find yourself in a financial crisis that could cost you most, or all, of your assets. Every year thousands of families are suddenly wiped-out. And it can happen to you!

How can you protect your assets from danger? How is 100 percent financial security accomplished? What must you do to get started?

These are important questions. That's why it's important to read this first chapter closely. You'll learn here the ten secrets to every successful asset protection plan.

SECRET #1

Why You're More Vulnerable Than You Think

No matter how safe and secure you feel today, the simple fact is that you can never be certain that your lifetime's accumulation of wealth won't suddenly disappear tomorrow. We all flirt with liability and financial disaster, no matter what our lifestyle or occupation, or how prudently we act. It can't be avoided. There are just too many ways to get into trouble today. Consider your own vulnerability. Tomorrow you too can be unexpectedly hit with:

- A tax audit and a whopping IRS assessment.
- A costly uninsured motor vehicle accident.
- A major damage suit for injury around your home or business.
- A negligence claim as a corporate officer or director.
- A lawsuit for breach of an important contract.
- A professional malpractice suit.
- Claims arising from business debts.
- Huge medical bills.
- A lawsuit with business partners.
- A fine for violating any one of thousands of federal or state laws–such as environmental protection.

- A suit for defamation or assault and battery.
- A divorce.

These are, of course, only a few of the many ways you can unexpectedly find yourself on the wrong end of a costly claim–and your assets and your family's financial security suddenly at stake.

Are you still unconvinced it can happen to you? Consider these eye-opening statistics:

- Over 40 million civil lawsuits are filed each year in America. Your chances of being sued next year are one in four. Statistically, you have nearly a 100 percent chance of being hit with one or more devastating lawsuits in the next 10 years. If you're under age 30 you can expect no less than five major lawsuits over your lifetime. At least one will be a killer lawsuit.
- Divorce? If you're now married there's a 50 percent chance you'll someday divorce. Sure those statistics are depressing, but so too are the probabilities that a divorce will cripple you financially–whether you are the husband or wife.
- Are you in business? Here's more unpleasant news: If you have been in business for under five years, there's an 80 percent probability you'll fail. What personal liabilities will you have? What assets will you lose?
- Tax problems? They're more common than you think. About four million Americans are audited each year, and many taxpayers are clobbered by big tax bills they can't afford to pay. There are also many other ways to get into big money troubles with the IRS. Once you owe the IRS, you'll see how quickly your assets can be wiped out. Over three million Americans are now running from the IRS collection corps. What will they lose?
- Unexpected bills? What about hospital or medical bills should you or a family member require catastrophic care—and you're inadequately insured? Or what would happen if you lost your job and couldn't handle your mounting bills? How safe are your assets then? Bankruptcies are at an all time high and are climbing steadily. About one million personal bankruptcies are filed annually. If the trend continues, more than two million bankruptcies will be filed annually by the end of the decade. Will you be among them? What will you lose if you are?

What these few dismal statistics prove is that everyone is vulnerable to a legal or financial disaster–including you. There's no surefire way to escape liability.

Adopt this wise philosophy: Don't ask if a financial disaster *will* happen. Ask *when.* Since you can't predict the answer, your only logical course is to assume a financial crisis will strike you tomorrow. This means you must create your powerful asset protection plan *today!*

Asset Protection Is 100 Percent Smart And Legitimate

Do you have difficulty with the objectives and goals of asset protection? Do you see it as illegal or immoral because its goal seems to cheat your creditors? Indeed, my one big concern in writing this book is that some "do-gooders" may see me as an advisor to all the certified deadbeats of the world. Rest assured this is not the case. I believe that people who want to learn what this book has to say are simply savvy souls with a strong survival instinct.

First, let me also assure you that asset protection–properly practiced–is not illegal. You cannot, of course, commit illegal acts such as perjury, violate bankruptcy law, conceal assets or issue false statements. In fact, a sound asset protection plan neither encourages nor permits illegal acts. Fortunately, you can implement an effective asset protection plan without violating a single law or regulation. This is the underlying principle on which we proceed.

Tackling the ethical question is more difficult. We each see things in a different light. While there are those who consider it improper to shelter assets from those who can make a rightful claim to them, others believe there is no obligation to expose assets where it is legally permissible to protect them. They also, with some perception, argue that not all claims are justifiable or equitable, whether support-ed by a court decree or not. Indeed, there is no shortage of cases where people fall victim to unfair claims. Such people recognize that life is not without its risks, but there is no compelling reason to participate in a legal lottery where they can lose all they own. This is the attitude you must adopt.

Asset protection is a form of self-defense. It will help you avoid frivolous and harassing lawsuits. Yes, many individuals are bombarded with shaky lawsuits only because they have exposed wealth. Individuals who are known to be protected face far less chance of being a target for a lawsuit. The bottom line: It's good to be wealthy. It's bad to have your wealth exposed.

You'll not be alone when you protect your assets. Hundreds of thousands of families undertake comprehensive asset protection planning every year. Attorneys readily assist them, as they should. Corporations, trusts and limited partnerships, for example, are routinely organized for no reason other than asset protection. Moreover, the law itself recognizes asset protection as a perfectly permissible activity, as evidenced by the many laws designed to indicate permissible from impermissible asset protection strategies. The distinction is much like tax avoidance and tax evasion.

Do you still have a problem with the ethics of asset protection? Consider this solution: Act now to protect yourself. Should a claim later arise that you feel morally bound to pay, you can then volunteer your assets. Asset protection at least gives you that wonderful choice.

How To Recruit Key Players

A sound asset protection plan requires understanding and support from those who have an interest in your financial affairs. Your spouse, for example, may rightfully be concerned when you suddenly redeploy assets in ways and for reasons your spouse does not understand. To allay fears or uncertainties, your spouse deserves to be told exactly why the family's financial affairs are undergoing radical change. With candid explanation will come understanding and cooperation. Also involve other family members, as well as trusted friends, who in one way or another have some interest in your financial well-being or role in the administration of your finances. Trustees of your trusts, executors under your will, and possibly even business partners or key associates when business assets are affected, are examples. Individuals involved in specific or limited aspects of your finances shouldn't be party to financial matters that don't involve them, but they certainly should be a party to those that do.

Caution: While you must involve the appropriate individuals, you must be careful about what you tell them. Your spouse may safely know that asset protection is at least one of your objectives, but there is no need to announce your asset protection objectives to involved friends or relatives. It's best they believe you have other goals, such as tax savings or estate planning. This doesn't imply that there's anything illegal about asset protection, it's only that intent

can be an important factor should an asset transfer be challenged. You gain no advantage in having a friend or associate testify about your asset protection objectives. You'll stand on more secure ground when other motives are suggested.

You need people you can trust if they are to play a role in your asset protection program. Not only must you evaluate the degree to which each can be trusted, but also whether they will remain trustworthy. You must then decide whether the level of trust is adequate for their responsibility. In asset protection planning your ability to judge others is as critical as your selecting the right legal strategies.

A well-designed asset protection program will have you retain sufficient control over your assets so that the trustworthiness of others who may hold title to these assets becomes less important. Nevertheless, there is no plan that can completely protect you against an individual who decides to violate your trust. That's why your objective assessment of each individual upon whom you rely becomes central to the success of your program.

How To Prioritize Objectives And Accept Tradeoffs

Asset protection has only one purpose: To deploy your assets in a way that they are most secure from creditors. As worthy a goal as that may be, what you do with your assets will also depend on your other goals and objectives. For example, how well will your asset protection plan achieve your tax objectives? Is your plan consistent with your estate planning? What about safety of investment? Are you willing to sacrifice some safety of investment for increased protection? How about control? The more control you have over an asset the less safe it will be from creditors. Less control, in turn, will give you greater asset protection. Since control and safety are inconsistent, you must bring to the planning process some idea of the trade-offs you are willing to accept. These are also the type issues you will want to explore with your spouse or others with an interest in your property. You'll also want to explore with your professional advisors the trade-offs, as well as the possible alternatives, that can more closely reconcile conflicting objectives.

Bear in mind that your advisors cannot easily sense your priorities, or what you believe to be most important, given all the possible considerations. How important is liquidity? Safety? Control? Taxes? Return-on-investment? To what extent is one factor more significant than another? While you may be forced to sacrifice some benefits to achieve a reasonable degree of financial security, most people believe it's a small price to pay for their peace of mind.

Your asset protection plan may also feature some undesirable consequences. Examples:

• Your safest strategy may be to gift an asset to a child, but this will cause both loss of control over the asset and impose a sizeable gift tax. How does your objective of keeping the asset safe from creditors compare in importance?

• You now hold an 18 percent mortgage note due you, but it is threatened by creditors. The advice: Sell the note at a 10 percent discount and hold the proceeds as cash in an offshore account earning five percent interest. Would you exchange the high interest you now enjoy for the added safety of the asset?

These two situations exemplify the point and well represent trade-offs that are part and parcel of asset protection. Read this book, and listen to your own advisors and you will see that you must frequently forfeit or relax control over property if you are to safely protect it. Still, I do not assume that you will allow total loss of control over your assets, no matter how much it strengthens your program. It is, however, my objective to explain how less control and more safety are directly related. It is you who must define what you will forfeit as other options appear. No two individuals, of course, will come up with the same answers. And how you answer today may change considerably with time, as your own needs, objectives and resources change.

Fortunately, asset protection does not always signify negative consequences. Asset protection maneuvers frequently produce higher investment returns, lower taxes, or more satisfactory estate plans. In many instances, asset protection planning is the catalyst for more effective total financial planning.

Anticipate both the advantages and disadvantages as you redeploy your assets. While your advisors can explain the advantages and disadvantages of each strategy. You must decide upon the game plan most in harmony with your various objectives.

SECRET #5

Why Asset Protection Must Be A Life-Long Process

Your financial picture constantly changes so you must constantly review and redesign your plan to keep up with those changes. Assets are added, others are sold or gifted. Your obligations change. So too the legal and financial hazards you face. With time your financial goals and priorities also change. Equally important, asset protection strategies of the past may no longer be the most suitable in light of more recent laws and court decisions that suggest more secure strategies.

For these reasons, make asset planning an ongoing process. Review your program at least annually, and more often if a major event–such as a windfall inheritance or threatening lawsuit–comes your way. Also review your plan if you move to another state. Its laws may dictate a new plan. Only a thorough update on a regular basis can ensure your plan is correct for your ever-changing situation.

Sound asset protection demands this commitment. If it's to remain an important component of your financial life, it will involve time, expense and effort to keep your protection strong. Your willingness to continually assert asset protection priorities and shun more attractive financial arrangements that offer less protection is part of that commitment. Don't let your asset protection erode over time because you no longer keep this objective in sight. Once a financial threat passes, you may see no further need for asset protection. It's then that you are most vulnerable.

SECRET #6

Design The Asset Protection Plan That Fits

There are any number of ways an effective asset protection strategy may be designed to achieve your objectives. Ask ten asset protection specialists and you'll be handed ten different plans. Why? Several reasons: Different state laws is one major reason. What offers ironclad protection in one state may offer absolutely no protection in another. Asset protection strategies are influenced largely by state laws. That's why a book such as this can only serve as a general reference rather than prescribe precisely the strategy best for you.

Your attorney's plan will also be influenced by his own background and experience–or how comfortable he is with each of the various options. For instance, your attorney may be inexperienced with several of the less-common trusts that are excellent asset protectors. Your attorney may instead recommend a less-effective procedure he is more familiar with.

Cost is another important factor to shape your plan. Asset protection can be expensive. Depending upon the size and complexity of your assets, a sound asset protection plan may cost tens of thousands of dollars. Even a modest estate can consume several thousand dollars in professional fees–fees beyond what you can afford to spend. A less involved plan, but one that matches your pocket book, may still offer you reasonable protection. Discuss fees with your attorney before you formulate a plan. With costs one of the first issues on the agenda, your advisor will know how complex a plan to design.

Timing is still another factor. A plan to defend against future liabilities will be a far different plan than when creditors are pressing. Asset protection strategy also depends upon the nature of the claims, the type creditors and what they are likely to do in pursuing your assets.

No two individuals share identical financial situations, family relationships or potential hazards. You want the one plan that responds best to each of these considerations.

You May Be Wealthier Than You Think

Asset protection planning requires careful preparation. You and your advisors need your complete financial and legal picture. You then know precisely what you must protect. Your advisors will want to see:

- Deeds and mortgages on real estate.
- IRA, Keogh, pension and other retirement plans.
- Life insurance policies.
- Last will and testament, codicils and any testamentary trusts.
- Pre-nuptial or post-nuptial agreements.
- Divorce decrees and property agreements.
- Savings and checking accounts.
- Wills or trusts where you are a beneficiary or grantor.
- Ownership interests in any closely held business, including corporate or partnership documents and financial statements of each business.
- Notes or evidence of other obligations due you.
- Notes or evidence of other obligations you owe others.
- Tax returns for three prior years.
- Leases.
- Outstanding major contracts.
- Inventory of valuable personal assets (antiques, jewelry, art).
- Titles, registration and appraisals on any autos, boats, planes or other vehicles.
- Lawsuits or evidence concerning contemplated suits against third parties.
- Lawsuits, judgments or potential claims against yourself.
- Malpractice or liability insurance.
- Applications for credit or loans issued within the prior five years.

If you own a business, and it is a significant part of your estate, your attorney will want to review:

- Corporate books and records, if incorporated, or partnership agreements, if a partnership.
- Copies of any notes or loans between yourself and your business.
- Corporate obligations to which you are a guarantor.
- Life insurance policies maintained by the company.
- Financial statements of the business.
- Tax returns of the business.

Critical to the success of your plan is that every important asset you own be accounted for and fully protected. It's remarkably easy to overlook valuable assets unless you systematically review this asset inventory:

- Cash on hand
- Checking and savings accounts
- Cash value life insurance
- Motor vehicles
- Residential real estate
- Investment real estate
- Stocks or bonds in publicly owned corporations
- Certificates of deposit
- Money-market funds
- Stocks or equities in any closed corporations, partnerships or other business entities
- Notes or mortgages receivable
- Savings bonds
- Accounts receivable

- Boats, airplanes or other recreational vehicles
- Options to acquire property
- Leases or leasehold interests
- Art, jewelry and antiques
- Beneficial interests in trusts
- Revocable trusts to which you are a grantor
- Licenses or franchise rights
- IRS, Keogh, 401K or other retirement accounts
- Tax refunds due
- Choses in action (actual or potential claims against third parties)
- Inheritances and future interests
- Safe deposit box inventory
- Copyrights, trademarks or patents

Estimate the approximate value of each item as closely as possible. Indicate how each asset is titled (singly in your name, jointly with spouse, in trust, etc.). Also specify your percentage ownership in assets owned with others. Finally, list liens or encumbrances against each asset to determine the equity to be protected. Repeat this exercise for your liabilities:

- Mortgages
- Tax liabilities
- Notes on car loans
- Unsecured loans
- Other secured installment loans
- Charge account balances
- Credit card balances
- Alimony or child support
- Business debts guaranteed
- Other guaranteed debts
- Outstanding judgments
- Potential or threatened claims

Compile your records so your advisors can quickly put your financial affairs into focus. The more prepared you are, the sooner and more easily you can put your plan into effect.

Also put together information on the sale or transfer of significant assets over the past three years. Your advisors can then decide whether these transfers may be challenged successfully by creditors. Finally, project ahead over the next year or two so you anticipate and plan for inheritances or other windfalls that may come your way and require protection.

How To Find And Use The Right Professionals

As you proceed through *Asset Protection Secrets,* you'll see that designing an ironclad protection plan is a complex process that requires the right professional team.

Asset protection must be a team effort. It's not the job for lawyers alone. Legal considerations serve as the plan's foundation, but other factors exist. For example, you'll want to temper safety with low taxes, so your accountant must be involved. You'll also have investment objectives–liquidity, rate of return, safety of investment and growth–so your financial planner or investment advisor must participate. Your banker may join your team, particularly if your plan contemplates refinancing assets or your bank's trust

department is to serve as trustee of your trusts. Your insurance agent? Another vital professional, particularly when assets are to be reinvested into insurance-funded annuities or other commonly exempt insurance-based investments.

Each of these professionals are needed to design a sound plan if you have a large net worth, a wide array of holdings, complex investment objectives and severe liability exposure. Do you have more modest wealth? You may possibly put together a basic asset protection plan with your attorney and accountant in one afternoon. An asset protection plan is as simple or complex as you make it.

The key to a successful asset protection plan is not the number of advisors but the right choice of advisors. Selection of a skilled asset protection attorney is critical. Few attorneys specialize in asset protection, so it's doubtful your family lawyer, while proficient in routine legal matters, can serve you well on asset protection.

Where do you find the right legal talent? The best qualified asset protection lawyers generally come from three legal specialties: Bankruptcy, corporate law and probate. Bankruptcy lawyers make their living in the tug-of-war between debtors and creditors, and typically spend their days either chasing someone's assets, or protecting assets from others in pursuit. Corporate lawyers have sound familiarity with many of the entities–corporations, limited partnerships, etc.–each useful in asset protection. Probate lawyers, on the other hand, are most expert in the use of the various trusts, gifts and other asset protection strategies comfortably combined with estate planning. An advantage in merging asset protection and estate planning is that you can build a stronger case that the transfers were for estate planning purposes, and there was no intent to harbor assets from creditors.

Look for a lawyer you're comfortable with. This is important because complete candor on your part is crucial to reach the level of communication you and your lawyer must establish. Together you'll discuss who within your family you trust. You'll candidly talk about marital relationships, your concerns, your vulnerabilities and myriad other personal issues. The right asset protection lawyer will know how to comfortably draw out the facts needed to prepare a safe and comfortable plan. Asset protection is very much a people business and the quality of your professional relationships is critical.

Where do you find such an attorney? Check with your local bar association. Ask the clerk of your local bankruptcy court. The clerk will know the veterans who can help you. Having worked with asset protection lawyers and consultants in many parts of the country, we can possibly refer you to specialists in your area.

Once you have attorneys to interview:

- Ask for references of other asset protection clients.
- Consider how well she answers your questions–or how insightful her own questions are.
- Discuss the estimated fees.
- Select an attorney who will not only design and implement your plan, but also one who will defend it if challenged. Ultimately, the test of an asset protection plan is whether it

will withstand a creditor challenge. Pick the lawyer confident she can win that contest.

A good financial planner is equally important. Even families of moderate wealth must today balance asset protection objectives with sound investing. Well-qualified financial planners make a valuable contribution to the process and often detect asset protection possibilities even your attorney may overlook.

The one difficulty with financial planners: As a newly emerging profession, it's difficult to determine those who are qualified. Check memberships or affiliations. The best credentialed in the profession are designated Chartered Financial Consultants (CHFC) and Certified Financial Planner (CFP). The financial planner you want has experience in asset protection planning and can usually list as references attorneys they worked with in this area. Your financial planner may even refer you to a good asset protection lawyer.

There are three national associations to call for a list of qualified planners in your area:

International Association of
Financial Planning (IAFP)
2 Concourse Parkway
Atlanta, GA 30328
(404) 395-1605

Institute of Certified
Financial Planners (ICFP)
2 Denver Highlands
10065 E. Harvard Avenue
Denver, CO 80231
(303) 751-7600

International Board of
Standards and Practices for
Certified Financial Planners
1660 Lincoln Street
Denver, CO 80264

Why A Low Profile Is Vital

Asset protection is largely knowing how to avoid liability and lawsuits in the first place. Asset protection planning can only safeguard your property from lawsuits and creditors. Whether you are sued has little to do with how well your assets are protected. More important is whether the would-be plaintiff perceives you to have enough wealth to make a lawsuit worthwhile.

Some people will do anything to transfer your wealth to their pockets. There's no shortage of lawyers ready to help them. They know most people will pay something rather than defend against a costly lawsuit. Unfair as it seems, these lawsuits most frequently target those with deep pockets: People who drive expensive cars, live in expensive homes and display the other trappings of wealth. Yes, you certainly have the right to live as comfortably as possible, and rightfully enjoy your prosperity, but the fact is that an ostentatious lifestyle waves the proverbial red flag before a bull: It attracts the wrong kind of attention.

Avoid this! Learn to lead a low-key lifestyle and keep your wealth confidential. This will help you avoid a rash of nuisance lawsuits. It will also help you settle lawsuits filed against you for considerably less than if the plaintiff believed you could afford more.

How can you develop a financial camouflage? You certainly should not live like a pauper, but you may consider a more modest home, or drive a less flashy car. Large charitable contributions also draw attention, as do flashy jewelry. Avoid boasts about your income or the property you own, particularly to your relatives. In sum, call as little attention as possible to your wealth. It is an important part of asset protection planning and in many respects the most difficult since it involves sacrificing a lifestyle you are entitled to.

Why You Must Act Now!

Safely insulate your assets and make yourself judgment-proof before trouble strikes. Courts look unkindly on people who attempt last minute transfers to defraud creditors. Sound asset protection depends on timely asset protection action before you have problems. That means you must anticipate the reality that you too can get into financial trouble. When you accept this fact you have come to terms with your own vulnerability. Only then will you give asset protection the sense of urgency that will force you to do what you must to successfully protect yourself for the future.

Most people with property to lose periodically think about asset protection. It may have been prompted by a lawsuit or some other temporary crisis, but the thought usually vanishes with the threat. The procrastinator eventually gets hit with a financial crisis that doesn't vanish. We then have one sorry individual about to lose hard-earned wealth.

Remember these two words: ACT NOW! They are the most important two words in this entire book.

Set yourself a timetable. Commit to see your attorney and other professional advisors as soon as possible, and stay on top of your advisors for rapid implementation of your program. This is the one commitment you must make to the preservation of your wealth.

Key Secrets To Remember

- You are more vulnerable to financial problems than you realize. Your assets are never safe until you make them safe!
- It's no crime to protect your assets. Nor is it immoral. As long as you obey a few simple rules, you'll find asset protection 100% smart and honest.
- Involve in your asset protection planning those individuals who will play a part in its implementation. You'll find the process proceeds far smoother.
- Know what you may gain, and what you are prepared to lose, when undertaking your asset protection program.
- Continuously review your asset protection program. As circumstances change, so too must your plan.

- Be comfortable with your plan. It must fit your situation, your psyche and your finances.
- Count what you own and what you owe. Your finances are the building blocks of an asset protection plan.
- Arm yourself with the professional advisors who know how to put together the one best plan for you.
- How you restructure your finances is only one part of the planning process. You also must look less vulnerable.
- Don't delay. Build your financial fortress before it's too late!

2 HOW TO MAKE YOURSELF 100 PERCENT CREDITOR PROOF

Your one all-important goal when protecting assets is to make certain that your creditors cannot reach them. Your creditors, however, may insist that even though assets are no longer in your name, they were either disposed of in such a way, or are now held in such a manner, that they are recoverable by your creditors.

Whether you or your creditors prevail depends on whether your creditors can convince the court that your transfer was nothing more than a sham attempt to place your assets beyond the reach of creditors. Whether you or your creditors win is the acid-test of your asset protection plan.

You may be one of the many individuals who scurry to hide or transfer assets once you're sued or creditors' press their claim. Foregoing sound asset protection planning well in advance, you now hurriedly undertake a futile last ditch attempt to salvage what you can from the grasp of your creditors through a helter-skelter disposal of assets to friends and relatives. Assets are sold for far less than their fair value, or are gifted and invariably end up in the name of some trusted friend or relative who can be counted on to dutifully return your property once the financial threat disappears. The classic example is the financially troubled businessman who quickly transfers all his assets to his wife the day before filing bankruptcy.

Simply transferring your assets to someone else may seem like a safe way to protect yourself, but it seldom protects against a determined creditor. Nor does a gift of property to a relative or friend usually work. Courts are seldom so naive as to allow you to escape your debts by simply gifting assets to friends and relatives, or through other equally apparent attempts to shield assets from creditors. Remember: Asset protection, by its very definition, means shielding assets in a way that they will be 100% safe from creditors. Will your plan pass this test?

Fraudulent Transfers Can Sabotage Your Plan

Creditors who successfully attack debtor transfers prove the transaction was fraudulent in that it hinders or delays their rights as a creditor to reach the debtor's property. In their attempt to classify the transfer as fraudulent, the creditor will rely upon either the Uniform Fraudulent Conveyance Act (UFCA), in effect in the majority of states, or the Uniform Fraudulent Transfers Act (UFTA), operative in the remaining states. The two laws, however, are nearly identical, and can be discussed as one.

Fraudulent transfers fall within two categories:

• Fraud-in-law or constructive fraud.
• Fraud-in-fact or actual fraud.

Fraud-in-law occurs when: 1) there is a gift or sale of the debtor's property, 2) for less than fair market value, 3) in the face of a known liability, and 4) the transfer rendered the debtor insolvent or unable to pay the creditor.

Each element must exist for there to be constructive fraud or fraud-in-law. But there is no need to prove that the debtor actually intended to defraud the creditor. The transfer may even have occurred before the debtor knew of a claim. The fact that the creditor had the right to make claim is sufficient to set aside a later transfer that renders the debtor insolvent and unable to satisfy the claim.

The theory is that property owned by an insolvent debtor constructively belongs to his creditors. When the debtor, however innocently, transfers property without receiving in exchange assets of approximately equivalent value, the debtor's creditors can recover the transferred property. This is true even absent proof the transfer intended to deprive creditors of the assets when the transfer was made. A fraudulent transfer occurs even if the debtor had charitable motives when transferring the property.

Two questions must then be resolved: 1) What constitutes fair consideration or fair value sufficient to make a transfer non-fraudulent? 2) When does a debtor become "insolvent" under the fraudulent transfer laws?

Fair consideration or the fair value of the property is what a reasonably prudent seller would be able to sell the asset for using commercially reasonable means. This doesn't mean the price must equal the precise fair market value. In the case of a home or other real estate, a payment of at least 70 percent of the actual market value is sufficient consideration. The law recognizes certain assets are difficult to market under distress conditions. Publicly listed securities can be sold for a known price any business day. If a debtor sells securities for considerably less, the courts can conclude there was no fair consideration. When less than fair value is paid, the transferee can be required to return the property, but only upon the repayment of what he paid. Alternatively, the debtor may be required to pay the difference between what was paid and the actual fair value of the asset as determined by the court. A transferee is protected if he acts in good faith without knowledge of fraudulent intent and pays fair value. This fair value does not have to be money. It can be the exchange of other property or even services. The court will, of course, closely examine services rendered to ascertain it was worth its claimed value. Consideration, however, cannot be for future services, but must be for services previously or simultaneously rendered.

The second question is when does a debtor become "insolvent"? Recall that a conveyance is not fraudulent if the debtor was left with sufficient other assets to satisfy creditor claims. The law says you are "insolvent" if the market value of your total property is less than the amount necessary to pay your probable liability on your existing debts as they become absolute and due. Liabilities include all debts whether now due or due at a future date, contingent or non-contingent, disputed or undisputed.

The important point to bear in mind is that you cannot transfer assets for less than fair consideration when your remaining assets (inclusive of any liability insurance) will not cover your probable liabilities as they fall due.

In sum, the law does not prevent you from making valid gifts of your property as long as you stay sufficiently wealthy to fully pay those debts you can reasonably foresee as due and payable in the future. When you transfer property without fair consideration, and the transfer makes your liabilities exceed your assets, the courts automatically infer the transfer was made with fraudulent intent.

In contrast, with actual fraud cases your creditor must prove you actually intended to hinder, delay or defraud your creditors.

Creditors cannot easily prove your state of mind or force you to confess fraudulent intent. They are, therefore, left to prove fraudulent intent through circumstances or factors that tend to prove intent. Such factors include the relationship between transferor and transferee, whether the transfer was for all or only a small part of the debtor's assets, whether the transfer was concealed, or whether the transferor had knowledge of the claim or possible claim.

These and other factors only infer fraudulent intent. They do not create the presumption of fraud. Often, the transfer can be successfully explained away as an attempt to achieve legitimate estate planning, investment or business objectives. The court may then uphold the transfer as proper even though its net effect was to hinder or delay creditors whose claims remain unsatisfied.

A creditor can, of course, more easily recover under a claim of constructive fraud, or fraud-in-fact, because the creditor can then ignore the issue of intent. Here the creditor need only show the claim existed (whether known or not), the transfer was for inadequate consideration, and the transfer rendered the debtor too insolvent to satisfy the creditor's claim.

It's difficult to understand fraudulent conveyances in the abstract. Consider several case examples to illustrate transfers that may be viewed as fraudulent, and others that are valid:

Case 1: Mark guaranteed a business loan to his bank for $500,000. Shortly thereafter, and while the note was in good standing, Mark made a gift of virtually all his assets to various family members. Several months later Mark's business failed and the bank looked to recover on Mark's guarantee. Would a court find the gifts to be a fraudulent transfer and order them set aside?

Probably not. There was no consideration since the assets were gifted. Moreover, the transfer did render Mark insolvent since he was left with too few assets to pay the bank note. Yet, this case will likely center on the third issue–was the bank note guarantee a probable liability? It was a possible liability, but that doesn't make it a probable liability. Lawyers here would focus on whether Mark could reasonably foresee the failure of his business and the need to pay on his guarantee. The bank's attorney would point to all the signs of business decline to show the probability of liability. Mark's attorney would take the opposite position, and he would *probably* prevail, but that's far from a definite statement because no definite statement can be made. As with so many areas of law, the final determination is subjective. For this reason you cannot expect your attorney to ever guarantee your assets are safe. Your attorney will instead give you a qualified "reasonably" or "probably" safe, or that it is the safest they can possibly be under the circumstances. That is your true goal in asset protection.

Case 2: Mark, who resides in Florida, transferred his home to his sister as trustee in trust for Mark's minor children. Homes in Florida are homesteaded and therefore exempt from creditor claim. At the time of transfer, Mark had a $200,000 lawsuit against him. Mark has no other assets to satisfy the claim.

This would not be a fraudulent conveyance because creditors had no right to the home to begin with since it was home-

steaded. Thus, the transfer did not prejudice their rights. This example underscores the point that creditors cannot assert a fraudulent conveyance unless their right to the asset had been hindered.

Case 3: Assume that Mark owned $500,000 worth of non-exempt assets, and in the face of several lawsuits acquired exempt property with the $500,000.

This is a more difficult case. Most courts hold that it is not a fraudulent transfer because there is a fair value exchange–even though the replacement asset is beyond the reach of creditors. This reinforces the soundness of an asset protection plan that exchanges non-exempt assets for exempt assets. Still, not all courts agree this strategy is valid. Decisions vary between courts. This highlights still another difficulty in asset protection planning–court rulings do vary. In fact, the same court may change its own position on an issue over time. This adds to the uncertainty whether your asset protection plan is totally safe. At the least, it requires your attorney to thoroughly research recent cases in your state to more accurately predict how the court will view your transfers, should they be challenged.

Case 4: What if Mark later deeded his home valued at $500,000 to a friend in payment of a $700,000 debt?

This would probably withstand creditor attack because cancellation of the debt was fair consideration for the transfer. Similarly, Mark could have granted his friend a mortgage on his home as security for the $700,000 debt. This would also withstand attack as a fraudulent transfer. When property is transferred or mortgaged to one creditor in satisfaction of, or as security for a debt, the transfer is not fraudulent even though it deprives other creditors recourse against the asset. The only remedy for these other creditors is to petition the debtor into bankruptcy within three months of the transfer and set aside the transfer as a preference under bankruptcy law. The axiom here is that transfers made in exchange for good and adequate consideration are not fraudulent.

Case 5: Suppose Mark transferred title to his home (non-exempt) to his new wife, who, in return, promised to care for him in his later years. What would happen if Mark later went bankrupt?

Whether the bankruptcy court would overturn this transfer would depend on whether the transfer took place before or after the debts were incurred. If the liabilities existed at the time, the transfer would most likely be set aside as fraudulent. This is because the consideration contemplated future services rather than services that have been previously or simultaneously furnished. This form of consideration is not sufficient. If Mark had no debts, the property could not have been recovered by later creditors. They could not logically argue the transfer was made to defraud, hinder or delay their rights to the property when they were not yet creditors.

These cases only highlight a few of the many possible situations, but nevertheless provide a general overview of fraudulent and non-fraudulent transfers. Observe how even a slight change in facts can greatly influence the soundness of your asset protection plan.

Your Transfers Are Never 100 Percent Safe

There is a time limit within which creditors must act if they are to challenge your transfers. The statute of limitations on a fraudulent transfer claim is four years after the transfer is made, or the obligation incurred, or one year after it was, or reasonably could have been discovered by the creditor, whichever event occurs last.

A judgment creditor cannot pursue property transferred four or more years after the obligation or transfer.

A fraudulent transfer action is frequently brought by a trustee in bankruptcy alleging the bankrupt fraudulently transferred assets before bankruptcy. Under bankruptcy law, the trustee has two years from the first meeting of creditors to commence a fraudulent transfer claim. This doesn't necessarily put the bankrupt or his transferee in the clear if an action is not commenced within two years. The trustee can elect instead to bring the fraudulent transfer action under state law rather than bankruptcy law and the longer state statute of limitation will apply.

Because a creditor can argue he had no prior knowledge of a transfer made years earlier, a fraudulent transfer claim can be commenced long after the transfer. You are not completely safe until all creditors existing on the transfer date have been paid or their debt discharged. Two additional rules:

- Try to avoid bankruptcy for at least two years following any transfer that may be considered suspicious. A bankruptcy trustee may contest earlier transfers under a longer state statute of limitations, but few trustees attack transfers made more than two years earlier.
- If you can choose the location for a questionable transfer then have it occur in a state with a short statute of limitations. This applies only to personal property since real estate is always considered transferred in the state where it is located.

SECRET #13

Three Essential Steps Before You Transfer Property

In a fraudulent conveyance case, the debtor's conduct receives closest attention. But what about the transferee who received the property? What are his rights in regard to the property now in his hands? Of equal importance, what liability can the transferee incur for participating in the fraudulent transfer?

The law is clear that if the transfer is found to be fraudulent, the transferee can be compelled to re-transfer the asset for the benefit of the debtor's creditors. If the transferee was an innocent party and unaware of the fraudulent intent, then the transferee can impose a lien on the asset for the amount paid for the asset. In sum, the transferee is reinstated to his original position

where he is repaid, but surrenders the asset and any other benefit of the bargain. What if the transferee previously sold the property? If the second transfer was in good faith, and the second transferee was also an innocent purchaser, then the creditors of the original transferor lose their rights against the property. Some cases to the contrary can be found. However, the property may now be innocently encumbered or significantly changed, such as a house substantially renovated. Here the court cannot realistically put the parties back into their original position so the creditor's claim may be defeated.

If the transferee acted in bad faith and with knowledge of the fraudulent intent, he may then be forced to return the property, and will not gain the protection of a lien for what was paid, as would an innocent transferee. Insiders, such as a spouse, close relative or business associate, are held by some courts as having imputed knowledge of the debtor's insolvency, and are thus never entitled to the protection afforded an innocent buyer who regains his money in exchange for surrender of the property. This emphasizes the wisdom of transferring property only to those who have no relationship or only a distant relationship.

What civil or criminal sanctions can a transferee in a fraudulent conveyance action face? A transferee can indeed get into serious trouble. A transferee innocent of fraudulent intent will generally be free of either civil or criminal liability. However, a transferee who acts in bad faith with knowledge of the fraudulent intent can face substantial sanctions. As a civil remedy, the courts can hold the transferee, along with the transferor, jointly and severally liable for all attorneys' fees and costs incurred by the creditor in pursuing the fraudulent transfer. If the transferee, again in bad faith, transferred the property once again for purposes of placing it still further beyond the reach of the creditor, the transferee is then accountable to the creditor for the value or equity in the property that would have been otherwise available to the creditor.

Severe criminal penalties can also apply. Generally, any party, whether as a transferor or transferee, who is a party to a transfer undertaken with the intent to defraud, hinder or delay creditors, can be found guilty of a misdemeanor. This applies even to an attorney professionally involved in the fraudulent transfer. An attorney found guilty of such practices also can be professionally sanctioned.

As a practical matter, criminal sanctions in fraudulent conveyance cases are extremely rare. There is a very fine line between lawful asset redeployment and what might be viewed as a fraudulent conveyance. While it is not always possible to guarantee that a transfer cannot be set aside as fraudulent, it would take an inept attorney to structure the transaction in such a blatant way that it would attract prosecutorial attention. Several rules flow from this:

- Never transfer property to someone who would not respond well to being in the "middle" of a fraudulent transfer claim. It takes a certain individual, both in terms of loyalty and personality, to attend depositions and court hearings without sacrificing "your" property to the creditors. Creditors may attack a transferee hoping for just that result. Pick players you can count on.
- Respect your transferee's position. Never ask friends or relatives to become involved, if you value their association. A nasty fraudulent transfers case can destroy relationships.
- Suggest that your transferee have his own attorney review the proposed transaction. Not only does this strengthen your case that the transfer was arms-length, but it helps insulate you from criticism should the transfer be attacked and the transferee encounter legal problems.

Creditor Remedies You Must Know About

A creditor who believes a fraudulent transfer occurred has several possible remedies. The specific remedies will depend on whether the creditor's claim has been reduced to judgment or is a pending claim.

A judgment creditor, upon discovery of a purported fraudulent transferee, can file suit directly against the transferee. Typically, the creditor will ask the court to: 1) Set aside the transfer and restore title to the original owner-debtor for access by the creditor. 2) Enjoin further transfer, encumbering or depletion of the asset pending the outcome of the fraudulent conveyance action. This essentially freezes the asset. The creditor may also: 3) Seek damages from the transferee and supplemental damages from the transferor. These damages would be equivalent to the legal costs necessary to recover the asset. 4) Seek the appointment of a receiver over the conveyed asset if the asset may easily disappear or be destroyed. 5) Seek to recover the proceeds received when the property was sold (but the creditor cannot void the sale to a subsequent good faith purchaser for value). As you can see, numerous remedies are available to a creditor in a fraudulent conveyance case. The law, to the extent practicable, attempts to put the creditor back into the position held before the fraudulent transfer. Whether this can be practicably accomplished depends largely on whether the transferee still holds the asset intact or whether it has been altered or even destroyed.

A non-judgment creditor has greater difficulty attacking a transfer. But this doesn't mean a non-judgment creditor is without remedies. A non-judgment creditor has the same right to challenge a transfer and freeze the asset in the hands of the transferee, if he can convince the court: 1) There is a reasonable expectation of obtaining a judgment, 2) There are no other assets available from which to satisfy the judgment, should it be granted, and 3) There is a reasonable expectation the transfer will be found fraudulent. The creditor's chances are greatly improved if the court sees a pattern of fraudulent transfers, and that the creditor will lose his rights unless the debtor's remaining assets are frozen.

How The IRS Tackles Fraudulent Transfers

The IRS has its own remedies for a fraudulent transfer. The IRS can assess and collect estate, gift and income taxes due from the transferor, directly from a transferee who receives property for less than fair consideration. Interestingly, the IRS is not required to go to court to assess the transferee. The liability of the transferee is essentially that of a jeopardy assessment, with the IRS proceeding directly against the transferee.

The IRS must bring a lawsuit against the transferee to impose liability for taxes other than income, gift or estate taxes. The IRS also often litigates claims against the transferee for estate, gift and income taxes, although it is not required. Through court proceedings, the IRS may: 1) Set aside the fraudulent transfer, or 2) Establish transferee liability. In the first action the IRS only requests the court to void the transfer and thus allow the IRS to seize the asset. In the second, the IRS requests a monetary judgment against the transferee for the value of the transferred asset at the time of the claimed fraudulent conveyance.

When commencing such actions, the IRS necessarily relies upon the fraudulent transfer law in effect in the state where the action is brought. This is because no federal statute or IRS regulation specifically provides for either action.

Despite its broad powers, the IRS seldom chases fraudulently transferred property. This is true even when the transfer is an obvious sham. Why is this so? The probable reason is that the IRS must undergo a long bureaucratic process to challenge a fraudulent conveyance. Of course, this is not so when the IRS had a lien filed before the transfer. Without a lien, however, the local IRS collection agent must forward the case to regional counsel to evaluate the case. Since the IRS is frequently short-staffed, only the more substantial cases are litigated. There is thus little chance a quick transfer to beat an IRS lien will be challenged, particularly when the amount owed is relatively small.

Fourteen Telltale Signs Of Phony Transfers

Fraudulent intent is based on circumstantial evidence. Courts must therefore look to relevant factors–or badges of fraud–to support a determination that a fraud-in-fact occurred. These badges of fraud are fragmentary evidence that when taken together allow a court to infer fraudulent intent.

Review fraudulent transfer cases and you'll discover a lengthy list of "badges of fraud" consistently relied upon by courts to set aside a transfer as fraudulent:

- Transfers that are not in the debtor's ordinary course of business, or do not fall within the debtor's prior pattern for disposing of assets.
- The transfer of assets for inadequate consideration when the transfer creates insolvency, or adds to the debtor's insolvency.
- Secrecy in the transaction.
- Undue haste in the transfer.
- Transfer to a family member, friend or close business associate.
- When the buyer of a business allows a seller to retain managerial control, or a buyer of a home allows the seller to remain in tenancy.
- The failure of the parties to use independent counsel on transactions where independent representation is normally expected.
- Unusual or superficial attempts to present the transfer as one of fairness or reasonableness.
- The unusual possession or use of the asset by the seller after the transfer.
- Transfer of assets outside the debtor's jurisdiction.
- Failure to promptly record deeds of conveyance.
- Mortgages or liens for services rendered much earlier, or where the services or their value are questionable.
- Failure of the debtor or transferee to keep accurate records on loans or advances for their transaction.
- Failure by the transferor to demand payments on overdue loans for which the property was security.

These badges of fraud give the appearance of a simulated transfer, or one not really intended to legitimately divest the transferor of his rights to the property. The most common example: A sale to a transferee who agrees to hold title in his name with the tacit understanding that title will be reconveyed upon request. In the interim, the transferee allows the property to be used as the transferor wishes.

Twelve Tips For An Ironclad Transfer

What can you do to avoid a claim of fraudulent transfer? How can you overcome such a lawsuit? Here are twelve important ways to help prove your transfer was legitimate.

Tip 1. Protect yourself before the claim arises. There cannot be a fraudulent transfer when the transfer occurred before the liability arose. That's why it's important to become judgment proof well in advance of financial or legal difficulties. Always judgment proof yourself before you undertake financial obligations. Be as liability-free as possible when you undergo your asset protection plan.

Tip 2. Make small, incremental transfers. They attract less notice than large transfers of significant assets. Undertake transfers over a period of time rather than all at once. Your motives will be less suspect. Similarly, don't transfer all or most of your assets to the same transferee, or the same asset protection entity, such as a trust or partnership. When you "put all your eggs in one basket" the transfer is more easily attacked. Conversely, when your assets are widely scattered, a creditor must bring a number of lawsuits to recover your assets.

The cost and effort involved may then discourage action.

Tip 3. Avoid insider transactions to family members or close business associates. Even when completely innocent, these transactions are suspect in the eyes of both courts and creditors. Use non-family members to serve as trustees, corporate officers or general partners. Use of a brother-in-law with a different last name is preferable to a brother with your same name. Always make the transaction appear as arms-length as possible.

Tip 4. Show that the transfer was made for purposes apart from sheltering assets from your creditors. Have your attorney prepare correspondence showing you were engaged in estate planning, for example, when your irrevocable trust was set up. Also have your documents state in its recitals or preambles its purpose and what the instrument was designed to accomplish. Such evidence of "innocent" purpose can be persuasive to a court.

Tip 5. Carefully document the consideration you receive in exchange for property. If you received services, then be prepared to show that the services were performed and were, in fact, worth their stated value. If you borrowed money, be ready to show cancelled checks or other documentation to prove the debt was valid.

Tip 6. Avoid circumspect actions. If you sell your home, think twice about continuing to occupy it as a tenant. People do not ordinarily buy homes without the intent to occupy it. If you sell your business, think twice about continuing to manage it. People do not ordinarily buy a business and let other people manage it. If you sell a boat, think twice about keeping it at your own dock. Those who buy boats usually plan to use it themselves.

Tip 7. Verify the value of your property so you can establish you received "fair consideration". Have your home appraised by local real estate agents. You can then prove you received 70 percent or more of its appraised value. If an asset is sold at a questionably low price, establish through photographs or appraisals the defects that justified the low price. Go on the premise that the market value of the transferred asset will someday be called into question.

Tip 8. Choose your transferees carefully. Creditors may attack your transfer. When they do your transferee will be called upon to defend the legitimacy of the transfer that placed the asset in his hands. The friend who was "only doing you a favor" by taking title to your property may not want the hassles of litigation. Your friend, then, may too easily surrender your asset, or otherwise be so uncooperative in the defense that you are forced to forfeit the asset. Choose a transferee who understands that a claim may arise and is one willing to defend against the claim should it occur.

Tip 9. Don't announce your transfers. Why put your creditors on notice when re-arranging your financial affairs? This only encourages creditors to move quickly before they lose their rights to your property.

Tip 10. Use multiple asset protection strategies. Before you deed your home to a trust where your brother-in-law is trustee, why not also mortgage to your friend who is owed $10,000? You see the idea. Now a creditor must counteract both the transfer and the mortgage. This may prove too ambitious and expensive for most creditors.

Tip 11. Don't overdo it. It's not always smart to be 100 percent judgment-proof. Creditors are more likely to look hard for something to recover, and may then go after your most valuable or most recently transferred property. Your objective: Detract creditors with more available but less significant assets. Adopt a "throw them a bone" philosophy.

Tip 12. It's never too late to try. Even when creditors are two steps behind, do what you can to judgment proof your assets. You may not be as successful as if you had started earlier, but you'll probably come out wealthier than if you did nothing and lost your assets by default.

Key Secrets To Remember

- The ultimate test of an asset protection plan is whether it succeeds in preventing creditors from seizing your assets.
- Creditors usually have considerable time within which to attack a fraudulent transfer. Still, transfer your assets as early as possible.
- Transfer assets to individuals who can be trusted with your assets, and also trusted to defend the transfer.
- The IRS may be the one creditor that will give you the least difficulty with a fraudulent transfer–although they have the tough laws and huge resources to be the most difficult.
- It is not always necessary for a creditor to prove you actually intended to defraud creditors.
- There are many factors that spotlight a fraudulent transfer occurred–and many steps you can take for a safer transfer.

3

HOW CREDITORS SEIZE YOUR ASSETS AND HOW TO STOP THEM

Fail to pay your obligations or incur liability, and you can expect a lawsuit, unless:

- The amount owed is too small for the creditor to be bothered with, or
- The creditor cannot find you, or
- You discharge the debt in bankruptcy, or
- You convince the creditor that you are judgment proof, and have no assets the creditor can seize to satisfy a judgment, or
- You negotiate a settlement either before or after a lawsuit starts.

A major lawsuit can be frightening, particularly if you have never gone through the process before. Even more distressing is the ordeal of judgment creditors scrutinizing your financial and legal records to discover assets they can grab to satisfy their claims. Most devastating is watching creditors actually seize your home, car, life savings, invest-

ments, or even your business. This, of course, is precisely the tragedy this book can protect you from. But to most effectively defend yourself, you must thoroughly understand what creditors can and cannot do in their attempt to recover from you, and what you can do to legally shelter your property.

SECRET #18

How To Negotiate Dime-On-The-Dollar Settlements

Faced with a claim, your first goal is to dispose of the potential lawsuit as quickly and inexpensively as possible. That means negotiating a settlement with your creditor. Your creditor may be persuaded to accept less than the amount she believes is rightfully due, but she will accept if she views the settlement as a more favorable resolution than can be gained from a long and involved lawsuit. A creditor can find good reason to accept a fair settlement, even if the settlement is for paltry pennies-on-the-dollar:

- The creditor avoids attorney fees, which can take from 25 to 50 percent of any recovery.
- The creditor is not sure of his legal position, or believes you may have a good defense.
- The creditor needs quick cash and cannot wait two or three years for trial to get paid.
- The creditor is leery of the legal process.
- The creditor questions the collectibility of any judgment against you, and thus considers your offer an attractive alternative.

Focus on this last point since it rests on whether you are judgment proof. Creditors accept pennies-on-the-dollar settlement only if they believe they cannot possibly collect more. It's your task to convince creditors of this fact. You accomplish this with a two-step process: 1) First, thoroughly judgment proof yourself so you can factually show you are without assets to satisfy the claim, and 2) Persuasively communicate this unhappy fact to your creditor. Carefully follow these nine tips:

- Decide first whether you must negotiate settlement with only one creditor, or whether you must resolve problems with several creditors. In the latter case you must resolve matters with all your creditors as a group.
- Sincerity, quick action and close contact with creditors is vital. This builds credibility, creates a less hostile atmosphere, and greatly improves your odds for a favorable settlement.
- Prepare complete and accurate financial statements in advance of negotiations. Make certain they are truthful, but show no assets, or equity in assets available to creditors. Conversely, list other creditors with claims against you. This is a particularly persuasive strategy if you have priority creditors such as the IRS. Creditors hesitate to stand in a long line with many competing creditors, or stand behind as formidable a creditor as the IRS who always gets paid first.
- Treat creditors equally. Offer each general creditor the same pro-rata share. This is critical when negotiating with creditors as a group. One creditor cannot get a better deal than the others.
- Stay flexible. Will you pay the full settlement at once or in installments? If you pay in installments, will you pay interest? Offer security? There are many points to negotiate so be prepared for trade-offs.
- Be realistic. Don't settle unless you're absolutely convinced you can live up to its terms. If you're uncertain, then bargain for a more conservative plan, but one you're more confident you can honor.

- Be persistent. You may not convince a creditor to accept your proposal on your first attempt. Several attempts may be needed. If you can't sell your creditor, perhaps your attorney can convince the creditor or his attorney. If you face a group of creditors, use more influential larger creditors to persuade the smaller holdouts. Employ others to be your spokesman when creditors turn a deaf ear to you.

- Negotiate with creditors for more than a release. Consider your credit rating also. Will your creditor agree not to submit a negative or late payment code on your credit rating? If a negative report has been filed with the credit bureau, will the creditor withdraw it? This can be extremely important to you long after the claim is resolved.

- Have your lawyer prepare settlement papers. You want your deal reduced to a legally binding agreement. This can be quite complicated when a number of creditors are involved.

SECRET #19

Pro's And Con's Of No-Cost Debt Adjusters

Fortunately, you need not be on your own when negotiating settlement with your creditors. Nor is it necessary to hire an expensive lawyer. Low-cost and even free credit coun-selors are available to negotiate settlements with your creditors. There are three types of credit counselors you can use: 1) Non-profit credit counselors, 2) for-profit bill paying services, and 3) for-profit "pro raters".

Non-profit counselors are preferred since they receive their fees from the creditors through a voluntary 15 percent rebate of the funds paid to creditors.

These counselors are reliable and credible with creditors, and can often negotiate set-tlements where for-profit agencies may fail. To locate the nearest counseling agency in your area, write the National Foundation for Consumer Credit, 1819 H Street, Washington, D.C. 20006, or check your yellow pages under "Credit Counselors" or "Consumer Credit Counselors".

You can obtain similar services through your labor union, the legal aid society in your city, the military if you are in the armed services, or through Family Service America. FSA offers credit counselling services in over 40 cities. Contact: Family Service America, 11700 W. Lake Park Drive, Milwaukee, WI 53224.

The for-profit bill-paying service and pro-raters can be discussed together. Their difference is only how they are paid. For-profit credit groups charge a fixed amount, or an hourly rate. Pro-raters usually take as their fee a percentage of what they save you.

For-profits and pro-raters receive constant bad press. This is often deserved as some within their ranks demand up-front fees, but never attempt to resolve their clients' financial problems. Others are quite effective, and out-perform the non-profit consumer credit counselors.

Your best bet: Stay with a non-profit consumer credit counselor. Use a for-profit agency only if it comes highly recommended from someone whose financial problems were similar to your own.

The one danger with the non-profits: They are paid by the creditors and always negotiate full-payment settlements. This may not be in your interests.

SECRET #20

Strategies When Creditors Bluff Lawsuits

Despite your best efforts it's not always possible to negotiate a favorable settlement and avoid a lawsuit. Lawsuits do happen. Don't let that discourage you. You may find it even more advantageous to negotiate settlement after litigation begins–or even after the creditor obtains a judgment. Only then may a creditor see how difficult it will be to collect from you and decide to settle on your terms. Since lawsuits are inevitable, know how to safely navigate around them. Here's a few points:

- A lawsuit is not a certainty simply because you're threatened with one. Many creditors bluff but never sue. This is particularly true with small or questionable claims, or with creditors who suspect you don't have assets worth chasing. Never let the threat of a lawsuit scare you. It may be a bluff.
- Collection agencies cannot sue you. All they can do is refer the claim to an attorney in your area. Many collection agencies bluff debtors into thinking a lawsuit is imminent. In reality, collection agencies are powerless. Similarly, out-of-state attorneys may threaten suit, but they also must forward the case to a lawyer in your state. When may a lawsuit be imminent? When the creditor's claim is already in the hands of a local attorney.
- Out-of-state creditors must usually file the lawsuit where you live or conduct business. This is an obvious disadvantage to out-of-state creditors. Keep it in mind when negotiating. Few creditors welcome the prospects of traveling to a distant city to prosecute a claim.
- In most states you can delay a case for years by claiming a jury trial. This may require you to transfer the case to a higher court, and this is not always possible with a small case. But remember: Time is always the defendant's best friend. Stall a lawsuit as long as possible and you greatly improve your negotiating position.
- Don't waste money on legal fees if you expect to go bankrupt. But don't ignore the lawsuit either. Your best bet: A local lawyer, for a small fee, can help you file your own defense to the case. You can then stall the case for months, or even years, until you do file bankruptcy.
- Are you now in bankruptcy? Tell the creditor immediately. A creditor cannot sue a debtor once bankruptcy is

filed. Be certain you list the creditor on your bankruptcy schedule or the claim may not be discharged.

When You Can–And Cannot–Be Compelled To Disclose Assets

When can creditors demand information about your assets? Creditors generally cannot demand information about your assets until a judgment is obtained. This is because your assets relate only to your ability to pay, and this is not relevant to a determination of liability. Under the rules of evidence, matters not relevant to the proceedings cannot be pursued. But it is up to you to object to a creditors improper attempt to use the discovery process to find out about your assets. Creditors may attempt to find out about assets during discovery. There's nothing wrong with this tactic as you may unknowingly volunteer information you're not required to furnish. Avoid this mistake. Keep your creditors in the dark about your finances for as long as possible.

There are two exceptions to the rule concerning pre-judgment disclosure of assets: First, if you are sued on a claim of wrongful conduct involving punitive damages, the court may compel you to disclose your assets in advance of judgment. This is because your net worth is relevant to your ability to satisfy a punitive damage award. Still, the plaintiff must show evidence of fraud or malice. These are not always easy to establish.

A pre-judgment creditor may also probe an alleged fraudulent transfer, and may even file suit to set aside a purported fraudulent transfer–even though the primary claim has not reached judgment. But even here, the inquiry and action must center only on assets purportedly transferred fraudulently. No inquiry can be made about other assets.

Aside from these two circumstances, a pre-judgment creditor cannot compel you to disclose your assets. A creditor can, however, independently investigate your assets to the extent the creditor does not breach your right of privacy. In fact, a creditor in a major lawsuit would be foolish not to investigate. After all, why should your creditor waste time, money and effort pursuing an uncollectible claim? Your finances, what you can lose, and what you can afford to pay is critical information to any creditor.

This is one big benefit of sound asset protection. Without it your assets are needlessly exposed. Investigators soon discover every stock brokerage account, parcel of real estate, bank account and business interest. Your wealth makes you vulnerable, and encourages the creditor to vigorously pursue a claim and stubbornly hold out for a big settlement. With your assets properly protected nothing is exposed. You and your attorney can use your "paper poverty" as the most compelling argument possible for the creditor to either drop the claim or settle cheap. That should be your message. Deliver it to your creditor as soon as possible and as forcefully as possible. Volunteer proof of your poverty. Remember: Poverty has its own power.

What Your Financial Paper Trail Reveals About You

A diligent judgment creditor will demand from you a long and revealing list of documents. This paper trail lets creditors know precisely what you own and what assets can most easily be levied upon to satisfy their judgment. What will your creditors want to see?

- Bank account records (savings, CD's, checking, money market, etc.)
- Stock certificates
- Bonds
- Motor vehicle (car, boat, plane) titles
- Promissory notes owed you
- Deeds to real estate
- Receipts for property held by third parties
- Insurance policies
- Patents, copyrights, trademarks
- Royalty contracts
- Bills of sale to personal property
- Tax returns
- Applications for credit within the prior three years
- Leases held by you as a landlord
- Trusts to which you are a grantor, trustee or beneficiary
- Statements from Keogh's IRA's and other pension plans
- Bankruptcy filings within the prior six years
- Bills of sale of sold property
- Alimony or support orders
- Documents regarding lawsuits against you and lawsuits where you are plaintiff
- Occupational licenses
- Books and records of your business, if it is unincorporated

Other documents may be requested, but this list anticipates the usual documents that will come under review. Strategy: Review these documents with your attorney well in advance to determine whether they disclose exposed assets. Go back three or four years because the inquiry may go back that far.

How To Keep Your Tax Returns Secret

Few taxpayers and even attorneys realize it, but tax returns are fully protected from involuntary disclosure to creditors. A judgment creditor cannot compel you to show your tax return since it may violate your constitutional rights against self-incrimination. This privilege can, however, be unintentionally waived if you either voluntarily produce your tax return or allow disinterested parties access to it. Disinterested parties are those without a compelling "need to know" the information on your tax return. Generally, this includes everyone but your accountant, banker, financial planner, attorney and spouse.

Many states protect tax records on file with a lender. A creditor serving a subpoena on your bank for copies of your tax records must give you advance notice of the subpoena. This gives your attorney the opportunity to go to court and quash the subpoena. You can protect your tax records on file with lenders, even in states without such notice provisions. Ask your lenders to notify you if they receive a subpoena for your tax records. With notice, your attorney can avoid its involuntary disclosure.

Corporate tax returns are unprotected from involuntary disclosure. This is because a corporation is considered a franchise, and thus waives the privilege when it accepts the state charter. This rule is slowly being replaced by the theory that a corporation, like an individual, should be constitutionally protected against self-incrimination. Lawyers have successfully protected corporate tax returns with this argument.

Because many lawyers (and some judges), are unaware of the special status of tax returns, they do demand their production. Your own attorney may inadvertently allow it. Enforce your rights to privacy of your tax records, refusing all creditor demands for their production.

How Court Records Expose Assets

Savvy creditors prowling for your assets check court records for other lawsuits against you. Divorces or child support cases divulge quite a bit of valuable information. Domestic disputes typically involve property, and the parties usually disclose detailed reports of their assets, liabilities and income. Even in uncontested divorces, each spouse must file financial information under oath.

Have you a recent divorce? What do the court records say about your fiscal fitness?

Other civil actions are less revealing, but can nevertheless disclose important financial information. Earlier cases, for instance, may refer to certain property. They may have involved examinations by your creditors seeking to collect on their judgments. This same information will be helpful to your current creditor.

Court records are public. A creditor cannot remove documents from the court files, but can review and copy the court record, except in those rare situations where documents are sealed. In a large city it will be more difficult for a creditor to find court files concerning your property since the creditor must check many courts. Tip: If you have recent court cases revealing your assets then ask the court to seal your file. This will keep it private from prowling eyes.

Why Loan Applications Are Dangerous To Your Wealth

Debtors frequently think creditors will never investigate their assets–until it's too late. That's when loan applications that irrefutably point out assets you now own–or recently owned–come back to haunt you. Most people proudly list every possible asset on a loan application. They sometimes exaggerate their values as well. They hope a portrayal of greater wealth will improve their chances for a loan.

What loan applications have you completed lately? What assets do they disclose? Are these assets you transferred or intend to transfer for asset protection purposes? If you made incorrect or misleading statements on a credit or loan application, can you now go back to correct it? Example: You listed real estate as a personal asset when you are only a trustee of a trust that owns the real estate on behalf of other beneficiaries.

You cannot easily disclaim title to an asset once it is claimed on your loan application. Think ahead. What you declare on a loan application can prove quite damaging in a later contest with a creditor seeking to seize the asset you say is no longer yours. Tip: Don't apply for loans or credit if you even remotely believe you will soon have creditors chasing you. What you say today can hurt you tomorrow.

SECRET #26

Information Your Creditor Will Demand

Judgment creditors in search of assets are allowed a wide inquiry concerning your property and financial affairs. You can best protect yourself if you can anticipate their questions about your finances. In addition to your present or past finances, you may be asked for information on future interests, contingent assets, expected windfalls and future employment prospects. Rehearse: How would you answer these questions?

- If currently employed, state your full compensation–salary, commission, etc.
- Do you have part-time employment? (Details)
- Is your spouse employed? (Details)
- What are your other sources of income? (Details)
- Are you or any family members an officer, director or stockholder of a corporation? (Details)
- State occupations or business interests held or owned over the past five years?
- What bank accounts, checking accounts, CD's, etc. are in your name or to which you were a signer over the past five years?
- What bank accounts are maintained by your spouse?
- Identify source of money deposited to your spouse's account?
- Do you and/or your spouse own a safe deposit box? (Details)
- Do you have access to any safe deposit box?
- Do you have any accident, health, disability, annuity or income insurance? (Details)
- Do you own any cash value life insurance? (Details) If so, are there any loans against these policies? (Details)
- Have you assigned any insurance policies within the past five years? (Details)
- Do you or your spouse own an automobile? (Details) If so, is it mortgaged? (Details)
- Do you or your spouse own a boat? (Details) If so, is it mortgaged?

(Details)

- Do you or your spouse own other vehicles? (Details) If so, are they mortgaged? (Details)
- Do you or your spouse own real estate, condominiums, time sharing, cooperative shares? (Details) If so, are they mortgaged? (Details)
- Do you or your spouse own stocks, bonds or other securities? (Details) If so, are they pledged? (Details)
- Do you or your spouse have mortgages or deeds of trust due you? (Details) If so, are they pledged or assigned? (Details)
- Do you or your spouse own promissory notes, drafts, or bills of exchange? (Details) If so, are they pledged or assigned? (Details)
- Do you or your spouse have judgments or claims against third-parties? (Details) If so, are they pledged or assigned? (Details)
- Do you or your spouse have insurance claims? (Details)
- Do you or your spouse own jewelry? (Details) If so, is it mortgaged? (Details)
- Do you or your spouse own antiques? (Details) If so, are they mortgaged? (Details)
- Do you or your spouse own stamp or coin collections? (Details) If so, are they mortgaged? (Details)
- Do you or your spouse own patents, inventions, trademarks or copyrights? (Details) If so, are they mortgaged or assigned? (Details)
- Do you or your spouse own musical instruments? (Details) If so, are they

mortgaged? (Details)

- Are you or your spouse a grantor, trustee or beneficiary to any trust? (Details)
- Have you or your spouse inherited any money within the past five years? (Details)
- Are you the beneficiary under any will? (Details)
- Do you own or have any type interest in any other asset or property? (Details)
- Have you transferred any property within the past five years? (Details)
- Have you made any gifts of property? (Details)
- What books and records do you and/or your spouse maintain? (Details)
- Did you and/or your spouse file income tax returns over the past five years? (Details)
- Are you entitled to any money from any governmental agency? (Details)
- Who is your accountant?
- What other liabilities do you owe? (Details) How many are reduced to judgment? (Details)
- What are your average monthly expenses, and how are they met? (Details)
- Are you now making payments to other creditors? (Details)
- Have you applied for a loan within the past five years? (Details)
- Have you served as an endorser, co-maker or guarantor of a loan over the past five years? (Details)
- Who have you issued financial statements or credit applications to over

the past five years?

- Have you granted anyone a mortgage or lien on any property within the past five years?
- Have you made an assignment for the benefit of creditors?
- Has a receiver over your property been appointed by the court?
- Have you filed for bankruptcy?
- Are there any outstanding orders for payment of money, or supplemental proceedings against you? (Details)
- Is anyone holding any property on your behalf? (Details)

You must answer these questions, but must your spouse? Ordinarily one spouse cannot be forced to testify against his or her spouse, as all states recognize communication between spouses as privileged. This privilege, however, does not extend to examination proceedings to discover assets. Most states allow a creditor to interrogate a non-debtor spouse about the financial affairs of the debtor spouse. This prevents the spousal privilege from being used collusively for the non-debtor spouse to conceal assets from a judgment creditor. Tip: Review probable questions and all documents with your spouse in advance to insure consistent answers. Make your spouse as well-prepared as you.

<hr/>

SECRET #27

How Creditors Make You Disclose Assets

A judgment creditor not only has wide berth in the information demanded from you, but the creditor also has available five powerful ways to obtain this information:

- **Court Examination:** Most states require the debtor to appear in court and testify about assets and income. The court then determines how much the debtor will pay each week or month. This procedure, commonly called supplementary process, is more frequently used in smaller cases.
- **Deposition:** The creditor can also depose the debtor for office interrogation. This is conducted in the same manner as any other office deposition, except certain states, such as California, require advance court authorization for the deposition.
- **Interrogatories:** The creditor may also draft written questions (interrogatories) for the debtor to answer in writing under oath. This procedure is less costly than conducting an oral deposition, but a debtor may be either unresponsive or provide vague answers. For this reason interrogatories are seldom used to discover assets.
- **Request for Production of Documents:** Here the creditor requires the debtor to deliver specified documents to the creditor for examination. This can be done as part of a deposition or independently.
- Subpoena Duces Tecum can be used to compel the debtor to deliver documents. Since it is more forceful than a request for production of

documents, most attorneys prefer the subpoena.

The subpoena duces tecum can also be used to compel third-parties to appear for examination and testify about the debtor's finances. The subpoena also compels the third party to bring requested documents to the examination.

These are not mutually exclusive procedures. A creditor may use any combination of discovery procedures. For example, a creditor may start with interrogatories and later advance to depositions. These strategic decisions depend upon the amount of the claim, the responsiveness of the debtor, costs, distance, and other factors that make some procedures more practical than others.

When You Can Be Jailed For Non-Payment

Only a century ago debtors worldwide were frequently imprisoned. It is now generally prohibited to imprison a debtor, but there are four situations where it is still possible:

- The IRS can jail you for willfully refusing to pay income tax. This rarely occurs, except where the taxpayer also willfully fails to file tax returns, understates income or enjoys too much press.
- A court can hold you in contempt if you willfully violate a court order. The court, for example, may order you to provide records to a creditor seeking assets, and you may refuse. Child support and alimony decrees are court orders. A number of debtor-fathers are jailed each year when they fail to make support payments without good reason.
- The court can jail you for concealing assets from a judgment creditor.
- You can also be imprisoned if you refuse to appear in court or at a deposition for creditor examination to discover assets.

Refusing or failing to pay a judgment is, in itself, not a criminal violation. A judgment only authorizes a creditor to collect from a debtor if he can find assets from which to satisfy the judgment. Frequently a debtor is examined in court concerning his ability to pay the judgment. If the court, upon hearing the evidence directs specific payments, it can be contemptuous to violate that order.

Debtors are understandably uncooperative to a creditor's attempt to collect on a judgment. You may, for instance, fail to appear for examination to discover assets, refuse to produce requested documents, or leave unanswered appropriate questions about assets. What can the creditor then do?

Procedures vary between states, but persistent creditors eventually get their way by calling upon the court to enforce their rights. Example: If you fail to appear for examination, the court will order you to appear at a second scheduled date. You may also be ordered to pay the creditors' legal costs. If you fail to appear again, you'll most likely face a bench warrant and be found in contempt of court. This can lead to a fine and/or imprisonment. While the court cannot make you testify or cooperate, it can make the alternative far less attractive.

You May Owe More Than You Think

What does a plaintiff win with a judgment? The answer depends on the nature of the lawsuit. The law provides for many different forms of damage. Certain cases, such as anti-trust or trademark infringement, specify recoverable damages by statute. Some statutes allow treble damages (or triple the actual damages sustained). However, in most contract cases (such as when you borrow money), damages are limited to the amount that remains unpaid.

There is also interest from the date the lawsuit is filed. This varies by state from five percent to 18 percent. Because cases are often delayed for years, the accrued interest may exceed the debt. Court costs are also added to the judgment. This includes sheriff fees in serving the lawsuit and court filing fees.

The defendant does not usually pay the plaintiff's attorney's fees unless provided for by agreement or by statute. Promissory notes usually provide that upon default the debtor shall pay reasonable attorney fees necessary for collection. Anti-trust laws provide by statute that the defendant pay attorney fees.

What this means is that you may well end up owing considerably more than you expect so factor this into any settlement.

When Creditors Must Stop Chasing You

A judgment creditor can try to collect for only a certain number of years. This time may vary between in-state and out-of-state judgments.

Most states allow enforcement of judgments for 20 years. Wyoming and Kansas gives a creditor only five years to collect on a judgment. Creditors can extend the judgment, usually for a term equal to the original. A 10 year judgment is thus extended to 20 years. Other states allow the creditor to continuously extend the collection period. A judgment in these states never expires. Thus a good rule to follow: Expect your creditor to pursue you through probate of your estate, unless you first discharge the claim in bankruptcy or by settlement. This means that you must take a judgment very seriously.

A common mistake to avoid: Never drop your guard and accumulate assets on the erroneous belief an old judgment creditor will no longer pursue you. Judgment creditors may stop pursuit once they realize you are without assets, but that doesn't mean your creditor forgot you and won't renew the chase once he hears of your new fortunes. Either discharge your debts in bankruptcy or by settlement, or maintain a strict asset protection program for your lifetime.

How To Sidestep Out-Of-State Judgments

You may be sued in a state other than where you reside. Eventually the creditor may obtain a judgment in that state. To enforce that judgment the creditor must first obtain a judgment in the state where you reside and have your assets. To accomplish this, the creditor petitions your state court to recognize the out-of-state judgment and to issue its own judgment for purposes of enforcing local collection against you.

You are given an opportunity to appear in court and object to your creditor's petition for a local judgment but this is generally futile. The United States Constitution compels each state to recognize valid judgments from other states. It is automatic your out-of-state creditor will win a judgment from your state court he can then enforce against your assets.

Should you own assets in still another state your creditor must obtain another judgment from that state before taking legal action to seize those assets. Courts in one state do not have the authority to order the seizure of property in another state. This gives you still another reason to deploy assets within several states. Assets dispersed in many states is a vital

debtor defense weapon–and a perfectly legal way to frustrate a creditor's collection effort.

Why Your Wages Can Be Your Most Vulnerable Asset

If your creditor cannot easily satisfy his judgment by seizing tangible assets, he will probably turn to a wage attachment remedy.

Unless you're self-employed, it's relatively easy for a creditor to attach your wages. Under a wage attachment, the court orders a portion of your wages to be paid directly to your creditor each payroll period. You continue to receive the balance. This wage attachment continues until the judgment is fully satisfied.

Each state sets its own limit on how much of your paycheck can be attached. Most states limit the amount to the lesser of 25 percent of your net earnings, or excess wages above 30 times the federal minimum wage. A state-by-state wage attachment chart can be found in the Appendix.

It is not a difficult process to obtain a wage attachment. A judgment creditor applies to the court for a writ of execution, or writ of wage levy, as it is called in some states. The sheriff then delivers it to the employer who must comply with the order.

Can you contest the wage attachment? You legally can object and demand a hearing. Because the debtor has a substantial portion of his wages protected, courts generally grant the wage attachment. Still, courts can either refuse or further reduce the attachment if the debtor can show the attachment would present a severe hardship for himself or his family.

Employers are not enthralled with a wage levy, nor the fact that an extra effort is required each payroll to issue creditors a check. Fortunately, you cannot be fired because of it unless there are two separate wage attachments against you. Your best move: Convince your employer that you are doing everything possible to resolve the creditor problem and that further attachments are unlikely.

Five Essential Steps Once Creditors Seize Your Property

Personal property is seized by judgment creditors through use of a levy. A levy can be used to seize money in your bank or safe-deposit box. It can also be used to seize motor vehicles, jewelry, antiques, a boat or other non-exempt personal assets. The sheriff then attempts to turn the asset into money (unless a bank account was levied with the funds in your account automatically turned over to the creditor). A sheriff's sale of your tangible assets, usually through public auction, is used for liquidating your assets.

You can object to a seizure or sale, but not successfully unless you can show a procedural violation or that the assets were improperly seized. The proceeds from the sale are first applied to the sheriff's fees and liquidation costs, and the balance to the creditor's judgment. Should the proceeds not fully pay the judgment, the creditor can have the sheriff levy on other assets until the debt is fully paid.

Seizure of secured assets requires the secured party to be first satisfied, and the secured party need not allow the sale unless fully paid from the sale. For this reason, the sensible creditor checks for liens against seized assets to verify there is sufficient equity to produce payment for the creditor.

Several remedies are available to you once your assets are seized:

- File bankruptcy (Chapter 7, 11 or 13) before the auction sale. The sheriff sale must then be discontinued. Test your timing. If you are to seek bankruptcy relief, do it before your assets are seized and sold at auction.
- Offer to substitute property under seizure. Will the sheriff accept from you property that has less importance to you but will generate equal proceeds for the creditor?
- Refuse entry. You are under no obligation to allow the sheriff to enter your home for purposes of seizure unless the sheriff has a special court order allowing entry. But be careful. Don't interfere with the sheriff, or prevent him from taking property, unless you are confident your acts are legal.
- Require the sheriff to conduct a commercially reasonable sale so the maximum amount possible is received (and less will then be owed

on the judgment). This means, for instance, the auction must be adequately advertised to attract a reasonable number of bidders.

- Buy back the asset yourself if the asset has value to you, since it is likely to bring far less than its true value at auction. Obviously, you cannot title the asset again in your name, as it would then be subject once more to seizure and sale. Acquire the asset through a corporation, or a friend or relative.

state law). Second, plan ahead and assign accounts receivables to another entity, such as a corporation or limited partnership. Alternatively, set up another entity to operate your type business and own the newly-generated receivables should your creditor attempt seizure. A third alternative: Factor commercial receivables. Here you would sell your receivables to any one of a number of factor organizations that specialize in the purchase of commercial accounts. You'll then receive nearly the entire face value of your current receivables before the creditor surfaces to seize.

Three Ways To Protect Money Owed You

Some property cannot be levied directly because the asset is in the hands of a third-party. These assets include funds due you. Accounts receivable fall within this category, and also tax refunds, cash value life insurance, and annuities.

Similar in procedure to wage attachments, these assets are reached by an "assignment order". As with a wage attachment, the creditor obtains an assignment order by application to the court. Notice of the assignment order is then sent to third parties who hold funds due you. Creditors usually learn of these third parties through asset discovery.

Use a two-fold defense to block an attachment order: First, reclaim all funds held by third parties as part of the judgment proofing process before the creditor obtains judgment. This means liquidating such assets as insurance or annuities (unless exempt by

When Creditors Can Get Pre-Judgment Attachments

Can your assets be seized even before a judgment? Sometimes. The purpose of the pre-judgment attachment is to secure collection of a future judgment by encumbering your assets so they cannot be disposed of by you to the detriment of your creditor.

The court, in considering whether to grant a pre-judgment attachment, balances two issues: 1) How likely is the plaintiff to win the suit, and 2) How likely is the defendant to dispose of the assets before judgment should the attachment not be granted?

The conflict for the court to balance is the right of a defendant to have full use and enjoyment of his property until a judgment is awarded against the right of the alleged creditor to obtain some assurance that there will be assets left to satisfy a judgment, should it be awarded.

Courts are more likely to grant pre-judgment attachments on contract claims, such as suits to collect on promissory notes or for unpaid goods or services. Attachments are normally not granted for more speculative claims, such as negligence cases. The creditor may also be required to post bond to reimburse the defendant for losses caused by the attachment should the plaintiff lose the case.

A pre-judgment attachment gives the creditor a preference over other unsecured creditors if you do not file for bankruptcy within 90 days of the attachment. You can thus set aside the attachment as a voidable preference with bankruptcy. That option gives you powerful ammunition to negotiate a reasonable settlement.

Key Secrets To Remember

- The best time to resolve a claim is before a lawsuit is filed.
- You don't have to negotiate your own creditor settlements. Besides your attorney there are several low-cost alternatives.
- Always negotiate from a position of strength. You have the most strength when you have no assets and are judgment proof. What you then offer the creditor is better than receiving nothing. Poverty is power!
- Stall tactics can delay a case for years. Time is the debtor's best friend and a creditor's worst enemy.
- Creditors have broad powers to investigate your assets–once they

have a judgment.

- A paper trail listing assets, or your disposal of assets, can come back to haunt you.
- Judgments have a long life. If you have sizeable judgments against you, either settle, go bankrupt, or live without assets in your name.
- Don't assume a creditor cannot attach your assets before obtaining a judgment. You may be surprised.

4 LITTLE-KNOWN LAWS THAT AUTOMATICALLY SHIELD KEY ASSETS

A considerable portion of your wealth may already be protected by federal or state laws that automatically place certain assets beyond the reach of creditors. These are the homestead and exemption laws. The purpose of these laws is to provide you some financial security no matter how impoverished you may become. These laws commonly apply to your retirement funds, annuities, insurance, wages and even your home.

This chapter will acquaint you with the homestead and exemption laws in your state. You will then know which assets are automatically protected from your creditors. You will also learn how to take advantage of these laws so they protect as much of your property as possible. You will find in the appendix a complete list of exempt assets for your state.

How To Take Advantage Of State Laws That Protect Your Home

Homestead laws are found in many states. They are intended to prevent loss of the family home to creditors. The homestead owner in these states thus enjoys some financial security, and the community a sense of stability knowing it will not have to shelter its homeless.

Consistent with that goal, homestead exemptions extend only to the real estate owned and occupied by the debtor as the principal residence. Still, it's not always clear what property is subject to homestead protection. Examples:

• Many states limit homestead protection to a single family home and exclude duplexes, triplexes or larger apartment buildings where only one unit is occupied by the debtor. Since the debtor's interest cannot be legally segregated from the tenanted part of the building, the entire property is disqualified for protection. Unless you own a free-standing single family home, check this point carefully.

• Most, but not all homestead states, extend homestead protection to condominiums, since a condominium is considered property that legally stands alone. On the other hand, ownership in a cooperatively-owned building, as is common in New York, may not qualify for homestead protection. This is because the debtor does not own a specific property, but instead owns shares in a corporation that owns the entire building. Although this arrangement carries with it the exclusive right to occupy a specific apartment, it may not satisfy the homestead definition.

• Homestead protection may even apply to mobile homes when used as a permanent home. This, however, also varies between states based on their own interpretation of their homestead laws.

The bottom line: Homestead laws are tricky, and you cannot take it for granted that your home is automatically protected. Also keep in mind that a few states do not provide homeowners any homestead protection. In these states, the family home sits fully exposed to creditors. Other methods must then be found to shelter the home.

SECRET #37

One Mistake That Can Lose You Your Homestead Protection

Investigate how to correctly claim your homestead exemption under your state law. Requirements are not uniform. In many states you must record homestead documents in a public filing office, ordinarily where all other real estate documents are filed. Other states, such as Florida, automatically grant homestead protection, provided you can establish the Florida home as your primary residence. Still other states impose a time requirement, such as residency for six months, before you become eligible for homestead protection.

Who can claim homestead protection? Some states say only the head of the household. More typically, either spouse can make the homestead declaration, and this is certainly the trend. Surprisingly, some states actually reject homesteads when separately made by each spouse. Cross-declarations against the same property may cancel each other out. Check with the appropriate public officials in your state to properly declare your homestead. Tip: Give careful thought to which spouse should claim the homestead, if you live in a state where only one spouse can file. Have the homestead taken by the more vulnerable spouse, or the spouse more likely to incur claims, because the homestead can most effectively be used to protect against the claims of that spouse.

SECRET #38

Beware Homestead's Loopholes

Some debts pierce your homestead protection. A few states grant total protection from all debts, no matter when incurred. In these states you can file for homestead the day of a sheriff sale, and the homestead would protect you.

Most homestead states, however, protect you only on debts that arose after the homestead was claimed. Earlier obligations, whether or not ripened into a lawsuit, can be asserted against the home. Your homestead, then, should be claimed as soon as possible, and certainly before significant obligations are undertaken.

Nor is homestead effective against every type claim. Homesteads generally protect against all private claims, but not necessarily governmental claims. IRS claims, for example, are not protected against under any homestead laws. Many people, with no serious debts other than delinquent taxes, lose their homes on the mistaken belief their state homestead laws insulate them from the IRS. State homestead laws do not protect against the IRS because state homestead laws cannot supersede federal authority. This includes the power of the IRS to lien, levy or seize property. The states may, however, grant homestead protection against their own state taxes, and many do.

Claims against homesteaded property can also be asserted by a spouse in a divorce action. Homestead laws are not intended to deprive one spouse in a marriage their rights to the property of the other under state divorce laws. Similarly, a wife, or children, unlawfully excluded from an inheritance, may file a claim against homesteaded property in an estate.

Finally, while homestead laws normally apply to contract and tort claims-such as negligence-they do not always apply to intentional torts such as deceit, fraud, or libel. Punitive damages, as well as fines, can also usually pierce homestead protection and thus jeopardize the home. Since there may be several important exclusions to the homestead protection you rely on to shelter your home, carefully check out your state law with your attorney. Obviously, homestead offers no protection against voluntary or consensual liens, such as mortgages or deeds of trust. A mortgage holder has the same rights against homestead property as against property that is not homesteaded.

Nor does homesteading necessarily provide you complete creditor protection against your home. Homestead usually covers only a limited amount of equity. This is ordinarily between $10,000 and $40,000. Example: If you live in a state that grants a $40,000 homestead and own a home worth $200,000 with a $100,000 mortgage, then your equity is $100,000. Of this, $40,000 would be protected and the remaining $60,000 would be exposed. If you lived in Massachusetts with a $100,000 homestead exemption, then your entire equity would be protected.

Several states limit homestead to properties under a certain size or value. Texas, for example, protects a homestead of 200 rural acres without regard to value. Additional land is not protected. Urban property, on the other hand, is protected only to the extent the land does not exceed one acre.

Florida is the state of choice when it comes to liberal homestead laws. Your home in Florida is protected without limit as to value. You may, for example, go bankrupt in Florida and still keep your mortgage-free $10 million home. This explains why relocation to Florida is oftentimes a smart asset protection strategy when you have creditor problems.

Since other states are less liberal than Florida, it's essential to know how much actual protection your state homestead laws do grant you. If you live in a state with too small a homestead exemption, then additional protection is essential.

To take full advantage of the homestead law, have it shelter as much equity in your home as possible. If your home is worth $200,000, with a $100,000 mortgage and $50,000 homestead exemption, then $50,000 in equity remains exposed. How can you safeguard this $50,000? Why not increase the mortgage from $100,000 to $150,000? Then no equity remains for creditors. Place the $50,000 proceeds in other exempt property such as exempt insurance or annuities. You may make gifts to your children. These are only two of the many possible strategies.

Conversely, you may have an unlimited homestead, as in Florida. As in the earlier case, what if you have a $100,000 mortgage? Why not reduce it through funds borrowed against your non-exempt assets. Borrow heavily against a vacation home, a car, a boat, or other non-exempt assets. You would then have a home, free and clear, but still fully protected by your homestead. Your other property that was fully exposed to creditors, would now be encumbered by $100,000 in loans. In sum: Maximize your protection by borrowing against non-exempt assets, and apply the loan proceeds to property protected by homestead.

Although homestead is intended to protect the family home, the homestead laws in your state may offer too little protection to be of practical value. This explains why homestead laws are not extensively relied upon in certain states. Investigate and you may find:

- Your homestead exemption is too small to provide adequate protection. This certainly is true if you have $10,000 or $20,000 exemption. Such small exemptions are meaningless today.

- Your homestead exemption does not protect you from specific debts of concern, such as IRS claims or pre-existing debts.

- Your homestead declaration creates more title problems and complications than it is worth considering its negligible benefits. For example, you may have to endure a complex legal process to temporarily lift the homestead declaration so you can re-mortgage your property. While these legal technicalities associated with homestead are usually not too burdensome, they can be inconvenient.

The real danger of homestead is that it may give you a false sense of security. While homestead may protect you today, it may not protect you tomorrow.

Consider your position if your home is now worth $200,000, with a $100,000 mortgage and a $100,000 homestead exemption. It appears that between the mortgage and the homestead exemption, your home is safe from a creditor owed $75,000. Now consider your protection in future years. For instance, within a few years your home may increase in value to $250,000, and your mortgage may be reduced to $75,000. Your home then has the $75,000 equity to be seized by your creditor. This underscores the one big pitfall of most homestead exemptions: You lose protection as your equity increases. To avoid this, you must continuously refinance to keep your exposure limited.

Another problem: An attachment by a judgment creditor may "cloud" your title to your home, even if there is no equity to satisfy the claim. This cloud prevents you from selling or re-financing the property unless you convince your creditor to discharge the attachment. This, of course, usually requires some payment. Some homestead states do not allow a creditor claim to be filed against homestead property, so this problem would not apply.

Review these eight points to test whether the homestead laws adequately shelter your home from creditors.

- Do you live in a state with homestead law protection?
- Does your residence qualify for homestead?
- Can you establish your home as a primary residence so you can gain homestead protection?
- Have you properly applied for homestead, if required? Is it in the name of the spouse with the greater potential liabilities?
- Does your mortgage and homestead exemption combined equal or exceed the value of your home or is there still substantial equity at risk?
- Were your debts incurred subsequent to your homestead, and are they debts homestead protects against?
- Will the homestead exemption protect you in the future when you may have more equity in the property?
- Will homestead allow you to sell or refinance your home should a creditor file a claim against the property, or will the claim cloud your title and prevent a future sale?

Remember: Homestead only provides valuable asset protection if it completely shields your home from creditors, both now and in the future. When the protection is inadequate, title your property in a manner that will provide greater protection even if it means forfeiting homestead.

Why You May Lose Your Homestead Protection

You will lose your homestead protection if it can be proven by a creditor that your property under homestead is, in fact, not your permanent residence or domicile. You can have only one domicile and that is the place where you generally reside with the intent to remain indefinitely. These requirements can be established only through certain facts that tend to prove your residence is your domicile, and thus eligible for homestead protection:

- Was an affidavit of domicile filed in the public records, if required?
- Where did you file your federal tax returns, and what address did you use?
- At what address do you generally receive mail?
- What address do you use for your driver's license and auto registration?
- Where do you and your family spend most of your time?
- Did you obtain a homestead property tax exemption on your real property, if available?
- Where did you register to vote? Where did you actually vote?
- What address is used in your will, living will, or similar legal documents?
- Where do you maintain checking or savings bank accounts?

The above list is not all inclusive, but the points do represent those most commonly considered by a court in a homestead dispute. Also consider the following two points:

- A homestead can only come about through the occurrence of both actual residence and the intention to make that your home.
- Once a domicile is acquired, it continues until it is replaced. The mere acquisition of a second residence does not, in itself, disturb the existing domicile, without strong evidence to the contrary. A new residence is not presumed to be your new domicile unless you abandon your first domicile.

How To Protect Your Paycheck

Did you know both federal and state laws exempt at least part of your income from levy by judgment creditors?

Under the federal wage exemption established by the Consumer Credit Protection Act (CCPA), a creditor may not garnish more than the lesser of: (1) 25 percent of your disposable income, per week, or (2) the amount by which the disposable earnings for the week exceeds 30 times the federal minimum hourly wage then in effect. "Disposable" income or earnings is the net compensation after deductions of amounts required by law to be withheld.

Because the Consumer Credit Protection Act is federal law, it supersedes state laws that may allow greater garnishment. The individual states, however, can pass more protective garnishment laws that restrict even more the rights of creditors to reach wages of a debtor. Two states, Florida and Texas (the two states with the most protective homestead laws) also totally prohibit wage garnishment. The specific income exemptions enacted by each state are listed in the Appendix. Also, wages of federal employees cannot be seized by creditors.

Under the Child Support Enforcement Act of 1975, the income exemptions do not apply to enforcement of alimony or child support orders. Alimony and child support payments are not exempt from garnishment by creditors of either the payor or recipient. Creditor garnishment commonly occurs soon after divorce, because divorce leaves in its wake many unpaid bills. Support payments do enjoy a limited exemption in several states.

Welfare payments to recipients are entirely exempt from garnishment by creditors of the recipient in slightly more than half the states. It is either partially exempt or not exempt in the remaining states. This applies to the most common form of public assistance–aid to families with dependent children (AFDC). Proceeds of these payments are unprotected once received.

Most states grant exemptions, in whole or in part, to other types of public assistance, particularly aid to the blind, the elderly, and the disabled. These laws not only prevent creditors from garnishing the state for payments to be made to the debtor, but also protects proceeds once received by the debtor, but only so long as the debtor keeps the welfare funds segregated from non-exempt funds. Once the money is spent on other non-exempt property it also loses its protection.

Social security payments, including disability income, cannot be taken by creditors, notwithstanding that social security is not deemed a pension under Employee Retirement Income Security Act (ERISA). But social security funds are not 100 percent safe. Creditors can attach social security funds when commingled with non-exempt funds. Caution: The IRS can levy social security payments. As a matter of collection policy, the IRS does not go after social security funds, except under the most extreme circumstances. Still, the danger is always there.

Remember: Creditors can take exempt or protected income, if it is seized after it has been paid to you and before you spend it. One solution: Set up a corporation, have the funds paid to the corporation, and write your personal checks from the corporate account. For tax purposes, income transferred to the corporation can be treated as a loan. The checks can be repayment. Unless the corporation accumulates large sums, this will be a safe and simple way to shield personal funds from creditors–particularly the IRS.

Another wage protection strategy: Grant a wage assignment to a "friendly creditor" who can then "loan" the money back to you. To work–the wage assignment must be in writing and be in effect before a creditor levies on wages.

Insurance Can Be One Of Your Safest Investments

Your insurance policy is one of the very best ways to shelter your cash from creditors. Every state grants insurance significant exemption from creditor attachment. Insurance exemptions can be traced back to 1841 since insurance protects dependents of the insured, and thus offers them financial stability without need of state support. Today, of course, life insurance offers more than security. It can also be an excellent investment. In fact, many life insurance policies are purchased primarily to fulfill investment objectives. Despite this trend, insurance remains an exempt asset, and in most states probably will remain exempt in the future. Still, variances do exist between states in the protection they afford insurance:

- All states bar attachment of insurance by creditors of the policyholder. A number of states also prevent attachment by creditors of the beneficiaries.
- In addition to exemptions for individual life insurance, most states also exempt term insurance policies as well as group life policies.
- The amount of insurance protected also varies between states. Some states exempt all insurance. Others, limit the exemption with a dollar ceiling on the face of the policy. Creditors in these states can only attach insurance above the ceiling.

The ceiling may apply to each policy, or to aggregate coverage over a number of policies. If the ceiling is per-policy, then spread your insurance over a number of policies so no single policy exceeds the amount protected.

- Insurance exemptions universally apply to the proceeds of policies payable upon the death of the insured, but some states also extend the exemption to the cash surrender value of the policy. If you own policies with a substantial cash value, check the laws of your state and withdraw the unprotected cash before a creditor attachment.

Where states provide total insurance protection, the exemption does not extend to the Internal Revenue Service. When the IRS is your creditor, use alternate strategies to protect your policies. One possibility: Have an irrevocable life insurance trust own the policies on your life. A life insurance trust may also offer certain tax benefits and maximize protection to both the cash surrender value of your policy and the proceeds.

Are you a beneficiary under a policy with IRS problems? Ask the insured to have the beneficiary changed to a trust, or alternatively, to your spouse or children. This same advice applies if you have general creditors and reside in a state that doesn't protect beneficiaries of life insurance.

When You Can Lose Your Pensions To Creditors

How about your pension and retirement income plans? Are they well protected from your creditors or can they be seized? Fortunately, the law on this point has been somewhat clarified by a recent U.S. Supreme Court ruling that held pension plans are not subject to creditor attachment and will not be lost by a debtor in bankruptcy. This decision applies to all private pension plans. Public retirement programs—those funded by federal or state governments—have always been exempt.

You must always keep in mind that while these retirement funds may be exempt from attachment, these funds can be attached once paid to you. Your creditor, for instance, can trace the funds to a checking or savings account subject to legal seizure. Property acquired with the funds is in equal jeopardy. Creditors are only restrained from interfering with your right to receive payment. They are not restrained from proceeding against money already received.

Less clear is whether private retirement programs–IRA's and Keogh's can be attached by creditors. The majority of recent court cases have held IRA's and Keogh's to be subject to creditor attachment. Certain states have passed statutes that protect the principal and/or income from private retirement funds. Use the Appendix to check the laws in your state and determine your protection.

Federal law provides that tax-qualified retirement plan trusts include a "spend-thrift" provision. The spendthrift clause prevents benefits payable to the participant from being assigned, attached or seized by creditors of the participant. The intent of the "spendthrift" requirement is to protect retirement benefits so that a plan participant would not jeopardize his future financial security to satisfy current obligations. This law seems absolute in its objective of securing retirement funds for its participant. Its only exception is a 1984 amendment that allows attachment of retirement funds for purposes of satisfying court ordered alimony or child support payments.

Notwithstanding the 1974 "spendthrift" law that seemingly protects all tax-qualified plans, there have been a number of challenges by creditors who nevertheless attempted to reach retirement funds of the participant. In almost all these cases the creditor was denied the right to reach the funds prior to the retirement of the debtor. Attachment was frequently allowed after retirement. The central issue in these cases was whether the debtor had the right to control and/or withdraw funds from the plan. Since the participant normally had no access to the funds before retirement, the creditor was deemed to have no greater right. Conversely, if the participant had access to the funds after retirement, the creditor had equal rights. Apparently, this no longer is a factor based on the recent case.

If the pension funds accumulated were above what was reasonably required to finance retirement, the excess could be reached by creditors. In these cases, courts concluded that the funds were no longer accumulated for retirement purposes alone, but for other financial purposes as well.

Here the courts concluded that the participant set up the retirement plan to obtain substantial tax benefits, but without postponing constructive use of the funds which the participant directly or indirectly controlled.

These cases shared several common factors: 1) The plan participant owned or controlled the plan, 2) The plan had unreasonably high balances in the retirement account, 3) The participant was the sole trustee of the plan, or controlled other trustee(s), 4) The participant received frequent loans from the retirement account before retirement, and 5) The participant, for all intent and purposes, enjoyed complete control over the amount, purpose and timing of distributions from the retirement accounts.

Based on these cases, the courts in the past have carved a large exception to the "spendthrift" provisions. They disregarded the security of retirement funds when the funds were beyond what was reasonably necessary for retirement, or if the participant failed to treat the retirement account different from personal funds. These cases caused disturbing uncertainty concerning the safety of retirement funds, particularly when the plan involves a small privately-owned company with the debtor the primary plan participant.

The influence of these cases is now moot by the Supreme Court ruling that clarify and confirm the creditor protection afforded by tax-qualified plans. For now, you can conclude that creditors cannot lay claim to your tax-qualified plans.

Although the safety of tax-qualified plans is now more clear, you can still more fully protect yourself if you follow these guidelines when establishing your tax-qualified plan:

- Appoint someone other than yourself and/or your spouse as trustee(s) of the fund. At the very least, use one unrelated co-trustee.
- Prudently invest trust funds in investments that are consistent with those of professional plan administrators. Do not use pension funds for personal use.
- Do not remove pension funds in advance of retirement as loans. Also avoid frequent distributions. Remember, the purpose of tax-qualified plans is to build a cash reserve for your retirement years.
- Have your pension plan cover other employees of the firm as well as yourself, or even a select group of professionals or executives.
- Avoid excess accumulations. The trust funds should not exceed what you would reasonably need to maintain yourself in your retirement years in the same style you are presently accustomed.

Follow the above guidelines and you can be reasonably confident your pension funds will remain free from creditor claims.

How To Protect IRA's And Keogh's

IRA's have less protection than tax-qualified pension plans. Prior cases hold that since the debtor can withdraw funds from his IRA account, although with a tax penalty, his creditors have equivalent rights.

Other courts have answered the question of creditor access to IRA's on the basis of whether the plan was voluntarily or involuntarily. If the IRA was voluntarily entered into, and not mandatory for employment, then the IRA funds can be taken by creditors. If an employee is required to contribute to the IRA as a condition of employment, then the funds are sheltered from creditors.

There is no federal protection for IRA's. They are always under the control of the debtor and are not held in custodial accounts, as are other retirement funds. Nevertheless, many states exempt all retirement funds, including IRA's, from creditors.

The Internal Revenue Service has specific authority to seize IRA funds. It is, however, IRS policy not to take IRA's unless absolutely necessary. You should, nevertheless, consider your IRA in jeopardy if you owe the IRS.

The bottom line: If you have substantial IRA accounts you are wise to consider it as vulnerable as cash in a savings or checking account. The prudent strategy: Take the money out of your IRA prior to creditor or potential creditor claims, and locate it so it can't be levied. You'll pay a 10 percent tax penalty, but that's far preferable to losing the entire account.

In terms of safety, Keogh plans lie between ERISA plans and IRA's. They are less vulnerable than IRA funds, but less safe than qualified retirement plans. If you participate in a Keogh plan with multiple principals, your Keogh will probably be as protected as an ERISA plan. Your Keogh funds will most likely remain safe, whether you face one creditor or bankruptcy with many creditors.

Sole participant Keogh's are considerably more vulnerable than multi-participant Keogh's. State courts routinely allow creditors to seize sole-participant Keogh funds, noting that the debtor can withdraw funds at will and that the debtor is his own trustee. Tip: You greatly increase the safety of a Keogh account if you appoint a co-trustee. Your spouse can safely serve in that capacity.

As with IRA's, it is safest to consider Keogh's vulnerable. They should be liquidated in advance of a creditor attachment or bankruptcy, despite the few cases that suggest Keogh's are safe.

Annuities: A Safe Harbor In A Storm

Several states exempt annuities from creditor attachment. Annuities are an ideal haven for threatened funds, particularly when your state does not limit the amount of annuities that can be protected. Florida, for example, sets no limit on exempted annuities. A debtor can invest any amount into annuities and it will be sheltered from creditors. Based on at least one case, this is true even if the funds are invested into an annuity after the claim arose and judgment entered. Moreover, annuities in Florida, and most other states, do not restrict you to a particular type annuity. Your annuity is protected whether it is for a fixed or variable amount, whether payments are deferred or immediate, or whether it provides for flexible or single payments.

Investigate the protection an annuity can provide in your state. If your state exempts insurance, it is likely that annuities are similarly protected. Your insurance agent or investment advisor can advise you.

Since annuities and life insurance, in many states, offer equal creditor protection, the investment decision will narrow to one of investment objectives:

- Insurance offers tax-free growth and income. Annuities offer tax-deferred growth and income.
- Insurance may require annual fees of 3 percent or more. Fees for managed annuities seldom exceed two percent.
- Insurance may require continued contributions. Annuities do not.
- Insurance gives death benefits dependent on age. Annuities provide return of principal payments at death.

How To Protect Proceeds Of Exempt Property

An important question: How do you protect from creditors the proceeds of exempt property? Example: If you sell your homesteaded home, how do you shelter the unprotected proceeds?

Your strategy: Have the funds go directly from one exempt asset into another. You may, for example, assign proceeds from the sale of your home to an irrevocable trust. You may also assign your interest in the property to your creditor-free spouse.

If you suspect that a judgment creditor is patiently waiting for you to "cash out", then use surprise. Mortgage the property to the hilt when your creditor is off-guard, and quickly redeploy the cash proceeds into other exempt assets.

As a practical matter, you are only vulnerable to a judgment creditor during that "narrow window" when funds are passing through your hands on their way from one exempt asset to another shelter. This vulnerability can be best overcome by either direct assignment of funds to your new shelter, or by a rapid transfer when your creditor cannot react in time to seize the proceeds.

Key Secrets To Remember

- Your home may be adequately protected by homestead laws in your state. Still, don't assume homestead gives you total protection. You may require additional safeguards.

- Wages, in most states, are partially exempt. Welfare payments are totally exempt, while social security payments can be seized only by the IRS.

- IRA's and Keogh's are generally not safe from creditors, however, tax-qualified pension plans generally are.

- Insurance and annuities are ordinarily exempt assets, and they may also prove to be good investments. They can be a wise investment alternative to stocks, bonds and savings that are all unprotected.

- In asset protection planning, a primary step is to convert as many non-exempt assets as possible into exempt assets.

- Proceeds from the sale or liquidation of an exempt asset should be directly transferred into another exempt asset, or an entity that provides creditor protection.

5 WEALTH-SAVING STRATEGIES WITH CO-OWNERSHIPS

Assets are commonly owned by more than one person. When more than one person holds title to property they are co-owners, and the property is considered under co-ownership. How you hold property with others can be an important asset protection strategy. Conversely, if you hold title incorrectly it can present dangers beyond those you face had you owned the property outright in your name alone, or through another entity.

Converting property you own into assets owned with another person, most probably your spouse, may be the simplest and most foolproof way to shelter your assets. Little effort is required to accomplish it, therefore, co-ownerships should be one of the first strategies considered in your asset protection plan. The strategy should be rejected only when it's unworkable in your circumstances, or it's unsafe under your state law.

Co-ownership is also an important way to avoid probate, since property jointly-owned automatically passes to the surviving joint tenant. Many families managed to save their assets from creditors only because they held their home, stocks and bonds, or other important assets under the correct form of co-ownership. Asset protection in such cases was oftentimes inadvertent, but nevertheless a welcomed benefit. Knowledgeable individuals widely use co-ownerships because it can be so effective a wealth insulator. For these individuals, probate avoidance is their secondary benefit, and asset protection their primary goal.

To fully understand the role of co-ownership in asset protection, you must first understand the various types of co-ownership, as well as the characteristics, advantages, disadvantages, and practical uses of each. Co-ownership takes one of three legal forms:

• tenancy-in-common
• joint tenancy
• tenancy-by-the-entirety

Each type co-ownership offers a different degree of creditor protection which can vary, depending upon state laws. Several other considerations, in addition to asset protection, will influence the type of co-ownership you select. These include estate planning, taxes, the type property, and most particularly the nature of the relationship between the prospective co-owners.

There is a fourth type of co-ownership called a tenancy-by-partnership. This is discussed in Chapter 7. Finally, property may be also held as community property, which is still another form of co-ownership. This form of co-ownership is covered in this chapter.

Why Tenancy-In-Common Can Be Hazardous

When two people own property under a tenancy-in-common, each tenant (owner) is considered to own a one-half divided interest in the property. Because the interest of each owner is divisible, each tenant can sell, mortgage, or dispose of his share of the property. The other co-owner would have no right to interfere.

There is an obvious disadvantage to this: Since a tenant-in-common owns an interest separate from the interest of the other co-owner, his creditors can reach his interest, but only his interest. The interest of the other co-owner is safe from all but his own creditors.

This does not mean that holding property under a tenancy-in-common is without other potential hazards. For example, if you own property as a tenant-in-common, the creditors of your co-owner can petition the court for approval to sell the property. It may only be through a forced liquidation that your co-owner's interest can be turned into the cash necessary to satisfy his debt. This means that instead of owning a one-half interest in the property, you end up instead with the cash representing your interest. Of course, you can always negotiate to buy your co-owner's interest from his creditors, but that is not always possible or practical. Moreover, the creditor or someone who buys or obtains the debtor's interest in the property, may not want to sell his newly-gained interest in the property. You'll then have a stranger as your new co-owner.

A tenancy-in-common is not necessarily limited to two individuals. There can be any number of co-owners, and they may each own a different share of the property. As a practical matter, it becomes too unwieldy to use a tenancy-in-common with more than three or four co-owners. When participants exceed that number, they should instead use a corporation, limited partnership or trust to own the property, while they become shareholders, limited partners or beneficiaries. There is then less chance that title to the property will be clouded upon the death of a co-owner, or by legal problems of one co-owner causing attachments against the property.

What should you do if your co-owner under a tenancy-in-common develops financial problems? It can be smart for a co-owner in financial difficulty to transfer his interest to the other co-owner before it is attached by his creditors. The transfer can be supported by a price representing a proportionately smaller percentage of the property's actual value since the interest represents only a fractional share of the property. Once the creditor threat is over, the property can be reconveyed. Obviously, the beleaguered co-owner may really be forced to go through an actual sale because it may be the only opportunity to raise some quick cash before the creditor strikes.

Because property held under a tenancy-in-common is so vulnerable and can be subject to forced liquidation to satisfy the debts of one co-owner, it is important that co-owners enter into the relationship confident of their respective financial stability. In too many cases this confidence is misplaced. One or both parties may have severe or chronic financial or legal problems. When their financial record is clean, they may still develop later problems that jeopardize the property. Co-owners should share with each other any foreseeable problems so they can work cooperatively to safeguard the property, as well as their respective interests.

A tenancy-in-common does not grant survivorship rights. The share of each tenant does not, upon death, pass to the surviving co-owner, but instead passes to his lawful heirs. This too can cause complications, since those heirs seldom share the surviving tenant's same objectives concerning the property. A buy-out agreement between the co-owners can be one solution, particularly if the buy-out price is funded by "buy-out" insurance, as is commonly used in multiple-owner businesses.

Married couples seldom use tenancy-in-common to title their home. This is because they usually do want survivorship rights, a feature usually not desired by other co-owners.

The Hidden Dangers Of Joint Tenancy

A joint tenancy is created when real or personal property is owned by two or more persons, in equal shares, with the express provision that title is jointly-held.

In most states a joint tenancy can only be established by written agreement. A verbal understanding is insufficient. This acknowledgement of joint tenancy may be stated in a deed or bill of sale, or evidenced on documents of title, such as a stock certificate. (Example, Mary Doe and Ann Smith, jointly, or as joint tenants.) A joint tenancy may also be designated as Mary Doe or Ann Smith. The inclusion of "or" indicates survivorship rights which does not apply to a tenancy-in-common. This means that upon the death of one joint tenant, the surviving tenant or tenants automatically become the owners of the entire property by operation of law. This is true even if the decedent bequeathed his interest in the property to someone else. Therefore, jointly-owned property does not pass through probate, and this is often seen as its chief advantage.

A joint tenancy conveys to each owner an equal or undivided interest in the property. The joint ownership can, however, be terminated by one joint tenant conveying his interest. Here the joint tenancy ends and the remaining joint tenant becomes a tenant-in-common with the new owner.

How effective is joint tenancy in asset protection? A joint tenancy usually offers very little protection more than a tenancy-in-common. A creditor of one joint tenant can attach the one-half undivided interest held by that joint tenant and then petition the court to "partition" the property and order its sale. The proceeds are then divided. In some states it is possible to prevent "partition" by agreement between the co-owners: This can be important in asset protection planning because it defeats the right of the creditor to liquidate the one-half interest.

A creditor who attaches a joint interest, but does not liquidate his claim through partition and sale, risks losing his claim to the attached property should the debtor-tenant die. This is because the debtor's joint interest would automatically pass to the surviving joint tenant upon death, and in this instance the survivorship transfer would wipe out the attachment against that interest. There is a corollary: If the non-debtor-joint tenant should die while the creditor holds the interest of the debtor-joint tenant, then the creditor gains full rights to the entire property. This is because the rights of survivorship work both ways. Some creditors with attachments purposely sit on these rights waiting for the death of the other owner in a "winner-take-all".

Because a creditor's rights against a jointly-held asset ends upon death of the debtor, it obviously follows that an attachment during the debtor's lifetime has questionable value unless that interest can be liquidated through partition and sale of the property while the debtor is alive.

Most states follow this general rule: During the life of a joint tenant, the share of that joint tenant can be reached by his creditors. The principle is that since each joint tenant is free to transfer that interest during his lifetime, his creditors should be allowed to reach that same interest to satisfy debts owed by that joint tenant. The creditor's forced sale puts the creditor, or his buyer, in the same position as one who buys directly from the joint tenant: The joint tenancy is destroyed and the creditor, or his nominee buyer, becomes a tenant-in-common with the remaining co-owner.

While it is essentially true that a creditor cannot go against jointly-owned property once the debtor-joint tenant dies, several exceptions should be noted:

- If the joint tenancy was expressly established for purposes of defrauding creditors, it can be set aside. This does not mean, however, that a joint tenancy, in itself, is evidence of fraudulent intent.
- Federal and state taxes owed by the deceased joint tenant can attach to the joint interest and pass with the property to the surviving tenant, although other debts do not.
- Certain states grant creditors' rights against jointly-held property that are contrary to prevailing rule. Washington State and South Dakota, for instance, allow a creditor of a deceased joint owner recourse against the transferred interest. North Dakota, for example, allows a creditor to sue a surviving joint tenant for debts of the deceased joint

tenant up to the amount of the deceased joint owners contribution to the property. Although such laws grant creditors of a joint tenant considerable protection, states with such laws are also exceptionally limited in number.

- Bankruptcy is the final exception. The rights of a creditor against a joint tenant are definitely expanded should that joint tenant file bankruptcy. Bankruptcy law specifically provides that all property of the debtor becomes subject to the bankruptcy. This includes property jointly-held as well as property under other forms of tenancy. The bankruptcy code also provides that the bankruptcy trustee may sell the property of the bankrupt co-owner, which may include the entire property. The non-bankrupt co-owner must then protect himself by claiming his share of the proceeds. If he fails to, the entire proceeds may be applied to the bankrupt's debts.

Joint tenancy usually applies to real estate, but it is not necessarily limited to real estate. Joint tenancy can also apply to:

- Bank accounts
- Safe deposit boxes
- Copyrights, patents and trademarks
- Stocks and bonds
- Notes and mortgages due
- Motor vehicles (cars, boats, etc.)
- Any personal property
- Beneficial interests in trust
- Interests in limited partnerships

Virtually your entire estate can be jointly-owned, and you can completely avoid probate if all assets are jointly held. But it is not necessary to rely strictly on joint tenancy for asset protection and probate avoidance. For purposes of probate avoidance, you can, alternatively, hold your property in a living trust if you want to retain control, or in an irrevocable trust if asset protection is more important to you than control.

Because of the very limited protection provided by a joint tenancy, it should not be relied upon for asset protection. It is best to title assets in another way, such as in a corporation, family limited partnership or in one of the more protective trusts.

SECRET #48

When A Tenancy-By-The-Entirety Gives You Absolute Protection

A tenancy-by-the-entirety is a unique form of joint tenancy reserved specifically for husband and wife. The concept of tenancy-by-the-entirety (T/E) originates from the premise that marriage unifies two people–husband and wife–so that their property is not owned by each individually, but by the two by the "unity" or "entirety".

Since such titled property is owned by the two spouses "in unity", neither the husband nor wife can singly transfer his or her interest in the property. Moreover, upon the death of either husband or wife, the surviving spouse automatically gains title to the entire property. In this important respect, a tenancy-by-the-entirety is similar to ownership by joint tenancy. A tenancy-by-the-entirety remains in effect until both husband and wife simultaneously transfer the property, until divorce, or until the death of one spouse.

About one-half the states have tenancy-by-the-entirety laws, although there is variance in these laws between these states. The trend is away from these laws, now viewed as antiquated, out of step with modern legal transactions and the individuality of husband and wife.

The important question is whether holding property as tenants-by-the-entirety protects it from creditors. The answer rests on state law and whether it treats tenancy-by-the-entirety differently from joint tenancy.

In the majority of states there is no distinction. A creditor of one spouse can attach the interest of that spouse and force a sale of the property to obtain the proceeds from that interest. In these states, there is little or no distinction in the degree of protection afforded by any of the three forms of tenancy—tenancy-in-common, joint tenancy, or tenancy-by-the-entirety. If you live in one of these states, then you will not want property in your name whether it is titled with another individual or not.

There are, however, a large number of states that protect property under a tenancy-by-the-entirety. Some of these states virtually immunize the property from creditors, particularly if it is the family home. Others partially protect the property. For example, in Massachusetts the family home is protected from creditors of the husband as long as the wife resides there. The reverse is equally

true. A wife's creditors cannot seize her interest as long as her husband is in residence. Florida is an example of a state that offers considerable protection to tenants-by-the-entirety. Florida protects not only the marital home so titled but also any other asset held under a tenancy-by-the-entirety. As with a joint tenancy, it is not only possible to safely hold real estate this way, but also any other property such as bank accounts, stocks and bonds, or even expensive cars and boats. Given Florida's liberal homestead law and the protection it affords T/E's, it is not difficult to see why this state is favored by debtors.

As you review the various states with tenancy-by-the-entirety, you see a patchwork of laws concerning the rights of creditors. For example, if the creditor is owed for necessities of life provided to the debtor, it may enlarge the creditor's rights in some states. Because laws concerning tenancy-by-the-entirety do vary considerably between states, it is not possible to generalize on the adequacy of this type of tenancy as a form of protection. You must therefore review this question carefully with your lawyer to determine whether this form of tenancy is available in your state, and whether it can give you adequate protection.

There are some near universal features of a tenancy-by-the-entirety. One is that it generally applies only to the marital home. Second, your protection against creditors cannot outlast your marriage. When the marriage ends, whether through death or divorce, the tenancy, and its protection, simultaneously end. If the spouse free of liability predeceases the spouse with liability, the home will be totally exposed to creditor claims. For instance, if the husband has a judgment against him, the marital home titled as a tenancy-by-the-entirety may be protected. Upon his death, his interest in the home will automatically pass to his wife free and clear of the claim against the husband. Had the wife died first, the husband's creditor could then levy on the entire home now titled solely in his name. Since the odds of a husband predeceasing a wife are about four to one–it may be a worthwhile gamble to keep the home under a tenancy-by-the-entirety where the husband has the greater risk of liability.

Bankruptcy offers still another concern. Under bankruptcy law, the trustee in bankruptcy can force a sale of the home should one of the spouses under a tenancy-by-the-entirety declare bankruptcy. The non-bankrupt spouse could claim his or her share of the proceeds, but this still doesn't preserve the home or any equity the bankrupt spouse had in the home. Of course, the homestead laws or bankruptcy exemptions may shelter a modest equity, but usually not a sizeable one.

The benefit of a tenancy-by-the-entirety can only be realized if one spouse incurs liability. If both spouses incur the same liability, then their creditors can in the majority of states, proceed against property held in the entirety. Except for mortgages on your home, the sound strategy is to avoid having your spouse incur obligations with you. This is particularly true with substantial business debts. If you do incur joint obligations, you significantly run the risk of losing jointly-owned property or property held in the entirety to those creditors.

It can be seen then that the right of a sur- viving spouse to own the entire property upon the death of the other spouse is one of the central advantages of a tenancy-by-the-entirety. The property passing to the surviving spouse becomes his or hers alone, usually free of the liabilities of the deceased spouse to which the surviving spouse was not a party. The property also avoids probate under which creditors of the deceased spouse must file claims. Once vested with full title to the property, the surviving spouse is then free to dispose of the property free and clear of any claims against the deceased spouse.

Should both spouses die simultaneously, a rare occurrence, the property would be distributed as if owned as tenants-in-common: One-half would go to the wife's estate and the other one-half to the husband's.

Thus, a joint tenancy and tenancy-by-the-entirety are exceptionally similar in concept with three important differences:

- A tenancy-by-the-entirety may exist only between husband and wife. Any number of persons may hold property jointly. While non-married individuals cannot claim a tenancy-by-the-entirety, married couples can, in many states, elect to take title either as jointly-owned property or as tenancy-by-the-entirety, or even as tenants-in-common. The distinction is important in those states that afford a tenancy-by-the-entirety broader protection–sometimes complete exemption from creditors. In these states it is vital that title expressly state that it is a tenancy-by-the-entirety, or it may be construed as a tenancy offering less protection.

- Any one joint tenant can terminate the joint tenancy simply by transferring his or her interest. Title to property held under a tenancy-by-the-entirety may not be transferred unless done by both husband and wife.

- In some states, the concept of tenancy-by-the-entirety relates only to real estate and no other form of property. Joint tenancy, on the other hand, can be used in any state and to title any type property.

SECRET #49

Why Joint Bank Accounts Are Risky

How safe are joint bank accounts? It is an important question considering their popularity between spouses, family members and even unrelated parties living or conducting a business together.

The major question is whether the creditors of one joint tenant to the bank account can seize a part, or even the entire account, to satisfy the debt. The answer rests largely upon state law.

In many states the creditor of one joint tenant can reach the entire bank account on the basis that the creditor's rights to the funds are equal to the rights of the debtor-joint tenant. Since the debtor-joint tenant can take all the proceeds from the account, his creditor has equivalent rights. Obviously, such a joint bank account can prove costly

since all the funds in the account are in jeopardy for the debts of either party to the account. Several states take an opposite position and limit the creditor of one joint tenant to his or her fractional share. This position is at least consistent with the rights afforded creditors who attach real estate. Here, only the interest of the debtor-joint tenant is at risk.

The Internal Revenue Service should be the creditor of greatest concern because only the IRS has the right to levy against a bank account without court approval. All that is required is a 30 day notice of intent to levy. Yet this notice doesn't always prompt the taxpayer to pay, at which point the joint bank account may be levied. The IRS can take the entire balance of a joint account. The IRS, however, as a matter of policy, will return up to one-half to the uninvolved party, but only upon proof that the individual contributed at least 50 percent to the account. This is not always easily accomplished.

There are many other ways to lose jointly-held funds. You may, for example, share a joint bank account with your married son with the objective that upon your death the account shall by-pass probate and automatically pass to your son. But what if your son goes through a divorce? The account will certainly be frozen until the divorce is concluded, and there is no way to know what portion of the account will be awarded to your daughter-in-law.

The dangers of jointly-held properties are not limited to bank accounts. What was said about bank accounts can generally be said about any other jointly-held property: Stocks and bonds, collectibles, life insurance or jointly-titled auto or boat.

There is added liability when you jointly-own property such as an auto. Who is liable if the auto is involved in an accident and you are uninsured? Both joint owners, of course. There's no need for expanded liability. Vehicles, and other assets that may create liability, should not be jointly-owned between spouses, but should be titled solely in the name of the spouse with the fewest assets.

SECRET #50

Why Co-Ownership Is A Dangerous Way To Avoid Probate

Joint tenancy, including tenancy-by-the-entirety, is simple and convenient. Most such arrangements are between husband and wife for purposes of avoiding probate, rather than for asset protection. But there are better ways to avoid probate. Placing property into a living trust is a preferable way to transfer wealth without probate. A living trust makes it more difficult for a creditor of one spouse to reach the entire property held in trust. This is true, except in states where tenancy-by-the-entirety property is fully protected.

Joint tenancies also reduce flexibility when transferring wealth. There may, for example, be adverse tax consequences when you transfer property through rights of survivorship. These taxes can be eliminated with a more creative use of trusts. Joint tenancies may also be inconsistent with your true intent as a joint tenant. You may,

for example, have children from a prior marriage. If you own property jointly with your second spouse, the property will automatically pass to that spouse and eventually to his or her family. Here the true intent may be to leave your property to your new spouse, but upon his or her death, then to your children. Joint ownership impairs such estate planning.

Whether joint tenancy is advantageous or disadvantageous to you can only be determined by professional evaluation of your financial situation and your wealth-transfer objectives. The point here is that you cannot simply assume such arrangements are advantageous either in estate planning or asset protection. There are too many instances where it is not advantageous, and where other strategies will more effectively produce the results you seek.

SECRET #51

How To Protect Community Property

Eight states have community property laws: Arizona, California, Idaho, Nevada, New Mexico, Louisiana, Texas and Wisconsin. Originating from Spanish law, which explains its prevalence in southwestern states, these laws have undergone change in recent years, and notable differences now exist in the community property laws between states.

To understand community property, you must first understand the law in non-community property states. If the husband owes an obligation, his property can be taken to satisfy the obligation. Conversely, the wife can lose her assets to satisfy her debts. Where husband and wife are joint and severally liable, the property of either or both can be taken. In sum, the fact that two defendants are married neither affects their liability for their debts, nor limits the property that may be seized by creditors.

Unlike non-community property states, marital status is the key issue in community property states when determining both liability for obligations as well as the property that may be taken to satisfy that debt. In community property states you can approach the question of creditor's rights by answering three questions:

- Is the debt one that arose before the marriage, during the marriage, or after the marriage ended?
- Is the debt a debt of one spouse (a separate debt) or a community debt for which both spouses are liable?
- Is the creditor seeking to claim separate property (property of one spouse) or community property (property of both spouses)? If the property is community property, is the creditor claiming a right to the entire property, or only the interest of the spouse that owes the debt?

Debts incurred prior to marriage are treated as the separate obligation of the spouse that incurred the debt. So, too, are debts incurred by either party after the marriage terminates. Community obligations are defined as those that were incurred during the marriage. But this is only presumptively so. For the obligation to be legally considered a community debt, the obligation must in some way have provided a benefit to the "community", or both spouses.

In most states a creditor's right to claim marital (or community) property is not determined by the purpose of the obligation. It does not matter whether a spouse contracts for himself or on behalf of both spouses. In either instance, the creditor can proceed against marital property. This is not so in California, Idaho and Texas, three community states that do not distinguish between community debts and separate debts. In these states, debts belong to spouses either individually or collectively. This again emphasizes the importance of becoming familiar with the specific laws of your community property state.

The second issue is the property targeted by the creditor. Property that each spouse owned prior to the marriage continues to be separate property thereafter. Gifts, bequests and inheritances specifically given to one spouse during marriage also remain separate property. All other property acquired by either, or both spouses during marriage is community property. Earnings of a spouse during marriage are ordinarily also considered community property, but some states exempt them from the other spouse's creditors. Commingling of separate assets during marriage so they lose source identity also makes them community property. Property acquired after divorce is treated as separate property.

With that background, we can focus on the specific rights of creditors. Creditors owed separate debts can proceed against the separate property of the spouse that incurred the debt. Generally, but not conclusively, community property cannot be taken to satisfy a spouse's separate debt. Because a spouse does not have the right to convert community property into separate property, the law holds a creditor should have no greater right to have the community property partitioned. Conversely, with the exception of contracts for necessities, neither spouse can by themselves jeopardize the separate property of a non-contracting spouse. Similarly, judgment creditors holding other type claims (negligence, etc.) can usually only proceed against the separate property of the liable spouse, and not the community property. The asset protection features of community property laws can be summarized:

- Property owned by you before your marriage (and after) is exposed to your creditors during your marriage because it remains separate property. These assets require protection, which may take the form of a trust, limited partnership or other safe haven.
- Community property (acquired during the marriage) is relatively safe from creditors of each individual spouse, but not safe from creditors with claims against both spouses. Here, too, the safest approach is to re-title your property, if both spouses routinely undertake the same obligations. When debts are not jointly undertaken, the community property laws offer adequate protection.

The Only Time To Hold Property In Your Name

This chapter wouldn't be complete without some discussion of the advantages and disadvantages of holding title in your own name.

The major advantage is that holding title gives you the greatest flexibility in working out an estate plan. The disadvantage: Such ownership gives creditors the best opportunity to seize the asset, unless it is protected by some specific law, such as the homestead laws.

It's only sensible to keep real estate in your name when you can take advantage of the homestead laws. Without such a benefit, the exposure is too great and the possible advantages too minor to justify holding property in your own name. You can easily find alternate ways to safely title your property where you gain similar or more important advantages–but without the corresponding disadvantages.

Key Secrets To Remember

- How you title property is important in asset protection planning.
- Tenancy-in-common offers no protection from creditors.
- Joint tenancies can, under some circumstances, provide limited protection in some states.

- Tenancy-in-the-entirety, between husband and wife can, in many states, partially insulate the asset from creditors. In some states it offers absolute protection.
- Joint bank accounts can be particularly dangerous because the creditors of one tenant may be able to seize the entire account. Joint ownership–as with motor vehicles–also produces liability against both owners. Ownership should be in the name of the less vulnerable owner.
- Community property laws can protect marital property from the claims of creditors of either husband or wife, but not creditors of both. Conversely, creditors of one spouse can proceed against the property of that spouse if purchased before the marriage.
- Holding property in your own name is almost always a mistake because it creates the greatest exposure to creditors. However, in some situations–as when real estate in your state is homesteaded–holding property in your name may be the safest strategy.

6

HOW TO TURN ANY CORPORATION INTO A POWERFUL WEALTH PROTECTOR

Your own corporation can be another powerful wealth protector as it shelters assets in two important ways: 1) Owners of a corporation are not personally liable for its debts. The corporation is therefore the safest way to operate your business and to protect your personal assets from business obligations. 2) The corporation can also safely hold your personal assets beyond the reach of your personal creditors.

Establish your own family corporation. You can then indirectly control your assets while they are safely titled out of your name. The mechanics are simple: Once you organize your corporation, give yourself some of the shares and issue additional shares to your family. Example: Your spouse and/or children may set up the corporation and acquire 70 shares of stock for a nominal amount. Two or three months later, in exchange for 30 shares, you transfer to the corpora-

tion the personal assets you want protected. Your creditors would now only have recourse to your shares of stock, not the property transferred. But since your shares constitute only a minority interest in the corporation, they would be of limited value to your creditor. Other strategies can fully protect your shares.

How effective an asset protector is a corporation compared to a limited partnership or a trust? A corporation is ideal for holding business or revenue producing assets. Its major advantage is its simplicity. It's more cumbersome to work with partnerships and trusts, however, attorneys may disagree on this point. A corporation, on the other hand, may present some tax disadvantages. Because it does feature some advantages, the corporation, like the limited partnership or trust, should always be considered for holding assets. Whether it's the vehicle of choice depends on many factors that must be decided case-by-case.

SECRET #53

How To Gain Corporate Protection When You're Unincorporated

Business owners frequently start their venture as unincorporated sole proprietorships and become concerned about the possible loss of personal assets only as their business heads for bankruptcy. If you're that business owner, here's what you can do now to escape personal liability for business obligations. Quickly incorporate your business and transfer the assets from the proprietorship into the new corporation. The corporation should then pay the oldest business obligations first. Since these would be obligations of the proprietorship for which you are personally liable, their discharge will free you of personal exposure. As your corporation pays the older debts it will incur new debts–usually with the same suppliers. However, these debts are now those of the corporation since they were incurred after the business was incorporated. Eventually all proprietorship debts will be fully paid and your corporation can be safely liquidated as the creditors will have no further personal recourse against you.

This strategy works well, but it demands careful coordination. For instance, you must keep your business operating as long as necessary to complete the transition and fully pay your pre-incorporation debts. You must also advise your creditors that your business is now incorporated. Finally, you must be certain your creditors apply your payments to the oldest balance–the proprietorship debts you want discharged. This is best accomplished by noting on each check how it is to be applied.

Do you now own an unincorporated business? Convert to a corporation before you're in serious financial trouble. Best advice: Incorporate before your start your business.

SECRET #54

The Friendliest State For Incorporation

In which state should you incorporate? Most people say Delaware, but they're wrong. Nevada is now the state that offers the most advantages to incorporators. Here's why:

- Delaware imposes an income tax on corporate profits. Nevada is tax-free. By comparison, Delaware could prove costly if you anticipate significant corporate earnings.
- Nevada doesn't share information with the IRS. All other states do, including Delaware. With a Nevada corporation, you are thus less likely to face an IRS audit since there is no state tax information to trigger discrepancies.
- Delaware has a franchise tax. Nevada doesn't. The Delaware tax is

modest, but it unfortunately requires voluminous annual disclosures–such as dates of stockholder meetings, places of business outside of Delaware, and disclosure of the number and value of the shares of stock issued. This is not the privacy you need in your asset protection program. Nevada requires none of this information. Nevada only requires a current list of officers and directors. The stockholders are not a matter of public record in Nevada, nor does the state ask who they are.

- Nevada not only beats Delaware in privacy, but Nevada also offers corporate officers and directors far broader protection than does Delaware. Example: Articles of incorporation in Nevada may eliminate or limit the personal liability of officers and directors for claims resulting from breach of their fiduciary duty. This is true in all cases, other than those involving the improper payment of dividends. In contrast to Nevada, Delaware has a longer statute of limitations to sue when improper dividends are paid. It also provides fewer creative options for director indemnification. Finally, in Delaware the right of director indemnification is at the discretion of the court, while it is an absolute right in Nevada.

- Nevada also allows creative financial arrangements to indemnify. Indemnification can be extended to any person serving the corporation who may incur liability. The corporation can make these arrangements regardless of its authority to indemnify. These financial arrangements include insurance in the form of trust funds, self-insurance, or granting directors a security interest or lien on corporate assets to guarantee indemnification. From an asset protection viewpoint, the absolute authority of corporate officers and directors to place liens against their own corporation for purposes of indemnification, provides them near-complete control over corporate assets. Unlike Delaware, and most other states, where such self-serving financial and legal arrangements are usually invalid, Nevada fully supports such protective arrangements. In fact, in Nevada, absent fraud, the decision of the board of directors concerning any financial arrangement is conclusive and is neither void or voidable. This is not true in Delaware, nor in most other states.

More good news! It's remarkably easy to incorporate in Nevada. Because so many astute business owners are establishing Nevada corporations, several Nevada firms offer complete incorporation services to nationwide clients. Laughlin Associates, in Reno, is one of the more popular. They offer a full range of incorporation services. More importantly, they are exceptionally knowledgeable about how to use Nevada corporations for asset protection. Laughlin and

Associates also offers excellent seminars on asset protection. They are listed in the Appendix.

A final point: The one best state for incorporating is probably the state where you will operate your business. If you incorporate in another state, including Delaware or Nevada, you must still file as a foreign corporation in your own state. Your corporation is then subject to the laws of your state, nullifying the advantage of incorporating elsewhere. You'll also be subject to multiple state taxes and filing requirements.

When does it make sense to incorporate elsewhere–such as in Nevada? When your corporation will not regularly do business elsewhere. This means that your corporation must remain relatively passive. A passive corporation can, however, still be an ideal shelter for certain assets you want protected, and in that instance, a Nevada corporation is preferable to incorporating in your own state, as your own state will undoubtedly be more creditor friendly.

How To Pick The Right Type Corporation

Does the "S" corporation provide the same limited liability protection as a regular corporation? This is a common question.

The "S" corporation (previously called the Subchapter S corporation), has become increasingly popular in recent years as more and more business owners elect the "S" corporation to avoid the double taxation of a "regular" or "C" corporation.

Because the "S" corporation is taxed like a partnership or proprietorship (depending upon number of owners), it is frequently thought that the "S" corporation also loses the limited liability protection of a regular "C" corporation. Fortunately, this is not true. There is no difference between an "S" corporation and a "C" corporation concerning the degree of liability protection each provides. Only consider taxes when choosing one type corporation over the other.

In asset protection planning, you will have greater flexibility with a "C" corporation, because trusts or other corporations cannot always be shareholders of an "S" Corporation. If you want the corporate shares owned by these entities for privacy reasons, a "C" corporation is necessary.

How To Finance Your Corporation For Maximum Protection

Funds loaned to your own corporation are easily lost. But you can greatly reduce your risk if you structure your loan correctly.

Let's start with the wrong way to finance your corporation: You put your funds into the business either for shares of stock or as a loan. If your business fails, you're at best an unsecured creditor and will probably reclaim none, or only a small portion of your loan. A bankruptcy court may even subordinate your claim to the claims of other unsecured creditors. Then, you would certainly recover nothing.

Be a shrewd owner. Put yourself in a position where your loan is fully secured by the business assets, and your claim superior to general creditor claims. Be careful. Your loan must be completely protected so your security interest against the assets of your business will not be voided by a bankruptcy court.

The strategy: Have a bank, rather than yourself, loan the funds to your business. Your business, in turn, would pledge its assets to the bank as collateral. Your bank is certain to make the loan because you would pledge as additional collateral a passbook or other personal collateral with a value equal to the loan. Since the loan would be 100 percent secured, the bank has absolutely no risk. Should your business fail, your bank as the secured party would be repaid first from the business assets. Once paid, your bank would then release to you your personal assets pledged as additional security. In this indirect way, you safeguarded your investment. Using the bank as a helpful intermediary, you're insured your investment would have priority from liquidation proceeds of the business.

Travel one step further with this idea. Recent bankruptcy cases say that where a lender is secured by the business owner's personal guarantee, repayments to the lender from the business within one year of its bankruptcy is recoverable by other creditors as an insider preference. The theory is that the burden for repaying the lender should fall upon the business owner rather than upon its general creditors. The solution: Have a friend or relative act as intermediary and guarantee the bank loan. You would give your cash collateral to your intermediary who, in turn, would pledge it to the bank. Since you are not the direct guarantor of the bank loan, bankruptcy would not prevent the bank from asserting first claim upon the business assets. With the bank repaid, it would surrender the cash collateral back to your intermediary, who, in turn, would return the money to you as its original source.

Before you invest or make loans to your corporation, review this strategy with your attorney. It is not nearly as complicated as it appears, and your attorney and bank can easily put together the necessary paperwork. Its two tactical advantages are obvious: First, a major portion of the money you invest in your business would be far better protected than if you simply invested the cash for shares of stock, or as an unsecured debt. Second, since you indirectly control the mortgage on your business, you can better protect your business from its creditors by asserting your rights as a lien holder of its assets.

Eight Surefire Ways To Lose Your Corporate Protection

If your corporation is to be an effective

liability insulator, it must function as a corporation, be treated as a corporation, and be recognized by its creditors as a distinct entity. You can lose your corporate protection when you relax these rules.

Beware the eight most common mistakes that can allow creditors to successfully "pierce the corporate veil" and impose personal liability for business debts on you as its owner.

- **You commingle funds:** Operate your corporation as a distinct entity separate from yourself in every respect. Keep the corporation's funds separate from your own. Funds transferred between yourself and your corporation must be properly documented. Example: Deposits of your funds to the corporation may be either a loan or a contribution to capital. Funds flowing from the corporation to yourself may be a loan, dividends, salary or expense reimbursement. Whatever the nature of the transaction, is it properly recorded on your personal records as well as the corporation's? The same advice applies to financial transactions between related corporations.
- You commingle assets: Prohibitions against commingling cash also apply to other assets, such as inventory. You can transfer inventory between corporations, provided accurate records are maintained. Creditors of one corporation frequently throw affiliated corporations into bankruptcy when they

see undocumented transactions between the bankrupt corporation and those affiliated corporations not in bankruptcy.
- You fail to sign documents in the corporate name: Avoid sloppiness when signing documents. Since you operate as a corporation, the documents to which it is a party should say so. Clearly state the corporate name. Designate your title aside or beneath your signature. This advice applies equally to checks. There are many cases where an individual is personally sued on a corporate obligation because she signed it in her name rather than the corporate name. Be disciplined. Always include the corporate name on all its documents and state your corporate title when signing on its behalf.
- You don't operate your corporation autonomously: If you operate more than one corporation it is important to operate each autonomously. This means, for instance, separate rather than duplicate or inter-locking boards of directors. Individuals who serve as officers of two related corporations should hold different offices in each. Corporate meetings should be held separately, and of course, separate corporate books must be maintained.
- You don't keep adequate corporate records: Creditors can challenge a corporate existence by showing no records, or inadequate records were maintained to document authority for corporate actions. Keep good

records of all director and stock-holder meetings. It is not difficult to keep accurate corporate records. Order the *E-Z Corporate Record Book* from Garrett Publishing, listed in the Appendix. You can also instantly prepare good corporate records with their companion *Corporate Secretary* software.

- You don't identify your business as a corporation: Let creditors know they are dealing with a corporation. This will discourage personal lawsuits from creditors and others who may believe they are dealing with a proprietorship or partnership. Place your corporate name on all signs, letterheads, billheads, checks and everywhere else a business name usually appears. If you use a fictitious name instead of the corporate name, then properly register the fictitious name according to your state laws.

- You haven't kept your corporation in good standing: A corporation dissolved by the state leaves you with no corporation, and in some states, no corporate protection. Pay all necessary taxes and corporate franchise fees to keep your corporation in good standing so it serves as an effective personal shield from business claims. Never voluntarily dissolve a corporation with debts, as these debts are then automatically assumed by you as the stockholder.

- You undercapitalized the corporation: Do you have too little invested in your corporation? Compare the amount you paid for your shares of stock versus funds you loaned to your corporation. A safe ratio? There's no absolute rule in most states, but most lawyers and accountants advise at least $1 invested as equity (for the shares) for every $4 in loans. Some states set minimum capitalization requirements, and you're safe if you follow them.

Set up your corporation so that it legitimately operates as a corporation. Apply these five tests:

- Does your corporation have an actual business address, as well as cancelled checks, to show the corporation paid for its overhead and own expenses?
- Does your corporation have a telephone listed in its name?
- Has a business license been issued to the corporation, if applicable?
- Does your corporation have a bank or checking account?
- Does your corporation transact some business with unaffiliated parties?

Compliance with these few simple points can help prove that your corporation is actually engaged in business and is a legitimate entity separate and apart from you.

Creditors may try to "pierce the corporate veil" and claim the corporation is nothing more than a sham or alter-ego of its principals, but a creditor who asserts this argument has the burden of proof. Courts are reluctant to dismiss the important protection afforded by a corporation, but they have been known to do so when its owners flagrantly ignore the most basic requirements of respecting the corporation as a distinct entity. More commonly, a creditor's lawsuit against its owner-rather than the corporation-is simply a bad faith effort to force the owner to personally defend against the suit, and thus hopefully encourage a settlement. If this happens to you, threaten a countersuit against the creditor and his attorney for frivolous bad faith litigation. Even with the most careful attention to corporate protection you may find yourself personally defending against "bad faith" creditor claims.

SECRET #58

How To Make Yourself An Invisible Shareholder

Shares of stock in a corporation are an asset that your creditors can reach. A good asset protection program will therefore conceal your identity as a shareholder. How can this be accomplished? To start, understand the several giveaways creditors always use to discover who the corporate shareholders are:

- Examination of corporate books-A creditor may subpoena corporate books to determine who the shares of stock have been issued to.
- Bank and credit records-frequently

contain the names of the stockholders of a corporate borrower. Major suppliers may also list the true principals on credit applications. Utility companies also request stockholder information as part of their credit inquiries.
- Licensing applications-are another giveaway. For example, pharmacies must be licensed by boards of pharmacy. Nursing homes, liquor stores, barber and beauty salons are other examples of licensed businesses where ownership disclosure is mandatory.
- Building permits, zoning variances and other municipal applications-frequently require corporate shareholders to be disclosed.
- Corporate tax returns-specifically ask for the names of each stockholder and the percentage of shares each owns. This, of course, is a dead giveaway.
- Personal tax returns-shows dividend income from the corporation. However, a small business corporation seldom issues dividends to its stockholders. More commonly, as evidence of ownership, sophisticated creditors will investigate personal tax returns hoping to find a "pass-through" profit or loss from an "S" corporation.

It is impossible to conceal your stock ownership in a publicly-owned corporation because accurate records are kept by the transfer agent. Here corporate shares are best owned by a "straw", or by a trust, limited partnership or another corporation. In the case of a privately-owned corporation where various records clearly show ownership, the stockholder's best defense is to claim the shares are pledged to a third-party, or that the shares have been recently transferred. Since either action may invite challenge as a fraudulent conveyance, the best course is to properly plan stock ownership before it is issued. A limited partnership or irrevocable trust are two good options. Where husband and wife jointly-owned property is exempt from attachment by state law, co-ownership as tenants-by-the-entirety is a good third option.

To avoid creditor hassles, do more than conceal or protect your stock ownership. When trouble looms, resign as an officer or director of the corporation. Courts are more likely to believe you are not a stockholder if you are not a principal officer or director of the corporation. When creditors discover you are an officer or director of a small closely-held corporation, you also invite investigation into whether you also own stock in the corporation.

Six Ways To Make Your Corporate Shares Worthless To Creditors

With creditors in hot pursuit, quickly sell your stock or bonds in any publicly-owned corporation. A judgment creditor can seize the shares of stock or bonds that you do own. The options open to you as a stockholder of a privately-owned corporation are more numerous:

- Impose transfer restrictions on the shares: Restrictions on transfer generally do not prevent a creditor from seizing your shares, but they may discourage less-knowledgeable or less-aggressive creditors.
- Assess your shares: If you can establish that your shares are not fully paid, or are subject to assessment, the creditor can only claim the shares subject to such obligations. A sufficiently high assessment will wipe out any value the shares may have to creditors
- Issue non-revocable proxies: The fact that the creditor will be unable to vote the shares will certainly diminish the creditor's enthusiasm, lessen the value of the shares, and give the creditor less control.
- Encumber the business: Your shares of stock have no greater value than the value of the business itself. Why offer the creditor a financially healthy company that can be profitably sold or liquidated by the creditor? Offer instead a heavily indebted business that would yield the creditor nothing. This is the "poison pill" strategy that works wonders. Place a "friendly mortgage" against your business assets and you have your "poison pill".
- Pledge the shares: Perhaps you borrowed using your shares as collateral. If the amount borrowed

approaches the value of the shares, the creditor would again be chasing worthless shares.

• Transfer the shares to a limited partnership: Set up a limited partnership and exchange your shares in the corporation for a limited partnership interest. Now the creditor would have to go after the limited partnership interest which is a difficult process. A victory here would give the creditor only a limited partnership interest in a partnership that is a shareholder in a corporation. The creditor gains nothing of value for this effort.

Tip: For maximum protection combine strategies. Best strategy: Keep the shares out of your name to begin with. Your most practical strategy if you now own shares in a public corporation and have creditor problems? Sell the shares. Cash is the easiest asset to protect because there are so many ways it can be spent.

SECRET #60

When The Professional Corporation Can Be A Liability Shield

Are you a physician, dentist, accountant, lawyer, architect, or other professional who operates through a professional corporation? Professional corporations owe their popularity to the fact that their principals can invest more into corporate pension plans than if they were unincorporated.

Since the professional corporation gained its popularity as a tax-saver, few professionals rely on it for liability protection. Professionals are generally unconcerned about ordinary business debts since they only provide services and incur few liabilities. As professionals operating their practice they correctly reason they can still be sued personally for malpractice, and therefore the corporation is of no consequence in protecting them. Malpractice insurance further reduces liability concerns.

The professional corporation can have significant value as an asset protector. A sole practitioner can be the target of a malpractice suit where he himself is negligent, but what about instances where a subordinate or another associate causes injury without negligence on the part of the professional? Here the corporation, not the professional-stockholder, would be the target of the lawsuit since the corporation is the principal who employed the negligent individual.

Large law, accounting, and physician groups that operate as partnerships, or "loose-knit" associations, can equally benefit from corporations. A corporation would insulate each "partner" from the unlimited liability they are exposed to as individuals. Rather than the individuals becoming partners, a safer arrangement would be for each professional to set up a professional corporation. Their respective corporations, in turn, would form the partnership, with each corporation becoming a partner. Should the partnership incur liability, creditors could only reach the assets of the respective partner corporations, rather than the assets of their principals.

Despite this advantage, the professional corporation is not always the corporation of choice. A regular business corporation offers a major advantage over the professional corporation–the professional need not be the stockholder as is required with the professional corporation. For effective asset protection, the shares in the regular corporation can instead be owned by the professional's spouse or another entity, such as a trust, or a limited partnership. This greater protection is possible only when you incorporate as a regular business corporation without restrictions on who its stockholders may be.

How To Escape Corporate Guarantees

Small business owners are frequently asked to personally guarantee corporate obligations. Your guarantees obviously reduce the usefulness of your corporation as a liability insulator. Certain debts, such as bank loans, inevitably require owner guarantees, but you can usually sidestep guarantees for other creditors. However, to avoid guarantor liability on corporate debts you must know how to avoid guarantees in the first place. You must also know how to escape liability on the few guarantees you mistakenly sign. Personal liability on corporate guarantees can be eliminated or limited if you combine common sense with a tough attitude:

- If one supplier demands a guarantee it doesn't mean they all will. A guarantee is only a bargaining point when dickering credit terms. Bluff. Most suppliers will extend some credit to your corporation even when your guarantee is refused. Should a supplier insist on your guarantee, shop around for another supplier with a more lenient credit policy.
- Understand your creditor's position and try to reduce his risk. Your creditor may then forego the guarantee. Example: Without your personal guarantee your supplier may be unwilling to ship $20,000 in credit, but may risk $10,000.
- Offer alternate collateral. Convince your supplier to accept a security interest on assets of the business instead of your personal guarantee. How about a guarantee from an affiliated corporation?
- If you must give a guarantee, negotiate a partial or limited guarantee in place of a full guarantee. Always try to limit your exposure. Will your creditor cancel the guarantee once your business has paid for a number of orders and established a track record? It's an important bargaining point.

Refuse guarantees on past indebtedness. Make it your unshakable policy never to guarantee an existing corporate debt. Nothing is to be gained. If your business falls behind in its payments, or shows other signs of decline, credit managers will plead, promise, threaten and cajole you for your personal guarantee. But why risk your personal assets to back up now shaky corporate obligations? Nor should you become victimized by assumptions your business will make good on its obligations. It may, but then again statistics prove that once a company runs into serious financial difficulty, it seldom revives itself to the point where its debts are fully paid.

Do you have partners? Make certain they also sign on any guarantee. Unless your partners have financial resources equivalent to yours, expect your creditor to most vigorously chase you for payment. Creditors logically go after those with the deepest pockets. It is consoling to know that your partners' pockets are as deep as your own.

Maybe you're one of the many struggling business owners who foolishly signed a few too many guarantees and now wonder how you can best extricate yourself from these obligations. Here are four strategies:

- Verify which obligations are guaranteed. Many individuals never realize they also signed a guarantee along with their original order form or credit application. Confirm with each creditor that no personal guarantee exists, and request copies of any that do.
- Terminate all outstanding guarantees. Guarantees can always be terminated concerning future credit, and all such guarantees should be revoked to prevent further liability once your company begins to falter. Also be certain to cancel your guarantees on future purchases if you sell your business.
- Rapidly pay-down personally guaranteed debts. Your objective: Have guaranteed debts fully satisfied before your company fails. If necessary, keep your floundering business operating until you can fully extinguish all guaranteed debts. Also secure your creditor with a mortgage on business assets. This will give him priority in payment over other creditors and thus reduce the odds he'll have to come after you for payment.
- Negotiate to have your creditor release you of your guarantee while you're in a position to offer concessions from the business. If the creditor is owed $20,000, will he accept $20,000 in return merchandise? Will he accept $10,000 in cash from the business? Will he accept the mortgage on business assets in lieu of your guarantee? If you owe your bank $500,000, will they release you personally if you help them to recover more than they otherwise would from liquidating your business? An important point: Secured lenders typically need an owner's cooperation if they are to recoup as much as possible from the collateral. That cooperation should be coupled with concessions to reduce or eliminate your personal exposure.

What if a creditor or lender who holds your guarantee will not release you in exchange for your cooperation? That creditor may be more responsive to certain actions that threaten his recovery. Example: A threatened Chapter 11 that forestalls foreclosure can quickly dissipate collateral. This is not to your creditor's advantage. There are many possible bargaining chips to coax a creditor to tear up your guarantee. Always use a "carrot and stick" approach when dealing with creditors.

Another strategy: Since you may be forced to pay guaranteed corporate debts from your own pocket, you then have a right of indemnification and reimbursement from the corporation. Why not have your corporation give you an indemnification and security interest on its assets as collateral for the indemnification? This would give you the right to recover reimbursement from the corporation ahead of unsecured creditors. Remember: Bankruptcy courts may set aside your mortgage as an insider preference if the business goes into bankruptcy within a year of the security interest. Secure yourself as far in advance as possible, and also try to liquidate the business under an insolvency proceeding other than bankruptcy. Only a bankruptcy proceeding can threaten your mortgage on the business.

SECRET #62

Nine Liability Traps For Corporate Directors

Corporate directors engage in a hazardous pursuit. Directors incur civil and criminal liability in a wide number of ways, most of which go beyond the negligent management of the corporation. Director negligence, however, still remains the most frequent cause of liability, particularly among directors of publicly-owned corporations. But in addition to possible negligence claims, a corporate director must also be aware of these ten trouble spots:

- **Improper dividends:** When dividends are unlawfully declared, the directors can be liable to creditors for any resulting insolvency of the corporation. Only Delaware permits dividends paid from funds other than earned surplus.

- **Loans to shareholders:** When directors allow the corporation to make loans to an officer or stockholder, the directors may become liable should the borrower fail to repay. The laws on this do vary between states, but directors must be most prudent in authorizing "insider" loans.

- **Unpaid taxes:** Corporate officers are not generally held to be "responsible parties" under the IRS Code, but certain states impose liability for unpaid state taxes on directors. That doesn't mean directors cannot also be liable for unpaid federal withholding taxes. If the IRS can show the directors controlled the funds and determined whether withholding taxes were to be paid, the directors will then be held responsible, along with the corporate officers.

- **Improper payments on dissolution:** It infrequently occurs, but directors can be liable to creditors should they authorize dissolution of the corporation and allow stockholders to receive the proceeds ahead of creditors.

- **Securities violations:** Directors seldom realize it, but they can be liable to investors for false and misleading statements contained in the corporation's prospectus. "Outside" or unaffiliated directors must be particularly scrupulous when verifying the accuracy of registration, as the SEC imposes this special burden upon them. Directors who resign before registration cannot be liable.

- **ERISA:** The Employee Retirement Income Security Act of 1974 imposes penalties against directors of between 5 and 100 percent of the funds involved in a prohibited transaction. Obtain legal counsel's opinion before undertaking any ERISA transaction.

- **Anti-trust violations:** Directors can be personally liable for anti-trust violations that they knew about, or reasonably should have known about, as directors of the corporation. Liability here can be particularly painful as recovery against directors may be triple the actual damages.

- **Civil rights and discrimination violations:** A comparatively new liability source for corporate direc-

tors. Directors, however, can be liable under these statutes when they approve or allow corporate policies that violate these laws.

- **Environmental law violations:** Another rapidly expanding problem for directors of companies committing hazardous waste violation. This is particularly true when the directors know of hazardous waste conditions and take no action to prevent further waste.

SECRET #63

Insurance Every Corporate Director Needs

Because corporate directors face potential liabilities from so many sources, a corporate director today must be adequately protected from any claim.

Knowledgeable directors insist upon indemnification by the corporation for any suit brought against them. To strengthen the indemnification, the company should obtain director liability insurance. Nearly 90 percent of all publicly-owned corporations do provide indemnification and insurance for their boards. A significant number of smaller, privately-owned corporations with outside directors similarly protect their boards. This is of necessity: Few outside directors will serve on corporate boards without insurance. Directors, however, seldom buy their own insurance. The defense of claims is less complicated, tax write-offs of premiums less questionable, and policies less expensive, when the corporation buys insurance for its entire board.

A director is assured of adequate protection only when he knows what to look for in the insurance policy:

- Amount of coverage: In today's litigious society, a policy should provide at least $1 million coverage per occurrence. $5 million or more is appropriate for larger corporations, or for corporations posing excessive risk, such as hazardous waste.
- What are the exclusions? Does the policy include or exclude claims based on dishonesty or fraud? Libel or slander? Violations of SEC law? Insider trading? Other exclusions may refer to pending lawsuits, ERISA, anti-trust and hazardous waste claims. These exclusions may be negotiable, or may be the deciding factor in determining the adequacy of coverage.
- What are the deductibles? Deductibles of $5000 per director, per claim, are common. But other policies use a split deductible approach–95 percent insured and 5 percent uninsured. On a $5 million judgment, this still represents a sizeable $250,000 loss to the director. A conservative fixed-dollar deductible is the only safe approach.

Even when these points are satisfactory other booby traps can exist:

- Is there required notification to the directors upon cancellation of the policy?
- Is there supplemental insurance to cover deductibles, exclusions and other lapses in policy coverage?
- Do the corporate by-laws provide for indemnification and company payment of the premiums?
- Is the insurance placed with a well-rated and financially-stable underwriter?
- Has the policy been reviewed and approved by both the company's attorney and your attorney? Remember, your interests differ from those of the company. Make certain you have the protection you need before you serve as a director.

SECRET #6

Little-Known Corporate Obligations That Can Snare You

Guaranteed corporate debts, or liability as a director, are hardly the only obligations for which you can be held personally responsible. Other debts can also impose personal liability on corporate officers, directors or stockholders:

- Unpaid withholding taxes: Corporate officers (ordinarily the president and treasurer) are automatically responsible for unpaid "trust" taxes–withholding taxes deducted from the employees' gross pay. There is no personal responsibility for the non-trust taxes–the taxes contributed by the business as the employer. There may also be corresponding liability for state withholding taxes, sales, meals and similar taxes. Check with your accountant or counsel concerning personal liability on the various fiduciary taxes. This will vary between states.

- Unpaid wages: Failure to pay all wages can also subject corporate officers to civil or criminal liability, depending upon state law. There may even be a duty to pay for severance pay, accrued vacation, and other "earned" time.

It would seem that these obligations would not cause significant personal liability, but that is not the case. Unpaid withholding taxes can quickly turn into a six figure personal liability for an officer of even a modest-sized business. Smart business owners realize the inevitable personal consequences of not paying payroll taxes and give these taxes top priority for payment.

If you cannot pay all of the withholding taxes, then at least send the IRS the funds to cover the "trust" portion. To insure that the funds are to be applied to the "trust" rather than "non-trust" portion, you must mark on the check that it is to be so applied. Unless you designate how your payment will be applied, the IRS will apply it to the "non-trust" taxes. This allows the

IRS to later proceed against the officers personally for the remaining "trust" taxes due, should the business not pay.

Because personal liability from unpaid withholding taxes is so common and serious a problem for owners of failing businesses, only one spouse–not both–should serve as an officer of the corporation. The IRS would then have recourse only against that one spouse. The other spouse can then remain a safe repository for the family assets.

- Bad checks: If you issue a bad check you may, in a number of states, be personally liable, even if you sign the check in your corporate capacity. Generally, these laws only apply to C.O.D. purchases rather than "on account" payments.
- Unemployment compensation: A number of states hold corporate officers responsible if the corporation has not made the required payments under unemployment law.

Check your state laws to determine whether you are individually responsible for these obligations, and, of course, give them priority for payment if you are. Some states hold corporate officers criminally liable for non-payment of unemployment compensation, sales and withholding taxes, wages, and bad checks. In these instances the court commonly orders restitution or payment. Review this with your attorney so you can determine which obligations carry the most severe sanctions, and thus require priority in payment.

How Your Corporation Can Shield Personal Assets

Business owners commonly throw a mortgage against their business assets to serve as a shield against creditor actions, but seldom are corporations used as the mortgage holder to shield personal assets.

This requires reverse-thinking. Your business corporation can legally secure itself with your personal assets if you owe the business money. The corporation may take a mortgage on your home, personal property such as a car or boat, or even accept a "blanket" mortgage on all your property. Should you later run into personal problems, the mortgage held by your corporation can effectively insulate your personal assets from other creditors. Of course, you must make certain the shares in your corporation are titled in another name so your personal creditor cannot take control of your corporation.

Caution: When you use this strategy, make certain your corporation remains financially strong. You, obviously, do not want your corporation going into bankruptcy, and your loan into the hands of a bankruptcy trustee who will chase you for payment. Use a shell or dormant corporation that has little chance of failure. This usually means one with relatively little business activity.

How To Take More Tax-Free Money Out Of Your Corporation

Asset protection is only one possible benefit of incorporating. But you may not know that the easiest and quickest way for a successful businessperson to save tax dollars may be to incorporate? How can incorporating help save you taxes and provide greater asset protection?

- Corporate tax rates are lower than corresponding individual rates up to $150,000 in taxable income.
- A salary for services is the usual way to get money from your corporation. But be careful that you don't draw too much as salary. The corporation has already paid taxes on its profits so you don't want to pay higher personal taxes as well!
- Fringe benefits are tax-free to the corporation's employees, but are deductible expenses for the corporation. Health, disability and life insurance, tuition, education and training, and travel and club memberships are only a few fringes with advantageous tax benefits for both the corporation and its employees. Company automobiles, airplanes, condominiums, and other benefits may also be tax deductible perks.
- Consider deferred fringe benefits. The corporation receives a deduc-

Asset Protection Secrets 83

tion for its contributions to pension and profit-sharing plans, and you get the tax-free trust funds for a wealthier retirement. These pensions are normally judgment-proof.

- Why not arrange interest-bearing loans from your corporation? A promissory note will establish that the loan was not a gift. Arrange for periodic repayment, and deal with the corporation as you would another creditor.

- Leasing can also save you significant taxes. A family partnership, for instance, may purchase property and lease it to the corporation at a fair price. The corporation deducts the rent paid to the partnership as a business expense. The composition of the partnership is also important. Taxpayers in higher brackets should be involved if the partnership can show a loss. Those in lower brackets and who can absorb a gain should be involved if the partnership is profitable.

- A corporation enjoying high past earnings, a promising future, and no plan to invest its earnings, should file an "S" corporation election. This will pass any gain or loss directly to individual taxpayers, and eliminates the double taxation of a regular corporation and its stockholders.

These few examples hardly cover all tax-saving opportunities. With the help of your tax advisor, you can plan your own best personal tax strategy for taking money out of your corporation, keeping the corporation financially solvent, legally avoiding excessive taxation, and insuring yourself greater asset protection.

SECRET #67

How Your Corporation Can Achieve Your Estate Planning Objectives

Long-term corporate planning goes beyond estate planning. Estate planning, by itself, is done in contemplation of death, and such planning has tax implications that don't apply with corporate planning or asset protection. Long-term corporate planning contemplates death of its principals, but also protects your shares of stock from your creditors–as well as helping you to avoid probate taxes. With proper long-term corporate planning, your estate is consumed by neither legal expenses nor taxes.

How is this accomplished? Since corporations do not cease to exist when a stockholder dies, a strategic long-term corporate plan can both protect your stock ownership and pass this ownership on to your heirs. Follow this plan:

- Organize a corporation, which when formed is a "corporate shell" without assets or liabilities. Its stock, of course, is worthless at this point.
- Sell this worthless stock from the corporation to your heirs for one cent per share (or other nominal amount). Since the stock has been

sold, it's not a gift and subject to gift tax.

- Form a limited partnership. You should be the general partner and your heirs the limited partners. The only purpose of this limited partnership is to own the shares in your corporation. Remember: In a limited partnership the general partner manages the business and the limited partners have no managerial authority, function or responsibility. Since the purpose of this limited partnership is to own the shares in this new corporation, this means you as the general partner must exclusively vote the shares on behalf of the partnership at any stockholders' meeting.
- The stockholders would next transfer their newly-acquired stock into the limited partnership. In exchange you become a one percent general partner and a one percent limited partner. Your heirs would become 98 percent limited partners. As the general partner, however, you continue to manage the business and vote the shares at any shareholders' meeting.
- The limited partnership has a fixed duration, and will exist for this period. Its duration depends on you. Specify a long-term so that when the limited partnership terminates you will no longer be in a position to control the corporation.
- The limited partnership should be drafted to end with the death of any general partner so upon your

death the limited partnership would terminate. Your other partners (your heirs) can then take their 98 percent of the shares in the corporation without probate. Only your small two percent of the shares will go through probate. Your heirs thus own the shares, but you, as general partner, completely control the corporation.
- Finally, transfer your personal assets into the corporation in exchange for a demand promissory note with a long maturity. You can then use corporate funds for note payments. Satisfy the IRS. Have your note provide that in the event of your death, any funds still due you by the corporation are cancelled. The demand promissory note should bear at least 10 percent interest. Pay yourself the interest when due. The corporation, in turn, obtains the funds to pay the interest from the personal assets you transferred to the corporation. The interest received by you will be taxable, but this is a small price to pay for such big benefits.

The bottom line: When you pass on your heirs already own what you want to leave them. Moreover, because the shares are owned by a limited partnership, creditors of any stockholder have no practical recourse to them. This is an intelligent strategy for anyone interested in combining creative estate planning with smart asset protection.

How To Avoid The Personal Holding Corporation Danger

The idea of a corporation formed primarily to hold assets for protection purposes rightfully concerns many accountants and attorneys who worry about the personal income and personal holding corporation trap that can cause you big tax problems.

This is a very legitimate concern, but it need not be a problem if the stockholders involved have the business savvy to follow a simple corporate strategy. The tactic simply involves two corporations. Whenever you are approaching an undesirable percentage of passive income (60 percent), have the other corporation transact some business with the passive income corporation. For example, they may purchase or sell certain items or services between them. This feeds active income into the corporation so that it cannot be classified as a personal holding corporation by the IRS. Ingenuity and some legitimate business transactions provide a simple solution to what appears an impossible problem.

A personal holding company arises when 60 percent or more of a corporation's adjusted ordinary gross income is personal holding company income. Personal holding company income (or passive income) may consist of dividends, interest, certain royalties, gains on sale of stock, income from personal service contracts and rents.

The tax on undistributed personal holding company income has been reduced in recent years, but there are still exceptionally high current taxes to pay when compared to holding your assets in a trust or partnership. This fear of "holding company" tax treatment often discourages use of the corporation as a vehicle to hold assets, but this need not be a concern. You can have your corporation safely protect your assets and at the same time provide you the tax and estate planning benefits you want.

Key Secrets To Remember

• A corporation is as useful an asset protection device as are limited partnerships and trusts.

• If your business is presently unincorporated, it may not be too late to incorporate and take advantage of the limited liability only a corporation offers.

• A corporation can be a safe harbor for virtually any asset, but it's best for business-related assets.

• Nevada offers many advantages over Delaware as a foreign state in which to incorporate, but your own state is usually your best alternative.

• You can intelligently and safely loan money to your own corporation, but you must know how to protect both your loan and your business.

• An "S" corporation offers as much liability protection as a regular "C" corporation. Elect your form of incorporation based on taxes, not liability.

- Treat your corporation as a corporation, otherwise you may lose its protection.
- Be an invisible shareholder. That means legally concealing your ownership interest from creditors.
- Avoid personal liability for corporate debts. Know what corporate debts you can be liable for, and how to sidestep these danger zones. This applies to you as a corporate director as well as a corporate officer or stockholder.

7 HOW TO GAIN TOTAL FINANCIAL SECURITY THROUGH A LIMITED PARTNERSHIP

Asset protection professionals agree that the limited partnership is one of the most effective devices you can use to stop creditors from pursuing your assets. They are absolutely correct. A limited partnership offers two unique and highly beneficial asset protection features: 1) As a general partner you retain total control over partnership assets, and 2) Assets placed in the partnership are safe from the creditors of any limited partner.

There are other advantages to a limited partnership. Estate planning is one. Example: If a parent serves as a general partner and owns a part interest in the partnership, then inheritance and estate taxes are assessed only in proportion to the actual partnership interest owned. This is true even if the parent as its general partner enjoys full control over the partnership and its assets. This, of course, permits maximum discretion and flexibility concerning investment decisions, while simultaneously limit-ing estate taxes on larger estates.

Partnerships are usually thought of as an entity to own and operate a business. As with a corporation, it is difficult to view a partnership as a way to own personal assets - such as a family home. But the fact is that the limited partnership, properly used and designed, is one of the safest, most effective asset protectors.

Asset Saving Features Of Limited Partnerships Over Regular Partnerships

To start, it is important to distinguish a limited partnership from the more common general partnership or regular partnership.

A general partnership is more popular

than limited partnerships. A general partnership occurs when two or more individuals engage in an undertaking with the agreement they shall share profits and losses, whether equally or not. In a general partnership the partners have equal authority to manage and act on behalf of the partnership interest.

The chief disadvantage of the general partnership? The partners are jointly and severally liable for all partnership debts. As a partner in a general partnership, you can lose all your personally-owned property to creditors of the partnership. The partnership creditors would have full recourse against your assets even if your partners had no assets from which to satisfy business obligations. Your partner may have caused the liability, however, this wouldn't diminish your financial responsibility to pay the claim.

General partnerships serve no role in asset protection. Creditors of a general partner can too easily reach their partnership interest. Moreover, because each partner can be held liable for all partnership obligations, the general partnership can create considerably more liability than it can protect against.

In contrast, a limited partnership has one or more general partners, and one or more limited partners. The general partners have total responsibility for the management of the enterprise. The limited partners, on the other hand, must remain passive and play absolutely no role in the management of the partnership. As long as the limited partners refrain from management participation they will be free from liability on partnership obligations. Their involvement in this instance is comparable to that of a corporate stockholder, except that a stockholder may participate in the management of the corporation.

The Revised Uniform Limited Partnership Act defines a person as a natural person, partnership, limited partnership, trust, estate, association or corporation. Any of these entities may serve either as a general partner or limited partner. Because a general partner, unlike a limited partner, is liable for partnership obligations, it is safest for a corporation to serve as the general partner. This insulates the involved individuals from personal liability and the possibility of lost personal assets.

Both general and limited partners can own interests in the limited partnership. The rights of a limited partner are also similar to the rights of a stockholder. The limited partner has rights to an accounting, to inspect partnership books, and obtain important information on partnership affairs. The limited partner also has the right to receive a proportionate share of the net partnership income when it becomes available for distribution as determined by the general partner. Finally, the limited partner has a right to a proportionate share of the net proceeds for partners upon liquidation of the partnership.

A limited partner, like a stockholder, has his liability limited only to the amount invested in the venture. A limited partner incurs none of the general liability of a general partner unless the limited partner assumes a role in the management of the partnership. However, even slight management participation can render a limited partner liable. Using the limited partner's name in the partnership can, for example, make the limited partner liable to creditors who relied on the representation to extend credit. To enjoy limited liability, the limited partner must undertake absolutely no involvement in the partnership other than those specifically enumerated in the partnership agreement.

SECRET #70

How To Organize Your Limited Partnership For Maximum Protection

It is comparatively simple to organize a limited partnership. To draft the articles of partnership you include:

- Name, address, purpose and duration of the partnership.
- The capital contribution of each partner.
- The percentile distribution of profits and losses among partners.
- The respective duties and responsibilities of the general and limited partners.
- General partner compensation.
- Provisions for death, retirement, incapacity or bankruptcy of general and limited partners.
- Provisions for the termination and liquidation of the partnership.

Once prepared, partnership articles are recorded in the public records in accordance with state law. Most states have adopted the Uniform Limited Partnership Act in its original or revised form, although several states have adopted their own limited partnership laws. California, for instance, drafted its law which differs considerably from the Revised Uniform Limited Partnership Act. In California, and several other states with their own laws, a limited partnership is treated more like a corporation. They tend to grant the limited partners the many advantages of corporate stockholders, but without taxing the partnership as a corporation.

How should your limited partnership be organized? If you are married, you may serve as general partner, and both you and your spouse may be limited partners. If you have children, consider giving them a gift interest. If you are unmarried, you may serve as general partner and your limited partners can be those relatives or friends who may be your intended beneficiaries. These, of course, are only suggestions. Remember: It is not necessary for natural persons to serve as either general or limited partners. A corporation, trust, or other general or limited partnership can be a general or limited partner. You have considerable flexibility to satisfy both your estate planning and asset protection objectives with a limited partnership. Obviously, you want to give the more vulnerable partner the smallest partnership interest. If it is the husband, then he may own a 2 percent interest while the other family members divide the remaining 98 percent.

"Family" limited partnership is a term you may come across. This is the same as a regular limited partnership. The name is simply a convenient way to separate a family-owned and controlled partnership as distinguished from the thousands of limited partnerships organized before the 1986 Tax Reform Act. Limited partnerships then were popular tax shelters for wealthy investors seeking tax losses, as substantial partnership losses were then available to the limited partners for tax deduction. Unfortunately, these benefits disappeared with the 1986 tax law revisions, and with it the popularity of the limited partnership. It is now regaining its popularity as an asset protection device.

How To Safely Transfer Assets To Your Limited Partnership

How do you transfer exposed personal assets from yourself to the limited partnership, or to your partnership from your other entities?

You can directly transfer to your limited partnership virtually any personal asset, such as a home, cash, investment securities, or even a 100 percent stock interest in a closely-held family corporation. In exchange, you would receive a limited partnership interest in the partnership. Cash contributions can also be treated as loans, but this offers no protection since a creditor can then reach the loan proceeds due you. Consider two other possibilities:

- Liquidate your operating corporation and donate its assets to the limited partnership. First, transfer all the corporation's assets to yourself in exchange for re-transfer of the corporate shares back to the corporation. Next, donate these same assets to the limited partnership. This increases the basis of the general partner's capital account in the partnership, and also remains a tax-free transaction, provided the corporation has a positive net worth.

- Alternatively, you may directly contribute your company shares to the limited partnership. This too presents no tax problems as the corporation remains intact while the limited partnership becomes its shareholder.

Partners in a limited partnership can allocate their percentage ownership interests in any manner they desire. This is a very important feature in asset protection. You may, for instance, contribute most of the assets to the partnership and receive in exchange the smallest partnership share. Think about it in terms of creditor protection. You may donate your home and other significant personal assets to the partnership, and accept in return only a negligible one or two percent partnership interest. The remaining partnership interest can be owned by your spouse and/or children, or one or more of the various estate planning trusts. Your advisors can help you to structure your partnership advantageously. The overriding asset protection strategy, is that you own only a negligible partnership interest. This gives negligible rights to any creditor who pursues that partnership interest.

How A Limited Partnership Protects Your Assets

In considering the limited partnership, the two central questions are: 1) How does a limited partnership protect assets? and 2) How much protection does a limited partnership provide? To answer these two questions, review again the position of the limited partner in the limited partnership. Only then can you fully understand the futility of a creditor who attempts to satisfy his claim through a limited partnership interest. This creditor of a limited partner has only three options:

- Seek to attach or levy upon the debtor's profits from the limited partnership,
- Try to reach the debtor's share of the partnership proceeds once the partnership is liquidated and the debtor-partner's interest in the partnership's remaining surplus, after payment of all partnership debts, is distributed to the partner, or
- Attempt to seize the partnership interest itself.

Let's examine each of these remedies. The first remedy is usually meaningless because partnership profits can be illusive, particularly when the limited partnership is a family affair and the interests of the participants are closely aligned. For example, the general partners can easily vote themselves a bonus, or pay themselves more salary, insuring no surplus is available to pay profits. A limited partnership in this respect is very much like the family-owned corporation. Dividends are rarely paid and can arbitrarily be stopped when they are. Surplus funds that otherwise would be paid to stockholders as dividends, can as easily be taken out of the corporation - or partnership - as salaries, bonuses, loans, or subcontractor or vendor payments. In sum: The creditor waiting for dividends to be paid can be in for a long, frustrating and profitless wait.

Consider the creditor's second remedy: Waiting for the dissolution of the partnership. It's no brighter. Since payment of liquidation proceeds to the creditor requires dissolution of the partnership, it is again a situation entirely beyond the creditor's control, and one entirely within the control of the debtor and his family.

Most partnerships have a perpetual existence and are only terminated when the partners decide to terminate. Partnerships are not frequently dissolved. The partners may even keep the partnership intact until the creditor's judgment expires. Bear in mind that a creditor can do absolutely nothing to compel partners to either pay dividends or liquidate the partnership and pay net proceeds to the partner - or his creditor.

The third remedy, seizure of the limited partner's interest, is an even more interesting remedy than the first two. In theory, a creditor has recourse against a limited partnership interest. A judgment creditor of a limited partner can obtain from the courts a so-called charging order. A charging order "charges" the limited partner's interest in the partnership with payment of the judgment.

A charging order's central purpose is to protect partners that are not involved in the debts of the debtor-partner. If the charging order does not produce payment, the court may, on request of the creditor, appoint a receiver to collect profits or liquidation proceeds due the debtor. The involvement of a receiver, however, does nothing more to extract payment than what the creditor could do on his own. This, of course, is virtually nothing.

What is a charging order that the creditor receives, and what powers are gained from it? The Uniform Limited Partnership Act, in effect in most states, makes provision for the "charging order". Where it is in effect, the charging order is the exclusive remedy of the creditor and can only be opposed by the debtor and no other partners.

The court can order the interest of the limited partner sold at public auction to satisfy the claim. But this remedy also has practical limitations: First, any one or more of the partners can purchase, with their own funds, the debtor-partner's interest. Alternatively, the remaining partners can purchase the debtor-partner's interest on behalf of the partnership using partnership funds.

To counteract the possibility of abuse, the court can fix the value of the limited partner's interest to prevent it from being fraudulently acquired by the other partners for an amount well below its actual value. Still, this amount may also be far less than the amount of the creditor's judgment. A family limited partnership generally has little value, and it is remarkably easy for general partners to dissipate the net worth the partnership does have. Moreover, the debtor would own only a small interest in the partnership. The debtor-partner - or his creditor - would hold nothing of great value, even if the partnership enjoyed a significant net worth and high profitability.

There are other defensive plays: The remaining partners may satisfy the creditor's claim by making payment to the creditor below the value of the debtor-partner's share, with the payment construed as a loan against the debtor's interest. The debtor-partner does not lose his partnership interest but must eventually repay the loan.

A more extreme measure is for a debtor-partner, with cooperative partners, to liquidate the partnership and re-purchase the assets at a low liquidation price through a new entity in which the debtor has no ostensible interest. Even when the partners do nothing to protect the debtor-partner's interest, the creditor may still be quite far from turning the partnership interest into payment.

At a foreclosure sale only the debtor-partner's interest is sold. But this has a limited value because the limited partner cannot assert management authority and must remain passive. Moreover, most limited partnerships are family affairs and this can create an uncomfortable environment for outsiders. Even if the creditor acquires the debtor-partner's interest, the creditor can still only obtain payments from profits that the general partners elect to distribute.

By acquiring the debtor's interest at forced sale, the creditor does gain the debtor's entire financial interest in the partnership. This extends to both dividends, when distributed, and any surplus upon winding up. But the creditor gains only these rights, and gains no other rights of the limited partner.

The debtor-limited-partner continues to be a partner in all respects except for the right to receive dividends or payment upon distribution. The creditor clearly has something, but whether it has any real value is doubtful.

From the debtor's position, the limited partnership shields the partnership interest from all but the most determined creditor. A creditor must overcome many barriers before there is even a possibility of some recovery. As a practical matter, few creditors are so determined. Most forfeit their claim rather than spend time and effort on a situation that produces so little in return.

The limited partnership also differs from most other asset protection strategies in another important respect: When property is put in trust or gifted to a third-party, the creditor may have a clear shot at the asset by claiming it to be a fraudulent conveyance. The creditor has good reason to challenge the transfer, because he wins 100 percent of the transferred asset should he prevail. With a limited partnership there is nothing worthwhile to attack. All the creditor has before him is a thicket of obstacles. Because a debtor-limited partner owns a very small ownership interest when compared to his contribution to the partnership, it does not mean that the transfer was necessarily fraudulent. The creditor, then, will have no chance of recovering the conveyed assets, but must settle for the limited partnership interest and a meaningless victory.

Four More Ways To Totally Frustrate Creditors

There are a variety of interesting ways to make a limited partnership interest even less attractive to creditors. Four highly-effective strategies to consider:

- Make the creditor aware that the limited partnership shall withhold all income distributions. The obvious result: The creditor will not receive any payment. Once satisfied this is true, the creditor will likely negotiate a favorable settlement. A creditor's attorney must oftentimes explain the hopelessness of the situation to the creditor, and a knowledgeable creditor's attorney will communicate that fact.

- A second creditor booby-trap: As assignee of the debtor's interest in the partnership, the creditor can be forced to personally pay all income taxes due from the seized partnership interest - even if the creditor received no payment. The creditor is then forced to pay money when his objective was to receive money. The partnership agreement should contain a provision that at the election of the general partners, the limited partners will pay their proportionate share of tax on any profit-whether or not they actually received the profit. This will greatly discourage a creditor who now sees the partnership interest as a *liability* rather than an asset. This strategy is even effective when the IRS is the creditor as they may find they're paying taxes to themselves on income they never received.

- Dissipate partnership equity *before* the creditor liens the partnership interest. Mortgage or sell the assets and make a distribution to partners. With little net worth in the partnership, there will be little net worth flowing to the judgment creditor. This tactic is advisable when all the partners are cooperative and the debtor has a sizeable interest.

- Investigate state law. Some states more completely protect limited partnership interests than do others. California, for example, prevents a creditor of a limited partner from seizing the partnership interest unless consented to by all other partners. This one law makes a California limited partnership a veritable fortress. Tip: You are not obligated to establish your limited partnership in your state. As with a corporation, you can establish your limited partnership in a state that offers greater protection. California is that state.

How To Avoid General Partner Liability

Because a limited partnership offers its limited partners complete safety from partnership debts, as a limited partner you will want to avoid any action that will change that status and expose you to unlimited liability. What can a limited partner safely do?

- Work as an employee or independent contractor of the limited partnership.
- Work as an employee or independent contractor of the general partner.
- Vote on amendments to the partnership agreement.
- Guarantee partnership debts.
- Vote on: 1) Dissolution of the partnership, 2) The sale, lease, exchange or encumbering of assets outside the ordinary course of business, 3) Changing the nature of the business, 4) Removing a general partner.

A limited partner cannot give orders or directives to the general manager, however, a limited partner can provide an advisory opinion. Finally, the limited partner's name cannot be part of the partnership name, nor can the limited partner in any other way create the inference the limited partner owns or is associated with the business, although the limited partner is, in fact, an owner.

If you are a general partner, then it is safest to incorporate for that purpose. Your corporation rather than you personally will then incur liability for the debts of the partnership. Concern over liability, is, of course, greatly mitigated if the partnership is to be used solely for purposes of owning, managing and investing family wealth. There is then little risk. But if you do contemplate business activities, confine these liability-producing activities to a separate limited partnership, or preferably a corporation where liability exposure would cause the least damage.

How To Maximize The Limited Partnership's Tax Benefits

As with general partnerships and "S" corporations, a limited partnership enjoys the benefits of profits taxed only once - upon its distribution to the limited partners who each pay income tax on the income. The regular "C" corporation has its profits taxed twice - once when it is earned as profits by the corporation and again as dividend income to the shareholders. A limited partnership, however, can lose its tax advantage and be taxed as a regular "C" corporation. The first situation is when the limited partnership violates its state laws on limited partnerships. Fortunately, state disqualifications of limited partnerships are rare.

A more common situation is where the limited partnership has a corporation as a general partner, and also has fewer assets than liabilities. To operate, confident it will not lose its single taxation status, the limited partnership must then have at least one non-incorporated general partner. The primary reason for using a corporation as a general partner is to avoid individual liability for partnership debts. A natural person as a general partner limits the value of the partnership in asset protection. However, the use of a corporation as a general partner is only necessary when the partnership engages in liability-producing activity. If the limited partnership is used solely to hold and manage passive assets and investments, risk is less an issue and individuals can safely serve as general partners.

Keep several other tax issues in mind when organizing and managing your limited partnership:

- The combined interests of general partners must be at least one percent of each - operating income and loss, and capital gain and loss.
- A limited partnership pays no income tax. All income and losses pass through to each individual partner - whether as a general partner or limited partner - who declares the profit or loss on his own return.
- Distributions to limited and general partners can be in any proportion desired. It need not coincide with either the amount invested or the percentage ownership. This can be a major plus in asset protection: You may, for example, agree to less income and grant other family members a disproportionately large share of the income.

• A partner's share of partnership operating losses, to be taken as a deduction on a personal return, are limited by the "at risk" provisions of the IRS Code. These provisions limit the deductibility of a partner's share of any loss to the amount invested, or what the partner could lose from the partnership - such as a guarantee on a partnership obligation.

Key Secrets To Remember

• A limited partnership is an excellent vehicle for sheltering both personal and family assets from creditors.

• Individuals with liability concerns should own only a small percentage of the partnership, as this is all that would be then exposed to his creditors. Other family members can receive the remaining interest. The debtor could still control the partnership by becoming the general partner.

• There are a number of possible strategies to frustrate the efforts of a creditor seeking debt satisfaction through a debtor's limited partnership interest.

• If you want to avoid the liability of a general partner, refrain from participating in the management of the partnership.

• A limited partnership can offer you tax advantages as well as liability protection.

• Investigate a California limited partnership. It can offer more protection than limited partnerships organized in other states.

8 TACTICS, TECHNIQUES AND STRATEGIES WITH ASSET PROTECTION TRUSTS

Trusts come in a wide variety and are used for many different purposes. Some trusts are used to keep assets private and out of the probate court. Others serve to hold property for minors or incompetent adults. Still others reduce or eliminate taxes. There are also trusts to protect assets against litigation, creditors, divorce, or other claims. These are the trusts we will focus on in this chapter so you can see how they can be used to your advantage in asset protection.

A trust is an easy legal concept to understand. Trusts are created by a settlor, grantor or trustor (the terms are interchangeable) who provides the funds, or other property, to be held in trust. As creator of the trust, the grantor also establishes the terms under which the donated assets shall be managed and eventually distributed.

The grantor also names a trustee(s). In some cases this is the grantor himself.

Finally, the grantor of the trust names beneficiaries who are to receive the benefit of the trust and eventually receive its assets. The grantor may simultaneously be both trustee and beneficiary. This, for example, is true with the popular living trust. However, this arrangement is not acceptable with trusts used in asset protection. Here the trustee must be someone other than the beneficiary.

Trusts can also be loosely classified. Living trusts, for example, as implied by its name, are set up during the grantor's life, and hence are classified as inter vivos trusts. Trusts that become activated upon death are classified as testamentary trusts.

Another way to classify trusts is either as revocable or irrevocable. A revocable trust can be changed or revoked during the grantor's lifetime. An irrevocable trust cannot. Let's investigate how each of these trusts can be used in your asset protection program?

How To Create A Creditor-Proof Trust

The irrevocable trust is the trust favored in asset protection because it provides a high degree of protection from creditors. To insure safety, the transfer of assets into the trust must also be made under such circumstances that it cannot be set aside as a fraudulent conveyance and thereby defeat its asset protection objective.

The irrevocable trust, as its name suggests, is one that cannot be later revoked or rescinded by the grantor. This means that once you establish and fund the trust, you forever abandon your rights to reclaim your property. In sum: With the transfer of assets to an irrevocable trust you lose both control and ownership of the property. These are serious considerations.

Because the irrevocable trust deprives you of control, you also lose the right to receive income, and also the right to sell or dispose of the property. For these reasons, consider an irrevocable trust only when you have sufficient additional assets or independent sources of income for financial security after you transfer your assets into the trust. Be objective. Carefully analyze your needs and resources before you act!

An irrevocable trust, like other trusts, can own any type property, but it should only hold property that adds value to the trust. The trustees management decisions must follow the prudent investor rule and be guided by the investment objectives stated in the trust. You can safely make an outright gift of property to the trust, or even sell assets to the trust if it has accumulated sufficient assets to pay you. But to be effective as an asset protector, the irrevoca-ble trust must be correctly organized and oper-ated in five important ways:

- The grantor cannot reserve any power to revoke, rescind, or amend the trust. The trust should explicitly provide that it cannot be rescinded, amended, or revoked by the grantor.
- The grantor can retain no rights, either directly or indirectly, to reclaim proper-ty once transferred to the trust. All con-veyances to the trust must be absolute and unconditional, with no strings attached.
- The grantor cannot assert any authori-ty on how the property will be man-aged or invested, or whether trust property should be sold or retained. These decisions must be delegated exclusively to the trustee.
- The grantor cannot assert any authori-ty over income generated from the trust property, or how the income will be distributed, except as initially pro-vided in the trust.
- The grantor cannot serve as trustee, nor appoint as trustee one who is not considered arms-length. Courts closely examine the relationship between grantor and trustee to determine whether the trustee is only the grantor's alter ego.

In sum, the protection provided by your trust will depend on the degree to which you relin-quish control. The more control you retain, the greater the likelihood creditors can reach assets transferred to the trust. Conversely, lesser con-trol means less chance your creditors can suc-cessfully attack the trust assets.

Why Your Revocable Trust Offers You No Protection

A revocable trust, or "nominee" trust as it is often called, is a considerably more common type of trust–only because it is revocable and thus allows the grantor the comfort of changing his mind. Such trusts are useful for estate and tax planning purposes, but a revocable trust is inadequate for asset protection. Creditors of the grantor can generally reach assets transferred to the revocable trust with the same ease they can attach assets in the name of the grantor.

The grantor, by reserving the right to revoke the trust, also reserves the power to take the property back from the trust. Therefore, the grantor's creditors, who literally stand in the grantor's position, can compel the grantor to re-transfer the trust assets for their benefit.

The rights of a grantor's creditors to property placed in a revocable trust differ among states. A few states provide that in the absence of a fraudulent transfer the grantor's creditors cannot reach the conveyed assets, even though the grantor reserved the right to revoke the trust and income from the trust.

In most states, the outcome depends on whether the grantor retained a general power of appointment as to the remainder, coupled with a life estate. This combination of powers has been viewed by several courts as tantamount to property in the name of the grantor. In these states, and probably all states, it's unwise to retain both powers.

Either a life estate or power of appointment standing alone doesn't trigger the same result. A life estate would nevertheless be an asset in a bankruptcy proceeding. It would then go to the creditors of the debtor. The bankruptcy trustee can also assert any other right, or claim to any other interest in the trust, whether present or future, actual or contingent, that the bankrupt grantor reserved.

If a grantor transfers assets into a revocable trust and reserves the right to revoke the trust, or control the disposition of principal and interest, the grantor's creditors, either by common law or statute, can reach the assets transferred to the trust. Generally, the grantor's creditors must first proceed against assets in the debtor's name. Only when these assets cannot satisfy the claims can the creditors look to the revocable trust property.

These situations assume that the transfer to the trust was not fraudulent. The rights of creditors, in these instances, are not based upon the circumstances surrounding the transfer, but upon the powers of the grantor in respect to assets now in the trust. The predominant number of cases allow creditors of the grantor to reach revocable trust assets. Avoid a revocable trust if you want conclusive protection from creditors. The irrevocable trust remains the only trust that affords you reasonable protection.

Two circumstances exist when revocable trusts can effectively be used as an asset protector. First, when the trust is used to shield property from an IRS lien. If property is transferred to the revocable trust before the lien is filed, the property will not be subject to the lien and can be later sold or transferred without the cloud of a lien.

Why can't the IRS recover property in the trust as can a private claimant? The answer is that the IRS can. The difference is that the IRS rarely pursues transferred property, even when there is a likelihood of recovery. A private litigant, less entangled bureaucratically, is far more likely to attack property exposed in a revocable trust. Notwithstanding IRS lethargy, shelter property, particularly real estate, in an irrevocable trust rather than rely upon the tenuous protection of a revocable trust–even when you owe the IRS.

The second possible use of a revocable trust offers considerably greater safety. Here you and your spouse each sets up revocable trusts but transfers into the spouse's trust his or her own property. You no longer control the property you previously owned, and your creditor can't easily reach assets in your spouse's trust.

Revocable trusts have become popularized with the living trust (or "loving" trust), which is, of course, usually nothing more than a revocable trust. The living trust is useful as a way to avoid the expense, delay and notoriety of probate. It offers neither tax advantages or disadvantages. Nor does it offer significant asset protection, other than in the two stated instances, unless it is an irrevocable living trust.

![SECRET #78]

Why You Cannot Trust Your Business Trust

Once popular, business trusts are no longer common either for transacting business or for asset protection. But since they have been around for many, many years they must be discussed. The business trust is designed to engage in a business activity and produce an operating profit. Other conventional trusts, in contrast, generally hold and invest assets for passive income.

By definition, a business trust is an association, (1) where trustees hold properties and business assets, (2) of an active, operating business that they manage and are responsible for as trustees, (3) under the terms of a trust agreement, (4) for shareholders who are the beneficial owners of the trust and share its income and sales proceeds. Therefore, the business trust more closely resembles a corporation than a conventional investment trust. What then, are the advantages and disadvantages of a business trust over a corporation?

One advantage of a business trust is that it may be more easily organized since it requires nothing more than formation of an agreement of trust. This is an entirely private agreement between the parties. A corporation, in contrast, is chartered by the state. While the process of incorporating is not difficult, it does place on public record the names of its officers and directors, and possibly the shareholders. Since the business trust does not involve public filings, its trustees and shareholders remain private. This is helpful in asset protection.

In terms of regulation and taxation, there's not always an advantage with a business trust over a corporation. Many states tax and regulate the two entities alike. In some states you escape corporate taxes with a business trust.

On the other hand, a business trust can

pose a considerable disadvantage to its shareholders: The shareholders may be personally liable for debts of the business trust. This, of course, is no minor disadvantage and one not likely to encourage use of a business trust over a corporation where shareholders are isolated from its debts. This problem may be easily avoided by a clause in the trust agreement limiting the shareholders' liability to the amount they invest.

Stock ownership in a business trust is subject to creditor attachment as are shares of stock in a corporation. The business trust offers no special advantage here. A small advantage is that it's more difficult to discover the identity of the shareholders in a business trust, because as a private entity it doesn't make the same public filings as a corporation.

With all factors considered, there is no compelling reason to use a business trust instead of a corporation (if it is to engage in business), or other type trusts (if it is to be a passive investor). Because the business trust is a hybrid entity, there's considerable uncertainty regarding the rights of creditors. Rely instead on entities that offer less speculation concerning the safety of your assets.

How A Minor's Trust Safely Transfers Assets To Children

A minor's trust can be an extremely helpful device to shield assets as a gift in trust to minor's is an irrevocable trust and takes control away from the grantor-and derivatively, the grantor's creditors. But to serve as an effective asset protector, it must be carefully drafted. Example: There can be no significant restriction on the rights of the trustee to either invade principal or accumulate income.

Minor's trusts, created under the Internal Revenue Code, also help you save taxes since they allow you to shift both assets and income to your children. The minor's trust has become particularly popular since the Tax Reform Act of 1986 when a number of income splitting strategies, such as Clifford Trusts, were eliminated. Similarly, custodianships under the Uniform Gift to Minor's Act have become less popular since they demand that earned income in excess of $1000, accruing to children under 14, be taxed at the same rate as the minor's parents. The minor's trust is a valuable alternative to continued tax savings since the minor's trust has a maximum 15 percent tax rate.

The one disadvantage of the minor's trust: It requires the beneficiary-the minor child(ren)-to receive distribution of the trust property at age 21. Assets then come under their total control when they may not be sufficiently mature to manage the assets wisely. In a very real sense this may put the assets at greater risk than had they remained titled with the grantor and potentially exposed to his creditors.

Insurance Trusts: The Ideal Way To Protect Insurance

The life insurance trust has proven to be still another valuable weapon in the asset protection arsenal. Life insurance–both the death benefits and cash value–are exempt from creditor attachment in a number of states, and nothing more need be done to protect your insurance policies in these states. Still, a number of states grant little or no protection to insurance. In these states an insurance trust is necessary. How can you effectively use an insurance trust?

- First, borrow as much as possible against the cash value of your life insurance. Don't leave the cash or surrender value of your policies exposed to creditors. Creditors have an absolute right to any cash values under your policies. Since the policies would then have no value, there are no gift tax consequences from their transfer to the insurance trust.
- Second, set up an insurance trust to receive your insurance policies. Name your spouse or other trusted individual as trustee. Do not serve as trustee of your own insurance trust.
- Third, with the insurance policies held in trust, continue to advance funds to the trustee to cover future payments on the policies.
- Fourth, decide upon the disposition of the insurance proceeds upon your death. You may designate a beneficiary under the trust as under an insurance policy. For example, the proceeds may be paid directly to your spouse and/or your children. You may prefer the funds administered for them to be under the same trust or a separate insurance trust. With an insurance trust you have full flexibility in the designation of beneficiaries.
- Fifth, insurance trusts can be either revocable or irrevocable. With a revocable insurance trust you can transfer the policies to the trust anytime during your life. Since the trust is revocable, you can also modify it during your lifetime. Similarly, you can cancel the trust and also cancel the policy at your election. You thus retain the flexibility to change the trust to coincide with your new circumstances and goals. However, upon your death the trust becomes irrevocable, and the insurance proceeds automatically flow through the trust to the beneficiaries. The irrevocable life insurance trust, in contrast, comes about when you irrevocably transfer your life insurance policies to the trust. Once transferred, you lose the ability to cancel either the policies or the trust, or change or modify the terms of the trust.

The irrevocable insurance trust offers the important advantage of insulating the insurance policies from creditor claims. Since this is the desired objective, the irrevocable insurance trust, rather than the revocable trust should be used.

An insurance trust may also be either funded or unfunded. With an unfunded trust, the policy is either fully paid when transferred to the trust, or provisions are made for the future funding of premiums. With a funded trust the grantor transfers to the trust, in addition to the policies, adequate income-producing assets to pay all future premiums.

Why Land Trusts Can Give You A False Sense Of Security

Land trusts are popular in Illinois and Florida. In these two states they are valued highly for asset protection because in these states land trusts have maximum privacy. Beneficiaries of the land trust cannot be easily uncovered because the trust property is recorded in the name of the trustee, not in the names of the beneficiaries. While this can also be true with other trusts, the land trust offers more secrecy since there is no public record of beneficiaries. Nor is it always easy to uncover the rightful beneficiaries using ordinary discovery processes. This doesn't suggest the beneficial interests of land trusts are beyond creditor reach. If a creditor can establish the debtor as the rightful owner, the creditor can take his trust interest to satisfy the debt. Beneficiaries of a land trust are still best protected by titling their beneficial interest in the name of their less vulnerable spouse or children.

Land trusts also present two disadvantages. First, it's often difficult to refinance property in a land trust. The trustees are usually banks who refuse to execute documents necessary for refinancing. This requires the trust property to be temporarily conveyed out-of-trust to its grantors or beneficiaries who complete the financing before reconveyance back into the trust. While out-of-trust, the property is dangerously vulnerable to creditors.

Second, if the beneficiary is to take advantage of a Section 1031 tax-free, like-kind exchange, the property must again be transferred from the trust. This is because a land trust is not considered an interest in real property, but an interest in personal property. All factors considered, the land trust has only marginal value in asset protection.

The Powerful Asset Protection Powers Of The Foreign-Based Trust

The foreign-based trust is a comparatively new type of trust, and is proving very useful in asset protection as it combines the powerful protection of both the irrevocable trust and the offshore haven.

The foreign-based trust is organized and operates similarly to more conventional trusts. The grantor conveys assets into the trust and names the trustee and beneficiaries. What makes the foreign-based trust unique is that it is used only in the Cook

Islands and the Isle of Man–two jurisdictions whose laws strongly favor the irrevocable trust as an asset protection device.

Does the idea of a foreign-based trust in either of these two islands cause discomfort? The Cook Islands is a dependency of New Zealand. The Isle of Man, located between Ireland and Scotland, is a British protectorate. Both havens are economically and politically stable and friendly to foreign investors.

With a foreign-based trust in either of these two Islands you can establish an irrevocable trust and name yourself as sole beneficiary. Your trustee must reside in the jurisdiction, however, many banks and professional trustees on either island are ready to serve. You can always replace an unsatisfactory trustee. Under this trust you can also require a trustee to obtain your consent to major decisions concerning trust investments. You thus remain in control of the trust through your ability to replace the trustee as well as approve investment decisions.

The one big advantage of a foreign trust: It prohibits creditor attachment of trust assets. Neither jurisdiction recognizes United States judgments on fraudulent conveyances. Creditors must bring their fraudulent conveyance claim in these jurisdictions. Unlike the United States, these islands are exceptionally protective of trusts and are far stricter about what constitutes a fraudulent conveyance than are United States courts. Nor do courts on these islands recognize a United States judgment. A creditor here would have to sue you again in their courts, even if they held a United States judgment. Few American creditors would

make the costly attempt to overcome these barriers.

Foreign-based trusts, despite their powerful asset protection features, can be costly. It can cost $5000 to $20,000 to set up a foreign trust in either jurisdiction. Also expect to pay up to $3000 for annual trustee fees. These costs, of course, make a foreign trust worthwhile only if you have substantial assets to protect. If you have significant wealth and want ironclad safety, carefully investigate the foreign-based trust.

How Medicaid Trusts Win You Free Nursing Home Care

The Medicaid trust is a special purpose trust used exclusively to shelter assets so the grantor can qualify for Medicaid for nursing home costs. Understandably, it is a popular trust with older Americans.

A Medicaid trust is created similarly to other trusts. The grantor (the individual or couple who want to qualify for Medicaid) transfers assets into an irrevocable trust. However, unlike most irrevocable trusts, the grantor becomes the income beneficiary, and the children or spouse are ordinarily the final beneficiaries to receive the trust's principal. Under this arrangement the grantor continues to receive income, but since the grantor is without assets he qualifies for Medicaid assistance.

The Medicaid trust is designed for this one special purpose. It is not useful for asset protection beyond what can be provided by any other irrevocable trust. If you, or a parent, are now approaching an age where nursing home costs are of concern, then consider the Medicaid trust. It is further discussed in Chapter 13.

SECRET #84

How To Turn Your Ordinary Trust Into A Wealth Trust

Take two additional steps and you can easily convert any irrevocable trust into a wealth trust. First, add a clause to your trust allowing the trustee the right to invest in residential real estate. Also give the trustee the right to allow the beneficiary use of trust property. Second, once the trust is funded, the trustee should invest in a desirable property. This property can then be used by the beneficiaries rent-free. If the property's value increases, it can significantly shift wealth from one generation to the other.

Wealth trusts also offer asset protection. Example: If your children (or grandchildren) who occupy the property go through a divorce, the property will remain protected from spousal claims. Creditors of either the grantor or the beneficiary are also unable to reach the property. The very wealthy have for years relied on this generation-skipping strategy to escape probate taxes. Their objective is to pass wealth from grandparents to grandchildren, by-passing one level of estate tax–while each generation has full use and enjoyment of the

wealth. The wealth trust is not only ideal for this purpose but can also meet your asset protection goals.

SECRET #85

How To Shelter Assets For A Favorite Charity With A Charitable Remainder Trust

One of the most effective asset protection strategies is to donate property to your favorite charity during your lifetime. Sound too extreme an asset protection measure? Yet, that's the essence of a charitable remainder trust.

A charitable remainder trust is a formal trust established by the grantor who selects a tax-exempt charitable organization as the beneficiary of the trust principal. The grantor can then take a tax deduction for the fair market value of the contributed assets. A fixed amount (not less than 5 percent of the contributed assets) must be paid annually to the income beneficiary, but the grantor can be that beneficiary.

This trust offers the advantage of insuring its beneficiaries a fixed income, even if it requires depletion of the assets. There are several disadvantages: A fixed income does not necessarily provide the beneficiary an adequate income during inflationary times. Also, once established, no further contributions can be made to the trust for purposes of increasing income.

How well does a charitable remainder trust protect assets? Drafted properly, this trust offers total protection from either creditors of the grantor or the immediate beneficiary. Income paid under the trust is subject to claims of the beneficiaries creditors, but only when it is received.

Why Popular Living Trusts Offer Absolutely No Protection

You can avoid probate by placing your assets into one or more trusts, commonly called living trusts. With a living trust, the grantor ordinarily names himself the income beneficiary. Upon his death, the trust assets are distributed to designated beneficiaries. For its duration, the grantor controls the trust and can freely revoke or modify the trust.

The grantor may elect to use one living trust, or several trusts may be set up to accommodate different beneficiaries or different types of property. It's also smart to make the trust the beneficiary of pensions, insurance policies, Keogh's or any other cash value resources.

The living trust has gained popularity because it allows you to avoid probate. Upon death the trust assets pass directly to the beneficiary. This reduces costs to administer your estate and also avoids delays in distribution. Moreover, since probate is avoided, privacy over your personal and financial affairs is main-

tained. This doesn't mean you can necessarily forget about a will. A will remains essential to dispose of assets that for one reason or another have not been transferred to the living trust. A will is also needed to name guardians of your minor children.

A living trust doesn't reduce estate taxes, although a husband and wife can use living trusts to protect up to $1.2 million from taxes. Conversely, other than for the small cost to prepare and administer a living trust, it poses no disadvantages. A living trust is worthwhile for anyone with assets to leave, but unfortunately the living trust usually offers no asset protection. This is because the living trust remains under the complete control of the grantor who also has a power of revocation that allows creditors of the grantor to reach the trust assets.

One type of living trust can be useful for asset protection. This is the irrevocable living trust. Its assets will remain beyond the reach of your creditors.

Millions of Americans have living trusts. In most cases they are revocable trusts only because the grantor never considered asset protection an objective. Others did not wish to lose control over the trust assets. Compromise! Set up two separate living trusts—one revocable and the other irrevocable. Let the revocable trust hold those assets you want to control. The irrevocable trust can include assets to be creditor-proofed. You can often satisfy conflicting objectives by use of two or more trusts.

Two Ways To Shelter Assets With Sprinkling Trusts

Sprinkling trusts are also gaining popularity. They are helpful in situations where the trust will be in force for possibly ten or more years, and the future income or tax picture for each of the trust beneficiaries is unknown. You can then modify the distribution of trust property through a "sprinkling" provision. This provision grants the trustee the authority to either disburse or retain principal and income over the duration of the trust, and thus determine what each beneficiary will receive each year. As the grantor, you must specify to the trustee the criteria used to determine the pattern of distribution. The grantor must also set the minimum income to be provided a spouse or dependent child.

Two key factors determine whether the sprinkling trust offers suitable asset protection.

- If you, as the grantor, retain the right to modify or revoke the sprinkling trust, you lose the protection of the trust. As with other trusts, it must be irrevocable and beyond your control as grantor if it is to shelter assets.
- Don't name a beneficiary as trustee. Although this is legally permissible, it nevertheless renders trust assets vulnerable to creditors of the trustee-beneficiary.

This is because the trustee can distribute assets to himself as beneficiary. His creditors thus stand in his place for purposes of reaching the trust funds.

Observe these two cautions and the sprinkling trust can play a very useful role in both estate planning and asset protection.

The Best Trust For Business Owners

The standby trust is designed specifically to protect the business owner who becomes unable to manage his business affairs. The trust activates once the business owner no longer can oversee his business. Anyone may be appointed trustee, but a close family member or professional advisor most familiar with the business is recommended. Until the owner becomes disabled the standby trust can be revoked. It turns irrevocable only upon the permanent incapacity of the owner. In this instance, the standby trust serves a purpose similar to a durable power of attorney.

A standby trust is one of the best methods to assure competent succession in the event of disability. It is also a reasonably effective asset protector because it becomes irrevocable at the same time it becomes operative. It can then, but not before, safely accumulate income or assets free from creditor claim.

When You Need A Spendthrift Trust

You cannot discuss asset protection without mention of the spendthrift trust. A spendthrift trust insulates a beneficial interest from the beneficiary during his lifetime. Upon his death, or other specified event, that interest is distributed to second-level beneficiaries. Ordinarily, all the spendthrift beneficiary receives during his lifetime is income from the trust. The amount of income may be specified in the trust or left to the trustee's discretion.

A grantor may not be as concerned about his own child being a spendthrift unable to responsibly handle an inheritance as he is about the child's spouse. The spendthrift trust also keeps principal intact should the child die and thus allows the remaining principal to be gifted outright to grandchildren or any alternate beneficiary selected by the grantor.

A spendthrift trust effectively protects trust principal from creditors of the spendthrift. Since the spendthrift cannot reach the principal his creditors cannot either. Spendthrift trusts are the ideal mechanism to fully protect inheritances intended for a beneficiary prone to financial difficulty.

What about the grantor's creditors? As with all other trusts, rights of the grantor's creditors are dictated by the control the grantor retains over the trust. If the grantor can modify or revoke the spendthrift trust, then the trust assets remain exposed to the grantor's creditors.

Seven Little-Known Ways To Improve Trust Protection

Your trusts will most likely be designed with asset protection as only one of several objectives. Tax savings, estate planning and asset enhancement are also objectives. While the asset protection characteristics of your trust must be balanced with your other objectives, you can greatly increase the asset protection powers of any trust with these seven strategies:

- Use multiple trusts with different trustees to hold your various assets. It is considerably more difficult for a creditor to attack several trusts as opposed to one. Moreover, the use of several type trusts will give you flexibility in accommodating your other objectives.
- Wherever practical, establish out-of-state trusts. This will also discourage litigation as the lawsuits will necessarily have to be brought where each trust is located.
- Transfer assets to the trusts gradually and over as long a time period as is practicable. This will argue against claims the transfer was made to defraud creditors.
- Have a preamble added to each trust stating its purpose–such as estate planning. This further supports contentions the trust was not set up with the intent to place assets beyond the reach of creditors.

• Add beneficiaries, other than yourself, to your trust. Some statutes say that a transfer in trust for the use of the grantor is void as against his creditors. But these laws usually apply only in instances where the grantor is the sole beneficiary. With two or more beneficiaries there can be less concern with these laws.

• Move cautiously when adding spendthrift provisions. Such a provision has no validity in respect to the grantor, and it decreases the chances a court will find other reasons for the grantor's creation of the trust.

• Remember–control is the central issue. The more control you retain over the trust and trust property, the greater the rights of the creditor to reach the trust assets. Use irrevocable trusts, not revocable trusts. Appoint others to be trustee, not yourself. Reserve no right to modify the terms of the trust or dictate how the assets or income will be used. And, of course, don't make yourself a beneficiary of your own trust. These mistakes can be fatal to your asset protection objective.

Key Secrets To Remember

• A number of trusts are useful in asset protection. Use trusts that not only provide you the asset protection you want, but also coincide with your general investment and estate planning objectives.

• Use as many different trusts as is practical. This not only gives you greater flexibility, but also makes it more difficult for a major creditor to reach significant assets.

• Control is the key factor in determining whether trust assets can be reached by creditors. The more control you retain the less protection you will enjoy. The less control you retain, the more protection you will enjoy.

• If you have considerable wealth, investigate the foreign-based trust. It can give you greater ironclad protection than any other trust.

9

HOW TO STAY INVISIBLE AND BUILD WEALTH SECRETLY

Now more than ever before you need financial privacy as a key ingredient in your asset protection plan. When people know you're wealthy, you're an easy target for lawsuits.It's difficult today to keep your wealth private. Your tax returns are more accessible than ever before. Your finances are locked in the computers of countless private companies and government agencies. Credit bureaus, banks, insurance agencies, health providers and virtually every other organization you do business with monitors closely your personal affairs. Your finances are no secret. And the greater your wealth, the greater your need to hide your wealth in private places, or invested in secret assets that cannot be discovered. In this chapter you'll learn about these two strategies to achieve complete privacy and financial protection with 1) collectibles and bearer investments, and 2) offshore havens. These two asset protection strategies can make you virtually invisible to and untouchable by any creditor.

Why It's Smart To Bury Wealth In Bearer Investments

One of the best strategies to gain privacy for your wealth is to convert titled assets–such as real estate or stocks and bonds into "bearer" investments. Bearer investments include gold, diamonds, art, stamp collections, coins and similar collectibles. These offer enormous asset protection because they're easily transported and are completely confidential and private. Buy and sell collectibles through a third-party, such as your own privately-held corporation, for even greater privacy.

An investment of many thousands of dollars in gold or diamonds occupies little space, can easily be transported as you travel, and is easily reconverted into cash–all in complete confidentiality and privacy. One major drawback: Security. Once your collectibles are lost or stolen, they are gone forever. Insurance is expensive and a give-away that you own these assets. This problem can be somewhat solved by having these assets held by a corporation that conceals your ownership.

SECRET #92

How To Buy The Best Bearer Investments

Bearer assets are not only a simple way to safeguard assets, but purchased wisely they can also be excellent investments. Diamonds, gold, art, coins and stamps can dramatically increase in price. Caution: It is equally easy to lose money with these investments. Consider their investment qualities:

- Gold is most popular among these investments. Fabricated as coins, bullion or even jewelry, gold is the basic international unit of value. Still, the market for gold is very unstable and it can rapidly and widely fluctuate in value. Gold can always be sold at its current market value and is easily liquidated back into cash. This is its one big advantage. Silver and platinum feature similar investment characteristics.
- Diamonds are more stable an investment than gold. Diamonds, however, greatly vary in value between appraisers, so your diamonds must be bought at the lowest possible price. This is the only way to avoid a loss on resale.
- Coins. Rare coins enjoy a relatively large demand. Thousands of international coin dealers insure your ability to quickly sell your coin collection. As with diamonds, unless you have inside sources, you will probably buy coins at near-retail prices and suffer a loss over the short-term.
- Stamps may be your best bet. Good stamp collections increased in value approximately 15 percent annually over the past 15 years. Stamps also enjoy a large market, so they too can be easily liquidated. The downside: Stamps require a sophisticated investor who can value and trade them profitably. This takes knowledge.
- General collectibles. Available to you are a potpourri of many different collectibles: Art, antiques, baseball cards, autographs, rare comic books, and even vintage wine. Each has exceptionally high profit potential, but there can also be large losses since their respective markets are controlled by so few players. Unlike other bearer assets, these collectibles are also less portable and more difficult to liquidate quickly.

The one best way to invest invisibly: Buy gold bullion or coins and store them in a safe deposit box registered in the name of a living trust or corporation. Keep each buy-sell transaction under several hundred dollars. Coin and gold dealers must report any suspicious transaction to the federal government, so large or unusual deals should be avoided. Finally, use cash to pay for your safe deposit box. Avoid any paper connection between yourself, your safe deposit box, and the gold.

Another good investment: Warehouse certificates for precious metals located in Zurich, Switzerland. Swiss certificates are registered to the buyer, therefore, use a corporate or trust intermediary. There's a steady market for Swiss certificates, and they are available through several precious metals wholesalers in Zurich. As the holder of the certificate, you can always demand delivery of your precious metals. This guarantees your liquidity.

What portion of your assets should you invest in collectibles? The answer depends on your savvy as an investor. If you are confident you can profitably trade and you are not risk adverse, then invest a larger percentage of your wealth. If you are inexperienced with these assets, then either find a professional to invest for you, or ignore collectibles as an asset protection option. Your wealth will be less safe than if exposed to creditors.

SECRET #93

How To Move Your Money Quietly

Keep a low profile when moving funds into secret investments. Your objective is to avoid government reporting requirements. But count on the fact your bank will have trouble keeping your secret from the government. Here's why: The Bank Secrecy Act of 1970 does everything possible to reveal your every banking transaction to the government. This law (the "Currency and Foreign Transactions Reporting Act of 1970") compels all U.S. depository institutions to maintain specified records as well as report various banking transactions to the government. How does the government make your bank keep tabs on you?

- Checks above $100 must be microfilmed and retained by your bank for at least five years. Most banks automatically microfilm all checks.
- Your bank must file a report of every deposit, withdrawal, exchange of currency, or other transfer or payment by or through your bank, of currency of more than $10,000. This applies only to cash transactions, and not check transactions. These reports also identify the parties involved.
- Your bank must report all transfer of funds over $5000, whether into or out of the United States.
- If you either own or control a foreign account, you must file a separate tax form identifying your account. Foreign account records must be kept available for five years.
- Your bank must keep a record of loans in excess of $5000, except for real estate mortgages.
- Your securities broker must keep a signature card showing your trading authority for your securities transactions. Brokers must also obtain your social security number.
- Financial institutions must record and verify your identity when you

complete a reportable transaction.
- Finally, the law requires your financial institutions to retain a copy of all transactions between themselves and you.

The scope of reporting that allows the government to spy on you compels you to come to one big unsettling fact: Your bank really can't keep a secret! The one best way to transfer large sums and keep it secret: Have your bank wire the funds or buy a money order.

No, you can't rely on U.S. banks for secrecy. A creditor, for instance, can find out about your assets by obtaining your checking account records for the past several years. The creditor need only subpoena your bank to turn over this information.

The federal government once had the absolute, unstoppable right to pry into your bank records. Recent laws make it slightly more difficult for government investigators to go after these records, but that doesn't mean it's either impossible or even overly difficult for the government. While the government can no longer go on a fishing expedition, government investigators can get a warrant if they can show probable cause that a violation occurred. Federal investigators routinely obtain search warrants, so there's no reason to believe the new laws give you meaningful protection or financial privacy. There are still plenty of myths on how you can keep your wealth strictly private. Here are the three biggest:

- Buy bearer bonds: Unfortunately they're no longer private. New issues of bearer bonds that don't dis-

close the owner's name have been outlawed since 1982. You can borrow the few leftover bonds issued before that date, but when you redeem it the IRS receives a Form 1099-B from your brokerage firm to advise them of your transaction.
- Send cash or bearer instruments overseas (cashier's checks payable to "cash", money orders, etc.): It's a felony to send $10,000 or more to a foreign country without reporting it to U.S. customs. You need not report less than $10,000.
- Buy stock with cash: Few brokers sell for cash, and all stock purchases above $10,000 are reported to the IRS.

Fourteen Safeguards To Build Your Wall Of Privacy

How can you gain more privacy for your asset protection program? Here are 14 essential steps:

- Don't disclose your social security number for identification unless required by law. No law actually requires you to either have or reveal a social security number. It's true, no bank will open an account for you, nor employer hire you, without one. The IRS also becomes annoyed with taxpayers without a SSN.

- Set up a company to handle sensitive transactions. Incorporate, so your business has its own taxpayer identification number. Do you have many sensitive transactions? Spread them through several different companies.
- Keep checking account transactions to an absolute minimum. Cash, money orders, or credit cards are safer to use.
- Be particularly careful when investing money abroad. Watch currency reporting limits.
- Never involve a bank in cash transactions over $10,000. Split the transaction into two or more smaller transactions. Then put them through your bank on separate dates so your bank won't consider it one reportable transaction.
- Limit the financial information you disclose on credit applications, or when opening bank or brokerage accounts. Supply only the essential information and nothing more.
- Conduct as many transactions as possible as bearer transactions since these are not reportable under your name.
- Use only accountants, financial planners and investment advisors who will hold your financial information confidential. The same is true when selecting banks. They should each agree to notify you should they receive a request or subpoena for information about you or your finances.
- Use a post office box or mail drop service to receive confidential or sensitive legal or financial documents.
- If you do incorporate, use a Nevada corporation. Nevada gives your corporation more privacy than any other state–including Delaware.
- Use private vaults or secure home or office safes for your cash and valuables. Bank safes are not as secure for financial protection.
- Use irrevocable living trusts to bequeath your property. Avoid probate and the inevitable financial disclosures and publicity that probate requires.
- Borrow from and do business with those who demand the least amount of information about you.
- Deploy your assets and investments in a way that requires the least amount of detailed information on your tax returns.

SECRET #95

How To Find Secrecy In Offshore Havens

Do visions of shady characters come to mind when you hear or read about money safely stacked in those sunny offshore havens?

More and more sophisticated Americans, most of whom are also quite law-abiding, know it's smart and legal to relocate assets in other countries. Particularly favored are those with rigid bank secrecy laws that insure investors exceptionally strict privacy and a strong shield against creditors. It is a smart strategy. Funds harbored in an array of foreign banks (as well as foreign finance subsidiaries of U.S. corporations), are generally safe from creditors in the United States. Offshore havens, in fact, can be the absolute safest way to protect your assets.

Consider that when you bank within the United States, your financial affairs are exposed to the IRS, other governmental agencies, and any creditor or litigant waving a subpoena for your records. It's far different when you bank outside the United States. Your financial records can then only be divulged with your express permission. Your best bet: An offshore bank (which is simply any foreign bank). This includes Canadian or Mexican banks, although you may prefer banking elsewhere. It's perfectly legal to bank offshore, with two cautions:

- You must declare to the IRS all income from offshore accounts, just as you declare income from an American bank. There are no income tax savings to investors who follow these reporting requirements. But unlike U.S. banks, foreign banks do not issue 1099 forms to the IRS, so the IRS has less opportunity to know about your offshore accounts.
- You must also declare when $5000 or more goes into or out of your foreign account. Smaller transfers retain their privacy.

As you can see, the purpose of a foreign account is not to avoid taxes, but to give you greater privacy and asset protection.

Foreign accounts have several small disadvantages: First, is inconvenience. You can bank by mail, and this is no more difficult than when you bank in another city or state within the United States. You must, however, wait longer for your checks to clear and to withdraw funds. Collection fees are also charged, but this can be avoided by having your offshore bank pay you in U.S. funds, payable through an American correspondent bank. Finally, your account will not be insured as are accounts with an FDIC insured bank. This is their major disadvantage.

A big plus with an offshore bank: Deposits smaller than $5000 will be undocumented. If you instruct someone to send you funds directly to your offshore bank, the IRS only knows about this income if you voluntarily report it. The IRS has even less chance to know about it if you spend your money offshore. Another advantage: Since offshore banks are not regulated by the more restrictive United States laws, they can and do offer substantially higher interest rates. Caution: If you have more than $400 of interest or dividend income from offshore accounts you must answer the question on Schedule B of your tax return (interest and dividend income) that asks whether you have an account in a foreign bank. Tip: You can legally answer "no" if your foreign accounts, in aggregate, do not exceed $5000. Another strategy to avoid reporting: Place your accounts with a U.S. Military banking facility overseas. This is an ideal solution if you're in the military.

Does risk make you hesitate to go offshore with your money? Foreign banks are generally healthier than United States banks. Still, it's difficult to have confidence in the banking system of another country, particularly those in small countries. The solution? Diversify. Spread your cash among several offshore havens. Absent a world economic crisis of unprecedented proportions, it's not likely they will all go through an economic disaster that could jeopardize your assets.

You have over 1000 offshore banks to choose from. You also have your pick of many excellent tax havens–the Bahamas, Barbados, British Virgin Islands, Cayman Islands, Hong Kong, Isle of Man, Netherland Antilles, Mariana Islands, Montserrat, Panama and Vanuata–as just a few. Banks in these tiny havens are as stable as those in Switzerland and other larger countries, and frequently offer more advantages. Investigate every haven before you invest.

SECRET #96

How Owning Your Own Offshore Bank Can Pay Big Dividends

Do you want to take fullest advantage of the privacy and asset protection an offshore bank gives you? Own your own bank. Sound ridiculous? Hundreds of Americans now own offshore banks. The entire set-up can be handled for under $25,000, often far less. How can you become president of your own offshore bank? You have two choices: Start your own bank from scratch, or buy an established bank. Starting from scratch takes more time and effort. Buying an existing

bank is less challenging but probably more costly. Either way you'll need professional guidance to keep you out of trouble.

Where do you start? The best place is with Jerome Schneider and his WFI Corp. They specialize in providing a low-cost program enabling investors to acquire offshore banks. Often within a few days, and at a surprisingly low cost. WFI can also help administer your bank once it's chartered. You'll find WFI listed in the Appendix.

Why own your own bank? One reason is that you guarantee your own privacy in case you're still concerned whether another bank will provide the secrecy you want. Most people think an offshore or foreign bank offers tax protection. As you now know, this is not true. What is true is that many offshore havens do not tax the interest earned in their accounts. Several countries, Switzerland included, impose a modest tax on interest paid to non-residents. But you are taxed in the United States for interest earned anywhere in the world. If you fail to report foreign income you are liable under IRS laws. Tip: If you want big tax benefits, then own the offshore bank and establish a bank account in your bank's name. This is not reportable to the IRS.

Not surprisingly, our government discourages U.S. taxpayers from setting up foreign corporations. Before 1962, a U.S. taxpayer could incorporate in another country and avoid U.S. income tax until interest or dividends were actually received. In 1962, the IRS made foreign corporations less attractive when it introduced the concept of a "controlled corporation"–a corporation where over 50 percent of the combined voting power is controlled by U.S. taxpayers. A

U.S. taxpayer is one holding no less than 10 percent of the shares.

The disadvantage of a controlled corporation is that U.S. taxpayers who hold stock in a controlled corporation must pay taxes on their proportionate share of corporate income–whether or not received. The controlled corporation is thus very much like the "S" corporation. A little-known way around the problem: The U.S. taxpayers should hold no more than 49 percent of the shares, even if it's held by only one stockholder. The other 51 percent should be held by another corporation or trust. Since less than 50 percent of the stock is in the hands of a U.S. stockholder, the company will not be a controlled corporation, and no income will be reportable by U.S. stockholders until actually received. This allows the profit to accumulate without tax.

How Offshore Havens Protect Assets

The primary purpose of the offshore haven is to protect your bank account from United States creditors. How is this accomplished?

Offshore banks operate with a high degree of secrecy concerning their depositors. No offshore haven will disclose the existence of your account under a civil lawsuit. This means that your U.S. creditor is absolutely powerless to find out about your foreign accounts unless you disclose it. Should the creditor discover the account, the haven won't cooperate with the creditor in enforcing the judgment. Thus, for all practical purposes, your creditors cannot reach your funds in offshore havens. There are two important exceptions: First, some offshore havens will disclose your account to a bankruptcy trustee. If you file bankruptcy you cannot automatically consider your foreign bank account safe. Second, your account can be disclosed, and even surrendered, under certain criminal proceedings. Each haven provides, within its laws, the circumstances when secrecy will not be honored. These laws should be thoroughly reviewed before you invest.

For maximum protection combine two asset protection strategies: For example, have a California limited partnership establish an account in an offshore haven. The creditor will be unable to discover the account. Moreover, the haven won't allow the creditor to enforce its judgment even if it should discover the account. If the foreign haven did fully cooperate, the creditor would still have to overcome the total protection afforded by a California limited partnership. These obstacles are insurmountable to any creditor. Another way to increase your protection: Diversify your assets among several accounts in different havens. It is virtually impossible for a creditor to overcome this barrier due to the enormous costs required.

How To Maximize Secrecy Offshore

Maintain as low a profile as possible in your offshore company if you want maximum privacy. That's why offshore firms frequently have nominees stand in for the actual stockholders. The nominees may even serve as officers and directors of the company while the true owner maintains control through proxies. This is a highly effective procedure if you want your affiliation with an offshore bank concealed. In most offshore havens this technique renders it impossible for a government agency or private litigant to discover the identity of the true owner.

There are other ways to achieve complete secrecy. You can use bearer stock certificates. Because "bearer" shares are not issued to a specific person, they are unregistered. The true owner claims title by possession of the certificates alone. Although the IRS cannot determine the true owners of the shares, American stockholders are still bound to pay taxes on profits.

Myths And Realities Of Swiss Bank Accounts

Whenever foreign bank accounts are mentioned, Switzerland immediately comes to mind. Swiss banking, like other offshore banking, is perfectly legal. Neither the United States, nor Switzerland, impose restrictions on Americans using Swiss bank accounts. But is Swiss banking really preferable to banking in other havens? Here are the pro's and con's.

- **Convenience:** You can as easily transact business with a Swiss bank as with an American bank. As with other foreign accounts, you must notify the IRS whenever you withdraw or deposit more than $10,000, whether in cash, checks or bearer certificates. Swiss banks are accessible, and you'll enjoy their proximity to all European markets.

- **Financial Stability:** Switzerland is one of the most stable tax havens. No exchange rules exist on precious metals or gold-backed currency, although reportedly the Swiss may prohibit these activities and restore foreign currency controls to help stabilize their economy. The reality is that Swiss accounts can be your best insurance against collapse of the American dollar.

- **Privacy:** It's a crime for a Swiss bank to disclose banking information to anyone-including the Swiss and American government. Disclosure of information under Swiss law is virtually impossible since accounts are numbered by code with the owner's name locked in the bank vault. Still, secrecy is not absolute. The Swiss can disclose information concerning criminal violations, particularly those involving organized crime and SEC violations. Disclosure may also be made in bankruptcy and inheritance cases. Note: Tax violations are not considered criminal under Swiss law so no disclosure is ever made to the IRS.

Which Swiss banks are safest? Union Bank of Switzerland (Zurich), Swiss Credit Bank (Zurich) and the Swiss Bank Corporation (Basel) are three to consider. But there are many other good banks in Switzerland.

It's easy to open a Swiss bank account. You can handle the matter entirely by mail, but it may be preferable to open the account in person, particularly if it's a large account. If you prefer mail banking, simply write the bank. They'll send you the necessary applications.

When opening a foreign account, also execute a durable power of attorney granting someone you trust authority over your account in the event of your death or disability. This insures continued management of your account if you are unable to act on your own. While this practice is strongly urged by the Swiss, it is equally good practice with any other offshore account as well as with your American accounts.

You'll receive a full range of services with a Swiss bank. Swiss banks offer savings and checking accounts as well as custodial accounts for your gold, precious metals, and stocks and bonds. Accounts may be in either Swiss or American currency.

How To Choose Your Ideal Offshore Haven

What country is best for offshore banking? Even investment specialists can't agree, largely because different criteria are used. Some offshore specialists give priority to privacy, others to security, and still others to interest rates. Convenience and ease-of-doing business is another factor worth considering, as are local income taxes. Finally, you must consider safety.

• Banks in the Cayman Islands and the Bahamas are favorites if you insist upon absolute privacy. Accounts held in these offshore havens are absolutely safe from prying eyes–particularly when they belong to the IRS. Nearly one-half of all offshore accounts from American depositors are sheltered in these two popular havens. Interest rates are competitive with those in the United States, but below those of several other havens. Convenience is good since both island groups are easily reached from east coast cities.

• Denmark and Austria rank high because they offer a good blend of high interest and privacy. Moreover, both countries are financially strong which translates into investment safety. Privacy is considered good but not as good as Switzerland, the Bahamas or Caymans. Two drawbacks: Convenience is sacrificed, although you can bank by mail. Also, deposits must be converted into their national currency.

- Scotland and the Isle of Man are known for their high interest rates. Security is also good. Privacy is not considered as secure as in other havens, but it is adequate in most cases. You can use foreign trusts in the Isle of Man, and this adds great protection.
- The least safe country? The Philippines. This country is spotty on privacy, inconvenient to deal with and least stable financially.
- Tax-free havens include the Bahamas, Cayman Islands, Turks and Caicos Islands and Vanuata.
- Low-tax countries are represented by Bahrain, Bermuda, British Virgin Islands, Channel Islands, Hong Kong, Liberia, Leichtenstein, Monaco, Monserrat, Netherland Antilles and Panama.
- Banking secrecy countries include Antigua, Bahamas, Bahrain, Bermuda, Virgin Islands, Cayman Islands, Channel Islands, Hong Kong, Isle of Man, Leichtenstein, Netherland Antilles, Panama, Singapore, Switzerland, Turks and Vanuata
- The most overlooked offshore haven is figuratively "right beneath our nose"-Mexico. Mexican banks are considered as safe as Swiss banks and offer equally good secrecy. Mexican accounts are not ordinarily set up as "numbered" accounts as they are in Switzerland, but they still enjoy the same privacy. Moreover, Mexican law makes it illegal for any bank to disclose banking information to third-parties. Also,

the Mexican government has no tax treaty with the United States, or any other government. Thus, your banking business will be kept beyond range of the IRS, other agencies or your creditors. Caution: Not all Mexican banks are safe. Deal only with the financiera, or government regulated banks.

Three Offshore Traps To Avoid

Most havens are reasonably safe and offer a valuable bundle of benefits to their depositors. Still, move cautiously. There are any number of scams and booby-traps to snare you:

- Some offshore banks are notoriously weak financially. This means you must investigate the financial condition of any bank you're considering. Review the bank's most recent financial statements. Your money is not necessarily safer in an American bank. In fact, the failure rate among American banks is considerably higher than among foreign banks. The big difference: American accounts are insured up to $100,000. Foreign accounts are uninsured. Moreover, banks in foreign countries are not always as highly regulated as U.S. banks. Investigate carefully! How can you locate offshore banks-and get the facts and figures to evaluate each? Write for Polk's Directory of International Banks, or find it at your local library.

- Hold your deposits in U.S. currency. Most foreign banks automatically keep your account in U.S. dollars. You thus avoid the risk of currency devaluation that occurs when your funds are in the currency of the offshore haven.

- Avoid offshore business trusts that promise financial privacy and a safe haven from the IRS and other creditors. Trusts do not give you the same protection as recognized, chartered banks. Business trusts not only cost you considerably more, but you'll also be more easily spotted by the IRS.

Learn as much as you possibly can about offshore havens. It will give you greater confidence in this very important asset protection strategy–and will also help you avoid costly mistakes.

SECRET #102

Know The True Costs Of Offshore Banking

Make costs an important consideration in your asset protection decisions. Offshore specialists frequently quote a flat fee of several thousand dollars to set you up in a foreign haven, but these fees fluctuate considerably, and seldom do they cover all the costs you'll encounter.

The true costs of offshore banking go beyond incorporation costs, if a foreign cor-

poration will be used. If you are a substantial investor, you'll want foreign counsel and a foreign accountant as well. Moreover, you will have travel costs and lost income if you personally conduct your banking business.

From an asset protection viewpoint, offshore banking should be considered whenever U.S. banking becomes too risky, but you'll probably not want to consider the cost and hassle of foreign banking unless you have at least $100,000 to put offshore.

Offshore havens are both a desirable and effective way to bury your money, but don't put all your funds offshore. No more than 50 percent of your cash should go into foreign accounts. While these accounts are generally safe, for maximum safety diversify and locate your funds in several havens. You can then enjoy thinking about all that money your creditors will never find.

Key Secrets To Remember

- Collectibles and offshore banking can be two extremely effective asset protection tactics.
- Collectibles give you secrecy of ownership plus easy portability. Their disadvantage: As with any investment, you must know how to buy and sell profitably.
- Be careful on how you handle your banking transactions. Banks keep a closer eye on you than you may think. And what they see they report to the IRS.
- Offshore havens are perfectly legal for hiding your money, but you must still pay U.S. taxes on interest earnings.

- Consider your own offshore bank. It's not cheap, but it does guarantee you absolute control over your money.
- Hundreds of havens await you. Interest rates, security, privacy and taxes are the four key criteria when selecting your haven. Choose the one with features you find most important.
- Investigate, investigate, investigate. You can fall victim to countless scams in the offshore haven game.
- Combine offshore banking with other asset protectors–such as trusts, corporations or limited partnerships. This gives you the added strength of two barriers between your creditors and your money.

10

BANKRUPTCY: HOW TO LEGALLY KEEP YOUR ASSETS AND LOSE YOUR DEBTS

Bankruptcy is an increasingly popular refuge for financially-troubled individuals and companies. Nearly one million individuals filed for bankruptcy in 1991. The statistics rise dramatically each year. Yet, this is not surprising. Once you take a closer look at bankruptcy, understand how it works and how it can protect your assets, you'll understand why more and more debtors are taking advantage of the bankruptcy laws.

SECRET #103

Why Bankruptcy May Be Your Wrong Move

If you have serious financial difficulties you may turn to bankruptcy for relief. But filing bankruptcy isn't always your right solution. Bankruptcy is only your answer when:

• You have too many debts to satisfy from either future income or from the sale of your assets. Example: It's foolish to declare bankruptcy if you earn $100,000 a year, but have debts of only $20,000. It may require short-term sacrifice to reduce your debts to a comfortable level, but that's certainly preferable to bankruptcy. A good rule of thumb: If your unsecured debts are less than 60 percent of your net annual pay–then try to avoid bankruptcy. You should be able to allocate 20 percent of your take-home pay to reduce excess debts. Creditors will patiently wait three years for full payment if you show good faith and systematic interim payments. Follow this formula and your financial problems will be over in only three years. You will also be proud you avoided bankruptcy. On the other hand, if you cannot realistically eliminate your debts within three years, then you should seriously consider bankruptcy.

• Bankruptcy may also be necessary to protect your assets. Once you file bankruptcy all civil actions against you must immediately stop. This includes lawsuits, seizures, levies, attachments, repossessions and foreclosures. Moreover, all creditors must obey the "automatic stay" of legal action imposed by the bankruptcy code. This includes your general unsecured creditors, the IRS, secured lenders, and even such creditors as landlords attempting to evict you, or a spouse suing you for alimony or child support. Bankruptcy becomes your valuable ally since it gives you the opportunity to resolve matters with creditors who may otherwise seize and sell your assets. Chapter 11 reorganizations and Chapter 13 wage earner plans are particularly well-suited for this purpose.

Bankruptcy *is not* your solution if:

• You filed bankruptcy within the prior seven years, from the date of the prior filing. This applies only to Chapter 7. There is no limitation on how often you can file Chapter 11 or 13.
• You primarily want to discharge debts that are not dischargeable in bankruptcy. Bankruptcy will discharge most debts such as court

judgments, household or business debts that you owe, rents, loans and charge card obligations.

Debts You Cannot Lose In Bankruptcy

Bankruptcy won't wipe out all debts. Not dischargeable in bankruptcy are:

• Federal, state and local taxes (less than three years old for federal income taxes),
• Child support and alimony payments,
• Recent student loans,
• Criminal fines and penalties (restitution and traffic fines, for example),
• Liabilities incurred through drunk driving,
• Withholding tax assessments,
• Otherwise dischargeable debts not listed in your bankruptcy filing.

Debts you cannot discharge in a previous Chapter 7 bankruptcy can be discharged in Chapter 13. The bankruptcy court can also rule other debts non-dischargeable in a Chapter 7 bankruptcy, if it is equitable based on the conduct of the parties.

Secured debts are dischargeable to the extent the debt exceeds the liquidation value of the collateral. Bankruptcy, however, eliminates your personal liability on the debt. The secured parties rights are limited to the collateral.

Another category of non-dischargeable debts are those incurred through fraud or misrepresentation. Because bankruptcy law is designed to assist honest debtors, the dishonest debtor is barred from such relief. Debts that fall under this category include last minute luxury debts owed any one creditor for $500 or more for luxury goods or services purchased within 40 days of filing. It also includes debts for cash advances in excess of $1000 obtained within 20 days of filing for bankruptcy. Oftentimes these obligations are owed to credit card companies (Visa, MasterCard, etc.). Credit card companies now contest discharges for debts in this category. Debts incurred through intentional fraud–such as the issuance of fraudulent credit applications are also non-dischargeable.

SECRET #105

How To Choose The Right Type Bankruptcy

There are several different types of bankruptcy for individuals and businesses. Each is designed for a different financial situation, so it's important to file the correct type of bankruptcy:

•Chapter 7 bankruptcy or "straight" bankruptcy erases all your debts other than those debts that are non-dischargeable. Conversely, you lose all your assets except those that are exempt. You can file Chapter 7 whether you are engaged in business or not. A corporation may also file under Chapter 7 and it will then be liquidated. Chapter 7 bankruptcy is by far the most popular form of bankruptcy, accounting for approximately 90 percent of all bankruptcies. Chapter 7 is for you if you have few, if any, assets beyond those that are exempt. The advantage with Chapter 7 is that once you are declared bankrupt your debts are forever gone. You can then truly start life again free of past debts.

•Chapter 13 or a so-called "wage-earner" plan differs from a Chapter 7 in that you keep all your assets. But rather than wipe out your debts, you repay your obligations in full or in part over three to five years. Under your repayment plan your creditors must receive at least as much as they would had you filed under Chapter 7. Certain priority creditors, such as tax agencies, must be paid in full. Secured creditors must be paid an amount at least equal to the liquidation value of their collateral. Chapter 13 is appropriate when you have non-exempt assets that you want to save, such as a home with an equity. If all your assets are exempt, it makes no sense to file Chapter 13. A Chapter 7 would still allow you to keep your exempt assets while eliminating your debts.

•Chapter 11 is similar in concept to a Chapter 13 since it contemplates that the debtor will keep its property and arrange a repayment plan with its creditors. While a wage-earner plan is limited to individuals who are not self-employed, a Chapter 11 can be filed by any debtor. There is another distinction between Chapter 13 and Chapter 11: Debtors under Chapter 13 cannot have over $100,000 in unsecured debt, or $350,000 in secured debt. There is no such limitation with a Chapter 11. Only recently have individuals not engaged in business been allowed to file Chapter 11. Many individuals with debts above what is allowed under Chapter 13 will find Chapter 11 a haven for keeping their assets while resolving their creditor problems.

It is also possible to shift from one type bankruptcy to another. A company, for example, may be involuntarily petitioned into Chapter 7 and then convert the case to one under Chapter 11. Conversely, a company in Chapter 11, or a wage-earner in Chapter 13, may be converted to Chapter 7. This most often happens when the debtor cannot arrange a satisfactory repayment plan, or defaults in its obligations under bankruptcy. Because it is so very important to elect the right type bankruptcy, the decision should be made only after consultation with an attorney well-experienced in bankruptcy.

Did you ever hear of Chapter 20 of the bankruptcy code? Probably not. This is because there is no Chapter 20. But it is possible for a debtor to file a Chapter 13 followed by a Chapter 7. This, of course, is why it's called Chapter 20.

The benefits are that it then becomes possible to keep your assets through the Chapter 13. You may then sell or transfer the assets, or convert them to exempt assets at your leisure. You can then rid yourself of the creditors you still have with the Chapter 7. This tactic is not very common, of course, but according to recent court decisions it is considered perfectly legal. If you think it may be the right strategy for you then check it out with your bankruptcy attorney.

Why You May File Too Soon Or Too Late

Timing is critical when filing for bankruptcy. Many people file too soon and would have benefited more from their bankruptcy had they delayed their filing. Others file too late and lose some of the possible benefits of bankruptcy. Six timing pointers to consider:

- Have you collected your tax refunds? If tax refunds are due you when you file, it will be taken by the bankruptcy trustee. If it is a sizeable refund, then collect it before filing.
- Don't file within 90 days of payments made on past debts, if you want the creditor to keep the money. Payments within that 90 day period are recoverable by the trustee as a preference.
- If you anticipate more debts in the near future then wait until they

arise and can be discharged in your bankruptcy. An example may be on-going medical costs due to extended illness.

- Claiming a homestead exemption? Make certain you have owned the property sufficiently long to qualify before you file for bankruptcy.

- If you owe personal income taxes then wait three years to file. Taxes owed less than three years are not dischargeable while those over three years are.

- Wait at least 40 days if you ran up some bills for non-essentials. Charges incurred within that time are not dischargeable.

Don't be too anxious to file bankruptcy no matter how indebted you may be. If you have few creditors you may be able to resolve matters without bankruptcy. Over time creditors do become more willing to settle accounts on favorable terms. You may also find this a perfect time to undertake some high-risk ventures. Should you fail, the debts from these ventures can also be discharged along with your prior debts. Caution: You can also delay filing too long. This is certainly true if you expect to save assets. Bankruptcy as an asset protector is of no value if the asset has already been seized and sold by your creditor. File before you lose your property–not after.

When You And Your Spouse Should File Separately

Spouses frequently file bankruptcy together, particularly when they share common obligations they want discharged. In fact, spouses can file together on the same bankruptcy petition. But there's one time when spouses should not file together: When they jointly own non-exempt assets such as their home. Here's why: If both spouses file together, the trustee in bankruptcy gets clear title to the entire property because the trustee receives the interest of both spouses. Since the trustee can claim the entire legal title to the property, the trustee can sell the property at its fair value as can any other seller. This would then make it difficult to keep your home unless you re-acquired it from the trustee at its fair market value.

Suppose instead you and your spouse own the property as joint tenants, or tenants-by-the-entirety, and file bankruptcy separately and at different times. The trustee, at any one time, would then control only the one-half interest of the spouse then in bankruptcy. The trustee would have extreme difficulty selling that one-half interest because ownership of the property would remain divided between the spouse and the buyer. Since the trustee could not sell more than the one-half interest, it would necessarily be at a distressed price. The husband and wife could then re-acquire that interest cheaply and repeat the process as the other spouse files bankruptcy.

But know this special rule: If you are married and you and your spouse plan a joint bankruptcy filing, you and your spouse are entitled to double the exemption. For example, if each of you is entitled to a $40,000 homestead exemption by state law, then you and your spouse would together have an $80,000 exemption on the equity in your home. If this double exemption adequately protects your home, then, of course, there is no reason to file separately and at different times.

SECRET #108

How To File Bankruptcy When You Can't Afford It

It currently costs $120 to file a Chapter 7 or Chapter 13 bankruptcy and $600 for a Chapter 11. Not surprisingly, many people are so impoverished when they need to file bankruptcy that they cannot even raise the filing fee, aside from the fee to hire an attorney. Tip: The bankruptcy code makes provision for installment payments if you cannot raise the filing fee. You must obtain court approval for installment payments, but this is routinely allowed once the court is convinced you are without funds.

Raising the money to hire a lawyer to handle your bankruptcy is another matter. A simple individual bankruptcy can cost you between $250 and $1000, although lower and higher fees are not unheard of. Most lawyers charge about $750 for a debtor not engaged in business. This has to be paid before filing. Few bankruptcy lawyers extend credit to their clients, although it's not unknown in these competitive times.

Check lawyer advertising in your local newspaper. Bankruptcy attorneys routinely advertise their fees in bankruptcy cases. Because these bankruptcy specialists handle many cases, they often charge considerably less due to their high volume and efficient use of para-legals to handle routine paperwork.

You can also handle your own bankruptcy. Consider it if you are without assets and need not concern yourself with the complicated exemption rules. Recommendation: Buy an *E-Z Legal Bankruptcy Kit* at any major stationery or office supply store. For under $20 you'll have everything you need to easily process your own routine bankruptcy. If you should run into complications you can always retain an attorney to resolve that specific problem.

SECRET #109

How To Go Bankrupt And Keep Your Assets

The key strategy in bankruptcy is to convert non-exempt assets into exempt assets before you file bankruptcy. Property held as exempt assets are fully protected in bankruptcy. Non-exempt assets will be lost under a bankruptcy.

A classic example: Suppose you live in Massachusetts and own $2 million in non-exempt assets (such as investment property, stock, bonds, boats, etc.). If you go bankrupt because you owe $3 million, then all your assets (except for the nominal $7500 exemption in Massachusetts) would be lost to your creditors. If you instead liquidated all your assets for $2 million and bought a $2 million home in Florida where homes of any value are exempt, you could safely keep your $2 million home while you go through bankruptcy in Florida. Once clear of bankruptcy, you could sell your $2 million Florida home, and return to Massachusetts with $2 million in your pocket. This strategy allows you to legally emerge from bankruptcy a full-fledged millionaire! Some cautions to observe:

- Convert your property as far in advance of your bankruptcy as possible. While conversion of non-exempt assets into exempt assets is perfectly legal, bankruptcy courts can frown upon it as inequitable and possibly set aside the transfers. Bankruptcy courts in Florida and other states have, however, upheld the right to convert assets even when done solely for the purpose of asset protection. This does not necessarily mean all courts will.
- Sell your non-exempt property at a reasonable price. If you sell at too low a price the court may question the legitimacy of the sale and set aside the transaction.
- Be prepared to account for the proceeds of your sale. If you sell a non-exempt asset for $50,000 and buy an exempt $10,000 item, the court will make you account for

$40,000. Total honesty is critical in bankruptcy.

It's really not too difficult to figure out how to use exemptions to your maximum benefit in bankruptcy. There are both federal exemptions and state exemptions. Your objective is to select those exemptions that will provide you maximum asset protection. Your first step is to know the federal exemptions available to you. These are listed in the Appendix.

Once you understand your federal exemptions, next determine your state exemptions. They are listed by state in the Appendix. Notice that some types of property are exempt regardless of value. Personal effects, furnishings and clothing are common examples. Most other kinds of assets are only partially exempt, that is, exempt up to a certain amount. Example: Washington state exempts automobiles up to $1200. Keep in mind that this refers to your equity in a vehicle. If your auto is worth $6000 and has a loan against it for $4000, the equity equals $2000 and $1200 of this will be protected. The balance of $800 is not protected and can be taken by your creditors.

In addition to an exemption on select assets, some states grant a general purpose dollar amount exemption. This is sometimes referred to as a "wild-card" exemption and can be used to protect any asset you designate (up to the stated amount). The wild-card exemption can be used to protect either partially exempt property or non-exempt property.

Finally, not all states give you the option to choose between federal and state exemptions. Connecticut, Hawaii, Massachusetts, Michigan, Minnesota, New Jersey, New Mexico, Pennsylvania, Rhode Island, Texas, Vermont, Washington, Wisconsin, and the District of Columbia allow you to choose either your state exemptions or the federal exemptions. California requires you to choose between two state lists or the federal list. In all other states you must use your state exemptions and you cannot use the federal exemptions. There is an important exception to this. If you file for bankruptcy and select the state exemptions, you may still take as exemptions your federal retirement benefits. Now let's briefly summarize the steps:

- Check to see the exemptions available to you under your state law, or allowed by federal law, when you can choose between the two.
- Profile the net equity in your assets (value less encumbrances) against the allowed exemptions to determine which assets will be protected in bankruptcy and which will not be protected.
- Convert non-exempt assets into exempt assets. Relocate to a state with more liberal exemptions, if necessary.
- File bankruptcy to discharge your debts.
- Once your debts are discharged, convert your exempt assets into assets you would normally own had you not filed bankruptcy.

How To Legally Dispose Of Assets Before Bankruptcy

A second way to protect assets in bankruptcy is to have them either transferred or encumbered *before* you file.

- *Transferring assets.* Most prospective bankrupts entertain the idea of selling or transferring assets before filing bankruptcy. Go back and review fraudulent transfers discussed in Chapter 2. Transfers that are without adequate consideration are voidable and can be recovered by the bankruptcy trustee. But you may, for example, sell your home to a relative for its fair value. Your relative may then lease the property back to you under a sale-leaseback arrangement. The cash proceeds you received from the sale, may, of course, be spent in a wide variety of ways. Two cautions: First, try to arrange for any sale or transfer more than one year before filing. Your bankruptcy schedules specifically inquire about transfers within the prior year. This does not, however, prevent the trustee from probing earlier transactions. Second, be absolutely truthful, both in your bankruptcy schedules, and to any questions answered under oath to the trustee or in court. Bankruptcy fraud is a very serious crime. There are other legal ways to protect your property in bankruptcy without need to violate any laws or commit perjury.

- Encumbering assets. Do you owe a friend, relative or business associate money? Do you want to protect that individual and someday pay that individual notwithstanding your bankruptcy? Here's how you can help each other: Give your friend a mortgage on as much of your property as is necessary to fully secure the debt you owe. Wait at least 90 days before filing bankruptcy because an earlier filing will make the mortgage voidable as a preference. If the mortgage is to a close relative, then wait one full year to file bankruptcy.

In bankruptcy the encumbered equity would be safe from creditors to the value of the encumbrance. As with all significant pre-bankruptcy transactions, expect it to be scrutinized by the bankruptcy trustee. The trustee will certainly want to determine the validity of the debt. Have the consideration for the mortgage well-documented.

It is more dangerous to gift property before bankruptcy. Gifts can be easily recovered as fraudulent transfers since they are without consideration. Transfers to family members, even at fair value, will be examined closely. Make it an honest transaction. Arms-length transactions won't appear as suspicious. In bankruptcy even the most innocent transaction can be wrongly interpreted and cause you needless aggravation. Make certain your major transactions over the preceding several years are reviewed by your attorney–before you file.

Five Tactics To Side-Step An Involuntary Bankruptcy

Not all bankruptcies are filed by the debtor. Your creditors can petition you into bankruptcy if they can prove you're insolvent. If you have fewer than twelve creditors then any one creditor with a claim of $5000 or more can petition you into bankruptcy. If you have twelve creditors or more then it requires three creditors with aggregate claims of $5000. There are, however, several ways to discourage or stop creditors from pushing you into bankruptcy:

- Create a preference: If you make small installment payments to any threatening creditors, they will probably not petition you into bankruptcy. Not only will they lose future payments, but you can also force them to repay, as a preference, those payments received within ninety days of the bankruptcy.
- Dispute the claim: Only creditors holding undisputed claims can file the bankruptcy petition. Show a dispute exists to the claim of any threatening creditor before a petition is filed. Document the dispute well with correspondence so you can show the dispute is valid.
- Threaten legal action: Creditors usually threaten bankruptcy before they petition you into bankruptcy. The threat, of course, is to coerce you into paying. Few creditors real-

ize it, but threatening you with bankruptcy is a crime. Title 18 of the United States Code says creditors cannot threaten you with bankruptcy. If you are threatened advise the creditor of this law, and also advise the creditor you will refer the threat to the United States Attorney should they carry it out. This tactic may bluff away your creditor.

- Are your assets heavily encumbered? If so, point this out to your creditors. The reality that they will see nothing from the bankruptcy may temper their enthusiasm for bankruptcy.
- Never disclose your creditors: Make it difficult for any one creditor to find two other creditors. You accomplish this by keeping your list of creditors to yourself.

Creditors seldom petition debtors into bankruptcy. They may bluff bankruptcy, but they seldom follow through. Why? A creditor may pay several thousand dollars in legal fees to prosecute a contested bankruptcy. This is usually a poor investment since general creditors seldom recover more than a few cents on the dollar. But don't take a chance on a premature bankruptcy. Be properly positioned before you go into bankruptcy by converting non-exempt assets into exempt assets, making all proper and timely transfers, and encumbering the few non-exempt assets that do remain in your name. Since creditors may strike first, it's always smart to defensively position yourself while you still have the opportunity.

When You Should Not Discharge A Debt In Bankruptcy

You may want to pay certain debts discharged in bankruptcy for a variety of reasons. This means you'll again be legally responsible for these debts as if you had not filed bankruptcy.

Reaffirming debts may be a noble idea, but it's usually a mistake. Bankruptcy gave you a clean start so it makes little sense to regain cancelled debts. You can legally reaffirm debts only with the approval of the bankruptcy court. The judge oversees these decisions to be certain you can safely handle the obligations without financial difficulty.

Creditors not listed on your bankruptcy schedules don't have debts due them discharged. These debts require no re-affirmation because they are still enforceable after bankruptcy. If you don't want a creditor to discover that you have filed bankruptcy, then it's wise not to list that creditor on your schedules. A substantial creditor not scheduled is counterproductive because you will remain legally burdened with that debt. Best bet: List all creditors. If you later become wealthy you can, as a moral gesture, pay those debts you feel a special obligation to pay.

When does it make sense to leave a creditor unscheduled? If you owe a small sum on a valuable credit card, such as American Express. Your strategy here is to continue to make timely payments. Unlisted creditors probably won't learn of your bankruptcy and will leave your credit intact.

Tax Benefits With Bankruptcy

People filing bankruptcy don't ordinarily think of the possible tax benefits. In fact, there can be important tax advantages with bankruptcy, and equally important tax disadvantages if you don't file bankruptcy. This is particularly true if you owe money to your own company or to your employer.

The main tax benefit: There are no tax consequences from debts forgiven under bankruptcy. On the other hand, forgiveness of debt without bankruptcy creates taxable income to the debtor on the amount forgiven. Example: If you owe $50,000 to your employer, or your own company, and you are voluntarily discharged from the debt without bankruptcy, you must claim the $50,000 as taxable income. This is not true if the discharge of the debt is through bankruptcy. Review the tax consequences of filing bankruptcy with your tax advisor. Your advisor may help you document the transactions properly so you can capture the maximum tax benefits when you do file bankruptcy.

How Bankruptcy Stops Foreclosure

Once a bankruptcy petition is filed, it operates as an automatic stay. All creditor collections or repossessions must halt. All lawsuits must also stop while the bankruptcy proceeds. One purpose of the automatic stay is to transfer all collection and debtor-creditor matters from other courts to the bankruptcy court. For example, your creditors cannot enforce prior judgments or liens against you or your property. Two exceptions: Criminal actions continue, as can the collection of back alimony or child support.

Although the automatic stay suspends a creditor's right to repossess collateral, a secured creditor can petition the bankruptcy court to relax this rule. This procedure is known as requesting adequate protection. A secured creditor is a creditor that holds specific property as collateral to secure repayment of a debt. It may be a mortgage on real estate, a security interest on personal property, or even a lease on equipment.

When a secured creditor requests adequate protection, the bankruptcy court must provide the creditor a remedy so the collateral is not impaired by the automatic stay. This is important where the collateral may lose value. Example: A boat will likely decrease in value over time. The bankruptcy court will require sufficient payments to the secured party to at least cover this depreciation. Conversely, the court will allow the creditor to repossess the collateral if there's no other way to protect the creditor. The automatic stay ends when the case is closed, dismissed, or the debtor receives a discharge.

Bankruptcy, as you can see, doesn't give you total protection against foreclosure or repossession. You must file bankruptcy with a workable strategy to deal with secured creditors who hold valid liens on assets you wish to keep. Of course, if you want to abandon assets to your secured creditor, you can do so any time during the bankruptcy. Any deficiency that results will be treated as an unsecured debt and discharged in the bankruptcy. However, if you want to keep the asset, and prevent the secured creditor from foreclosing, you may have more rights than you realize:

• The mere filing of the bankruptcy will halt any further foreclosure actions. Not uncommonly, a bankruptcy is filed the day before an important asset, such as a home, is scheduled for auction. To continue your restraint on the secured creditor be prepared to show the court that the secured creditor is not prejudiced by his inability to foreclose. You will probably have to at least pay interest on the loan so it doesn't increase the loan balance. You must further show the court that the asset is not losing value and that the secured creditor would recover as much later as today. Your protection will be short-lived unless you can convince the court that the delay won't hurt the secured party. In many cases a debtor files bankruptcy to stop foreclosure, but the court quickly allows the foreclosure. If you file bankruptcy to stop a foreclosure, then do it with a reasonable certainty that the bankruptcy will give you the opportunity to solve your loan problem. File bankruptcy with a reasonably good understanding about how you are going to emerge from bankruptcy with the property you want.

• Use your one big weapon against secured creditors–the cramdown. A cramdown petition requires the bankruptcy court to reduce the amount of a secured debt to an amount equivalent to the liquidation value of the secured collateral. Any balance is treated as unsecured debt. Example: If you have a $200,000 mortgage on real estate and you can show the court that the property would only bring $100,000 under foreclosure, the court can reduce the mortgage to $100,000. The balance will be treated as unsecured debt. There are technical considerations best left for the lawyers, but it's vital for you to know that bankruptcy can be your ideal remedy when you are over-financed and the secured lender wants to foreclose.

• Bankruptcy is also your opportunity to cure defaults on mortgages or secured loans. Chapter 13 bankruptcy gives you five years to bring current any past due secured debts. This is important, if, for example, you lost your job and fell behind on your mortgage payments but can now stay current. Under Chapter 13, you can pay the arrears over five years–and the lender could not foreclose provided you stayed current and made the arrearage payments punctually.

How To Protect Your Assets In Bankruptcy Without Filing Yourself

Here's a common problem. Suppose one of your real estate properties is under foreclosure. How could you stop the foreclosure? One answer is to file Chapter 11. But assume you are solvent and except for this one distressed property you personally have no need for the bankruptcy court. How can you then put your property into Chapter 11 without putting yourself into Chapter 11?

Answer: Transfer the property to a new corporation that you organize and then have that corporation file Chapter 11. Since the property is now owned by the corporation protected by bankruptcy, the lender will be automatically restrained from foreclosure. The Chapter 11 will delay the foreclosure and give you the opportunity to sell or refinance the property, or develop a plan of reorganization to resolve the problem loan.

Another strategy: Set up a Nevada corporation as a holding company to own all the stock in the subsidiary corporation that now owns the troubled property. Since the parent corporation is in Nevada, the subsidiary corporation can file its Chapter 11 in Nevada. The big benefit is that it will help you avoid the embarrassment of a Chapter 11 where you reside. It will be inconvenient for your lender to contest the Chapter 11. You can set up a holding company in any state, but Nevada is recommended because if offers the most privacy.

The Little-Known Bankruptcy Alternative For Troubled Businesses

Do you own a business with few assets and too much debt? It may be a waste of time and effort to attempt either an informal workout with creditors or a Chapter 11 reorganization. It's easier, less costly, and more sensible to liquidate your business and purchase back its assets while you conveniently leave behind the debts of your former company.

The tactic is absolutely legal. Correctly handled, your creditors will receive at least as much as they would under a non-bankruptcy workout, Chapter 11, or straight Chapter 7 bankruptcy. You, in turn, win back a debt-free business for pennies-on-the-dollar. You then have a fresh start with a minimum of inconvenience, disruption, aggravation and cost. Consider the advantages. A liquidation and buy-back is:

- Less costly than an expensive Chapter 11. It usually takes only several hours of professional time to orchestrate a buy-back. A Chapter 11 may cost tens of thousands of dollars–an expense prohibitive for the smaller business.
- Faster. You can complete a buy-back in a few days. A workout or Chapter 11 can drag on for years and distract you from your primary goal of making money.

• More controllable. With Chapter 11 your business is under the close supervision of the bankruptcy court and your creditors. The bankruptcy court can replace you with a trustee. If the reorganization fails, you lose control over your assets. A buy-back gives you more control because you determine how your business is liquidated, when it is liquidated, and finally who the liquidator will be.

• Much cleaner and less complex a process compared to Chapter 11. For instance, with a liquidation buy-back, there's no need to resolve contested claims or engage in protracted litigation since all debts are left behind.

Large, publicly-owned corporations can't take advantage of the buy-back strategy, however, the smaller family-owned venture or the mid-sized privately owned company will find it a practical solution to their creditor problems. These are businesses not burdened by outside stockholders. These firms also enjoy low-visibility and the flexibility to take a few perfectly legal and smart short-cuts on their way back to solvency.

The strategy is simple: Step one is to liquidate your business. Step two is to buy-back the assets through a new corporation at a commercially reasonable price–usually a small fraction of its real value. Step three: You're back in business but without your creditors.

You can voluntarily liquidate an insolvent business in a number of ways. In many states you can appoint an assignee for the benefit of creditors. This usually does not involve a court. The assignee is empowered to sell the assets with the proceeds paid to creditors. You can also have the state court appoint a receiver who, like the assignee, sells the assets and distributes the proceeds to creditors. Unlike a bankruptcy where you have no control over who is appointed trustee, you usually can influence who becomes the liquidator in a buy-back. You can even use a friendly mortgagee who can foreclose on your business and re-sell its assets to you.

No matter how your business is liquidated, the liquidator will entertain your offer for the assets provided you offer more than could be reasonably obtained at auction. This is usually determined by a professional auction value appraisal. Because you are re-acquiring your business assets for pennies-on-the-dollar, you are guaranteed a bargain and one more opportunity to start again with a debt-free business.

Keep it an honest transaction. Avoid even the hint of impropriety. Make certain you pay a commercially reasonable price for the assets or the creditors can and should set aside the transfer as fraudulent.

Do you want to learn more about this buy-back strategy? Order *How to Save Your Business From Bankruptcy*, available from Garrett Publishing listed in the Appendix. You'll see how this strategy saved over 2000 failing businesses from bankruptcy.

Key Secrets To Remember

• File bankruptcy only after careful thought. There are alternatives to your financial problems–and some may be more advantageous.

- Test your timing. Don't file bankruptcy too soon or too late.
- File the right type of bankruptcy. Match the bankruptcy to your own financial situation.
- The key to protecting assets in bankruptcy is to convert unprotected non-exempt assets into fully protected exempt assets.
- Another key strategy is to sell or encumber non-exempt assets far in advance of bankruptcy.
- Filing bankruptcy to stop foreclosure? Be realistic in whether your efforts will be successful.
- If your business is heading for bankruptcy, consider instead the non-bankruptcy alternatives–particularly the buy-back strategy. It can save you time, money and aggravation.

11

POWERFUL WAYS TO STOP THE IRS FROM PLUNDERING YOUR ASSETS

Is the IRS after you? Do you have nightmares of losing your home, savings, business and all those other worldly possessions you worked so hard to accumulate? Yes, it can happen. No threat to your financial well-being is as serious as the IRS. Only the IRS has such awesome powers to collect.

There's a bright side. Most taxpayers resolve their IRS problems losing only some hard earned money. While the collection corps at the IRS are tough (they do have a tough job to do), they can also be cooperative and reasonable–if you are cooperative and reasonable. The IRS has powerful laws to help them collect, but you the taxpayer have a few laws of your own to protect your assets from the IRS. Understand and assert these rights. It's your first-line defense against the IRS.

SECRET #117

How The IRS Tracks You Down

Hiding is no answer when the IRS is on your tail. The IRS has many devious ways to find you no matter where or how often you move. Their weapon? A powerful IRS computer linked to 50 state computers, as well as to social security and every other federal agency you have contact with. You are also easily tracked via state tax agencies, motor vehicle departments, unemployment offices, public welfare agencies, professional licensing boards, and even voter registration records. It's indeed difficult to hide.

Despite this vast spy network, the IRS computer works slowly. It can take the IRS a year or more to find you. So while moving around can forestall the day of reckoning, it is not a way to avoid it. Your best bet: If you owe taxes, deal with the IRS as soon as possible. Delay only costs you additional interest and penalties. You'll also receive far less cooperation from the IRS if they believe you intentionally avoided them. Caution: Delay long enough to protect your assets–so you can bargain with the IRS on your terms not theirs!

How To Keep Your Financial Records From The IRS

Soon after the IRS assesses a tax against you, they will request that you complete a financial statement. This "Collection Information Statement" (IRS Form 433) requires you to disclose all your property as well as sources of income. It's obvious purpose: The IRS then knows precisely what property and wages are available for seizure and levy. The IRS also has the information to work out a payment plan with you if you have too few assets to quickly pay.

What if you refuse to provide the information? The IRS will summons you to the IRS office to provide the information. Fail to appear and the IRS can have the federal court compel your appearance. The court can jail you and also impose a fine for your failure to honor the summons.

The IRS can compel your appearance to answer questions, but that doesn't mean you must actually answer IRS questions about your assets and income. Taxpayers have successfully refused disclosure of financial information by claiming their rights under the Fifth Amendment. This involves technical questions of law, so follow the advice of your counsel. You certainly are within your rights to refuse information if you have a reasonable basis to believe you are under criminal investigation by the IRS or any other federal or state law enforcement agency.

What is clear is that you must protect your assets before you give financial information to the IRS. The IRS will quickly lien or seize any listed assets, so time is not on your side. The key rule: Never lie when completing an IRS financial statement. Always be truthful because your statement is under perjury. It is far smarter and safer to refuse information than it is to falsify information. Keep in mind that the IRS will check out your assets from other sources. They cannot easily find cash, bearer investments, or collectibles such as gold, jewelry or artwork, but they can easily discover other assets you own.

Plan ahead so you can honestly answer the IRS asset inquiry and at the same time disclose nothing to lead the IRS to your assets. Review the IRS collection statement before you must complete it. You can then deploy your assets in a way to both honestly answer while revealing nothing of great value to the IRS.

The IRS will demand new collection information on your assets and income about once a year. The IRS is tracking your financial condition and your ability to pay. While the IRS may request annual information, more and more taxpayers are triggered for renewed collection efforts when their income increases as picked up by IRS computers monitoring tax returns.

What The IRS Already Knows About You

You can't conceal much about your financial affairs from the IRS. The IRS already knows virtually everything about you both from your own tax returns and information obtained from third-parties. Your tax return alone tells the IRS about your:

- wages
- interest income
- dividend income
- tax refunds
- rental income
- royalty income
- capital gain distributions
- moving expense payments
- vacation allowances
- severance pay
- travel allowances

Other third-parties you deal with, either through their own tax returns or via mandatory reporting, reveal:

- mortgage interest received
- funds received from barter and broker exchanges
- unemployment income
- tax shelters
- fringe benefits received from your employer
- distributions from pension and profit-sharing plans
- cash payments of over $10,000 made to your bank account
- cash payments of over $10,000 received in a trade or business
- gambling winnings over $600
- payments made to you if you are a health care provider under an insurance program.
- fees paid to you as an accountant, attorney or entertainer

With this data-base of information, your financial past and present can be accurately reconstructed by the IRS. A seasoned IRS agent will do the necessary homework to find your assets rather than rely solely on what you voluntarily disclose. Review your own tax records, as well as the possible information provided by third-parties. Make certain you can explain the disposition of assets that may be disclosed through these records.

How To Side-Step The IRS Jeopardy Assessment

A jeopardy assessment grants the IRS the right to lien and seize your assets even before proceeding through the usual collection procedures.

The IRS can simply assess the tax and begin immediate collection under a jeopardy assessment, however, certain procedures must be strictly followed both before and after the assessment. First, the IRS must have good reason to believe the taxpayer: a) is planning to leave the country, or b) planning to avoid payment of the taxes by concealing, transferring or dissipating property, or c) otherwise has his or her financial solvency imperiled.

Once the request for jeopardy assessment is reviewed and approved by the IRS District Director, the taxpayer is served with the jeopardy assessment. It is now immediately collectible by the IRS through enforced collection. How do you avoid a jeopardy assessment?

- Be extremely circumspect in your transfer of assets once the IRS begins its ordinary collection process.
- Avoid unusual or protracted foreign travel that the IRS may become aware of. It's unwise to even apply for a passport.
- Continue to work cooperatively with the IRS.
- Make absolutely no pronouncements about your financial affairs or intentions concerning your property.
- Do not suddenly close your bank accounts–but do reduce them to a negligible balance.

In other words, do nothing that seems out of the ordinary or could strike the IRS as a plan to take flight or render yourself insolvent. The bottom line: While the IRS expects you to remain a "sitting duck", you must in your own circumspect way strategically protect your assets without arousing suspicion.

Even though it seems jeopardy assessments are directed against ordinary folks only trying to protect their assets, in reality

the IRS uses jeopardy assessments chiefly against suspected drug dealers and those in organized crime. Still, that doesn't mean it won't be used against you. The mere fact that the IRS has the power to lien and levy upon your property with little or no warning should again reinforce the need to judgment proof your assets before you incur a large tax liability. Caution: Taxpayers often assume they have ample time to insulate their assets from the IRS, only to be hit early with jeopardy assessment tax liens. Delay in protecting yourself from the IRS can be very costly.

SECRET #121

Your One Key Move Before A Tax Lien Hits

Should you leave your assets in your name exposed to a forthcoming tax lien, or instead transfer or dispose of your property before the tax lien is filed?

Taxpayers often beat the IRS by conveying assets before they are encumbered with a tax lien. Transfer of your assets is absolutely your wisest strategy. Timing is critical. Conveyance after the tax lien is filed does not prevent the IRS from seizing the property now in the hands of a third-party, since a tax lien automatically follows the attached property. If your property is conveyed before the lien, the transferee takes it free and clear of the later lien.

The IRS, as any other creditor, can go to court to recover property fraudulently conveyed. The burden is on the creditor. The IRS may also file a "nominee lien" against the property now in the hands of the transferee. The IRS must then successfully litigate whether the transfer was a fraudulent conveyance. The IRS, as a giant bureaucracy, seldom goes to such great lengths to recover fraudulently transferred property unless the tax liability and the value of the transferred property is significant and the entire transaction blatant. Transferring property in the face of a tax lien comes under the adage of "nothing to lose and everything to gain".

How To Cope With A Tax Lien

What impact will a tax have on you and your lifestyle?

An IRS tax lien remains in effect as long as the IRS has the right to enforce collection. Since the IRS has ten years under the current statute of limitations, a tax lien remains alive and enforceable for ten years. Commencement of a tax claim in court, or time out of the country, will extend the lien for an equal length of time.

The immediate effect of the tax lien is that it automatically encumbers all property owned by the taxpayer. This prevents the taxpayer from selling or borrowing against the property. But there are still other effects. Once a tax lien is filed against you, it will be virtually impossible to obtain significant credit or finance larger items such as cars and homes because the tax lien will remain superior to debts owed other creditors. A new lender will not have clear rights to the collateral in the event of default. One solu-

tion: Have your spouse take title if your spouse is free of tax problems (one of the benefits of filing tax returns separately). Even safer: Set up a corporation to take title to any new purchases. Clearly, you do not want to list yourself as a stockholder. This still may not alleviate your creditor problems if you are asked to guarantee financing since your credit won't pass the credit test. The bottom line: Keep future assets out of your name and depend on others to guarantee your future financing.

A tax lien can also precipitate foreclosure by existing lenders who may become concerned the IRS will attempt to dispose of assets that they hold as collateral. One common situation is when accounts receivable is the collateral. The IRS gains a superior lien against a lender on receivables generated more than 45 days from the date of the tax lien. This poses a critical problem for businesspeople with receivables pledged to a bank. Since the bank would lose their priority rights to receivables generated 45 days or more from the lien date, the bank would rightfully insist upon a release of the tax lien (which would, of course, only occur if the taxpayer fully paid the taxes), or payoff on the bank loan. Alternatives may be substitution of other collateral for the receivables, or filing Chapter 11 within the 45 days. Any of these actions would keep the bank secure and in a first position. If none of these occur, the bank would be forced to foreclose on the pledged receivables to protect their priority rights to the receivables. This is one reason why so many companies with tax problems (usually unpaid withholding taxes) do file Chapter 11.

Another point to check: Although the IRS

should automatically file a release of lien when the tax liability is paid or the statute of limitations runs, the IRS does not always follow through. If you're entitled to a lien release, check whether it's filed with the public records. If not, personally demand a release of lien from your local tax office. Also have your credit report reflect that you no longer have a tax problem. Unless you're diligent on this you will have continuing credit problems long after the tax lien has been satisfied.

How To Settle With The IRS On Your Terms

You can be hit with a tax bill you cannot possibly hope to pay now or in the future. Your solution is to either:

- Remain a "paper pauper" until the statute of limitations on the tax lien expires.
- Stall the IRS for three years and then file for bankruptcy, thus discharging the income tax liability.
- Settle with the IRS through an offer and compromise.

Since the first two alternatives are discussed elsewhere, let's focus here on the offer and compromise.

An offer and compromise is a little-known IRS procedure that allows the IRS to accept a portion of the tax owed as full payment and discharge of your tax liability. If the IRS believes you will have high future earnings, the IRS may also bargain for part of your future income. An offer and compromise can also extend payments over time.

Tip: You'll only successfully negotiate a favorable offer and compromise when the IRS is convinced your settlement proposal is better than what they could hope to collect on their own. Follow these five additional pointers if you really want to improve the odds of convincing the IRS to accept pennies-on-the-dollar:

- Let the IRS chase you before you make your offer. The IRS must be convinced that regular collection efforts won't work on you, and the IRS is never quite convinced until they try.
- Have your offer clearly exceed any possible recovery from your assets at auction. Be asset-poor if you want a low offer to work.
- Since future earning power is a factor, do not portray too successful a future. Make your offer when you're between jobs or wrestling with what may be a chronic illness that may prevent you from working altogether. Watch this point, particularly if you are young and have good earning years ahead. Under these circumstances you won't get much sympathy from the IRS who can wait a long time to get paid.
- Start with a low-ball offer. As with any negotiations, expect the IRS to counter-offer no matter how reasonable your initial offer may be.

•Retain a seasoned accountant or tax lawyer to handle the offer and compromise. It's a tricky procedure, and one you probably will not be successful with unless you do have the right professional assistance.

The big benefit of a successful offer and compromise is that you reduce the tax liability to an amount you can handle. The second big benefit of an offer and compromise is that it usually suspends collection activity while the offer and compromise is under consideration. This is if the IRS believes you are acting in good faith and that the offer and compromise has a reasonable chance of approval.

The two disadvantages of an offer and compromise? 1) You must reveal all your assets in considerable detail, and 2) The time the IRS spends considering your offer and compromise is added to the ten year collection period.

How To Win The Time You Need To Pay

You may owe the IRS more than you can write a check for, yet not enough to warrant an offer and compromise. How can you convince the IRS to accept payments in installments over several months, or perhaps even a year or two?

The IRS has a procedure, less formal than an offer and compromise, whereby a taxpayer may submit to the IRS a financial statement and formally request permission to pay the past due tax in installments over a number of months. Caution: If your financial statements show assets that can be readily liquidated, the IRS will push for their sale rather than accept your installment proposal.

Strategy: Tell the IRS agent you will try to sell or borrow against some assets, but in the meantime you will pay a part of the tax each month to show good faith. As a practical matter you can probably win 8-12 months to pay the tax even though such a lenient payment plan would not have been openly agreed to by the IRS. But don't count on more than a one year installment plan. Revenue agents hesitate to keep cases open longer and may insist you file an offer and compromise or bankruptcy should you need more time. Nevertheless, installment plans of 18 or even 24 months are not unheard of. Contrary to popular belief, the IRS will agree to a reasonable installment plan if you do not have the readily available cash to pay your delinquent taxes in less time.

The IRS Code does not stop an IRS agent from accepting an installment arrangement. The IRS guidelines, in fact, recommend an installment arrangement if it would "facilitate collection" of the owed taxes. Once the IRS agrees to an installment arrangement it must honor it unless:

•You miss a payment.
•You fall behind on other taxes due the IRS.
•You fail to give the IRS updated financial information, when requested.
•You gave the IRS false information when negotiating the installment plan.

• Your financial condition significantly improves (such as with a large inheritance).

Why may the IRS refuse to give you time to pay your tax liability over time?

• You have sufficient assets to quickly pay the liability. For example, you may have ample stocks or bonds that can be liquidated within a few days. Remember-the purpose of an installment plan is to arrange for the orderly discharge of the tax obligation when other reasonable means are unavailable. When assets are available, you can expect the IRS to pressure you to use those assets to satisfy the debt.
• You have proven unreliable in staying with similar installment plans in the past. (On the other hand, if you have been reliable in the past, then use this as a selling point.)
• You request a repayment schedule over too long a period of time.

Another tactic to take. File IRS Form 911, the Taxpayer Assistance Order. Its purpose is to give you one more clear chance to resolve the tax problem with other IRS officials-before the IRS can levy upon or seize any property. This procedure can delay seizure for several weeks but you shouldn't count on relief for longer.

Assets The IRS Targets First

An IRS collection officer has wide discretion when choosing property to seize for purposes of satisfying a tax claim. In making the decision, the IRS considers several factors:

• The amount of the tax liability compared to the property needed to satisfy the claim.
• The ease of seizure and disposal of your various assets.
• How necessary each asset is to the taxpayer.

Assets the IRS targets-in descending order:

• Bank and checking accounts,
• Cars, boats, airplanes, and recreational vehicles with a high equity,
• Accounts receivable,
• Stocks, bonds, and other obligations due you,
• Investment real estate,
• Home,
• IRA's, Keogh's, and other pension accounts,
• Wages.

The IRS is most reluctant to seize a home, pension accounts or wages, and generally do so only when the taxpayer is uncooperative. Threatened seizure of the home may also be attempted when the agent believes it will spur the taxpayer to refinance the home to pay the taxes. The IRS will not hesitate to file a lien against all your property.

The IRS has its own guidelines concerning the seizure of social security payments and retirement funds. According to the IRS collection manual, levy of these sources of income should be made only in flagrant and aggravated cases, and then only with the prior approval of the authorized IRS supervisor who must sign the notice of levy. Contrary to popular belief–these two assets are not beyond the reach of the IRS.

SECRET #126

Assets The IRS Can't Touch

The IRS does not have to leave you with very much, but the IRS still cannot take everything you own. Exempt from IRS seizure is:

- Fuel, food, furniture and personal effects up to a total of $1650,
- Undelivered mail,
- Tools and books needed for your job, business or profession–up to $1100,
- Income needed to provide court-ordered child support,
- Unemployment, worker's compensation, public assistance and job training benefits,
- Clothing and school books,
- Pension payments of retired railroad employees, military disability benefits, or benefits from individuals on the Armed Forces Honor Roll.

Note that Social Security, IRA's, Keogh plans and 401K Qualified Pension Plans are not protected. That doesn't suggest the IRS will quickly seize these assets, and in fact they are seldom seized by the IRS. But if you have a large tax liability you should not keep IRA's, Keogh's or other pension accounts. Liquidate these tax deferred accounts to shelter the funds–even it it means incurring a tax penalty for early withdrawal. As a practical matter, the penalty may be treated much like the original tax liability, since it will be of little or no consequence if you do not intend to fully pay your tax liability.

Another caution: If you believe your home is protected from the IRS by your state homestead laws, you will be in for a rude surprise. The IRS is the one creditor that can totally disregard your homestead protection.

SECRET #127

How To Keep Your Assets From The Clutches Of The IRS

The IRS code makes it a felony to remove, deposit or conceal any property upon which an IRS levy has been authorized and when done with the intention of defeating the collection of taxes. This does not, however, mean that you must actually turn over to the IRS assets subject to seizure. In fact, IRS agents do not have the authority to force a taxpayer to produce any property for seizure.

Example: You may continuously move the location of a car or boat under threat of seizure. But if you volunteer the location of the asset to an IRS agent, the disclosure must be truthful. As with the bank account subject to constant relocation, the car or boat can be continuously moved to defeat seizure. Still, this tactic is not recommended, no matter how desperately you may want to keep the asset. Eventually the IRS locates and seizes the more significant assets. Safer strategy: Convey, sell or encumber the asset before the collection process reaches the point of lien and seizure. For example, it is considerably smarter to sell your car and then lease it (or another car) back. Here the IRS would have no car to chase and you would avoid a "hide-and-seek" game you are bound to lose.

Nor can the IRS enter either residential or business premises for purposes of seizing property unless you either voluntarily consent to such entry, or the IRS agent has obtained a warrant or a court order, "writ of entry".

You do have the right to examine the writ of entry. You can also confine the agent to the specific premises described in the writ. However, this only applies to private areas. The IRS does not need a writ of entry to seize assets on public property. An automobile in a public garage, for instance, can be seized by the IRS without a writ of entry, while the same auto in your garage cannot.

Property in another state can also slow the IRS. The local agent must then transfer your file to an agent in that state. In sum:

- Sell or transfer what you can before the lien.
- Redeploy other physical assets to distant locations.

- Close out and liquidate all bank accounts, securities or other easily seized liquid assets.

How To Win Release Of Your Seized Property

The IRS can seize your home, but it cannot throw you out. As a practical matter you have about 90 days between the date of seizure and a public auction or sealed bid sale of the property. You have another 180 days where you can stay in possession, after your property was sold to a successful bidder. During this six month period you can redeem or re-acquire your real estate for what the buyer paid, plus interest. Once the 180 day redemption period passes, the buyer can commence eviction proceedings, but this may take another several months. This means you have approximately one year of rent-free living from the date of seizure.

There's no similar right of continued possession with personal property. The IRS can take possession of cars, boats and other property from the date of seizure. Moreover, you have no right of redemption with personal property, as you do with real property. How can you win the release and return of your seized property? Any time prior to sale the IRS may release seized property, if:

- You enter into an acceptable payment agreement. Quite often the real motive of a seizure is to prod the taxpayer to solve their tax problem by selling or refinancing property. Taxpayers can be lax until they are about to lose valued assets, then they often do find money.

- Release will facilitate collection. This would apply, for example, to business assets. Presumably business assets in operation generate more than they would at auction, and this income can be used to pay the tax bill.
- The tax liability is satisfied or no longer enforceable. Payment in full will obviously bring about a release, but so too will passage of the statute of limitations. In either instance the IRS must release seized property.
- Bankruptcy is filed. A bankruptcy filing (whether under Chapter 7, 11 or 13) automatically stays any further action by the IRS unless and until they have approval to proceed by the bankruptcy court.
- You file a bond equal in value to the seized asset. You may also substitute collateral of equal or greater value.

SBA or have other federal funding. After all, it makes little sense for one federal agency to collect its money at the expense of another federal agency that will no longer have the opportunity to collect.

- Businesses that are minority owned, or have a high-percentage of minorities employed.
- Businesses that are engaged in defense work, or other activities of particular sensitivity or importance to the federal government.
- Businesses that are high-profile within a community, or employ a large number of people from the community.

If you own such a business you may find the tax collector will show greater restraint. Two points to bear in mind: First, this is not official IRS policy. It does, however, appear to be unofficial policy based on the observations of many tax specialists. Second, leniency in collection should not be taken as immunity. No matter how important your business may be, the IRS will expect payment for overdue taxes.

Why The IRS May Not Touch Your Business

Did you know the IRS moves less swiftly in seizing certain businesses? Who are these lucky entrepreneurs that are favored by the IRS?

- Businesses that are financed by the

How To Buy Your Assets Back From The IRS

IRS auctions often fetch as little as 40 percent of the actual value of the seized property. Sometimes less. Your best strategy then may be to allow the IRS to sell your home, car, boat or other property at public auction. If you can raise the money to cover the high-bid, why not buy your property back through a third-party or straw? This is a practical approach, for example, if the IRS has a $300,000 lien on your $100,000 home. Let it go to auction and you may possibly re-purchase your home for $50,000.

The IRS must establish a minimum price bid. It can then sell the property at public auction, or through sealed bid, at a price equivalent to or greater than the minimum price bid. Watch the minimum bid established by the IRS. They usually accurately predict what property will bring at a distressed sale. To calculate this bid amount, the IRS first establishes the fair market value of the property under a normal sale. They then deduct 20 percent, and then another 25 percent, representing the distress sale influence on the price. Thus, a home valued at $150,000 would end up with a $90,000 minimum bid requirement ($150,000 less $30,000 less $30,000).

An unreasonably low appraisal value may help you to literally steal your property back. On the other hand, it would also allow the IRS to sell your property too cheaply to outside bidders. This may not produce the proceeds necessary to eliminate your tax bill or give you a surplus. Once you know the minimum bid, try to convince the IRS to release your property to you for that amount. Remember–all you have to pay is the equity the IRS has attached. This might be quite nominal. This can make sense to the IRS since they

can avoid the expense of an auction sale. Caution: Should you re-acquire the property, take title through a corporation or trust, rather than in your own name.

SECRET #131

How To Safeguard Your Bank Account And Safe Deposit Box From The IRS

The IRS maintains a record of your checking and savings accounts and can automatically levy these accounts. In fact, funds in any bank account under your name are unsafe as long as you owe the IRS. The IRS routinely levies all known bank accounts of a delinquent taxpayer. It is their favorite collection weapon. How can you protect your money?

- Set up a corporation. Place your funds in the corporate account and use the corporate account to pay your personal debts. You could, for example, put the money into the corporate account as a loan and withdraw it as repayment of the loan–all without taxable consequence.
- Alternative: Keep your money in banks the IRS is unlikely to know about. Use small, out-of-the-way banks, because the IRS sometimes "shotguns" and levies all banks in your area. Since the IRS will periodically make you complete a

financial statement listing your bank accounts, it will be necessary to open a new account elsewhere immediately after disclosing your present account. There is absolutely nothing illegal about this. It is, however, illegal to lie to the IRS about bank accounts (or other assets) when asked. IRS agents frequently levy bank accounts either to find no funds on hand or that the account was closed. The IRS then searches for a new bank account and/or seek other assets to seize.

Your safe deposit box is no safer. If the IRS suspects you have cash or other valuables secreted in a safe deposit box, the IRS can compel you to disclose its location. The IRS can then demand that you open the box in the presence of an IRS agent, or lacking your cooperation, the IRS seals the box and denies you access. They assume that eventually you will want access to your box and then be forced to permit IRS examination. The IRS frequently waits until the safe deposit box rental contract expires and a bank officer is then authorized to open the box and display its contents to the IRS.

One solution: Never store cash or other valuables in a safe deposit box. Yet, this is not always convenient or desirable. Quite frequently, a safe deposit box is the only safe place for your valuables. Your best strategy: Rent the safe deposit box in the name of a corporation you organize. Since the corporation is an entity apart from yourself, the IRS cannot legally gain access to the corporation's safe deposit box to collect on your tax obligations. Another advantage: Even if

you are not a tax delinquent, the IRS can seal your safe deposit box upon your death. A corporation, on the other hand, has perpetual life. Your death will not invite IRS attention to the corporate safe deposit box. A spouse, or other designated individual may have corresponding authority to open the box.

Besides the opportunity to collect on overdue taxes, there's good reason for the IRS to be snoopy when it comes to cash hidden in safe deposit boxes. Absent proof to the contrary, the Internal Revenue Service considers cash found in your safe deposit box to be undeclared income. You're then taxed on the money, together with interest and penalties. You can submit evidence to the IRS that the money is either exempt from taxation or is previously reported funds. For example, you may have notified your accountant, in writing, that the cash represents proceeds from the sale of your home. The basic rule: Never stash cash without third-party documentation as to its source. It's money you just may end up paying tax on twice.

IRS Perils For Trusts And Jointly-Held Property

Property held in trust is not ordinarily subject to seizure for payment of the tax liability of the grantor, but this rule can be ignored under two circumstances:

- When the grantor conveyed the property to the trust solely to defeat the rights of the IRS, and the transfer constitutes a fraudulent conveyance, or
- When the grantor retains control over the trust property, or has the right to revoke the trust, as is commonly the case with a living trust.

If you conveyed the property into the trust well before you incurred the tax liability you should have no problem. More important, however, is to use an irrevocable trust so you do not have control. The IRS closely examines trusts to determine if the taxpayer has sufficient control to allow the IRS to reach the trust assets as an alter-ego of the taxpayer.

Another problem area is jointly-owned property. Creditors of one spouse can force the sale of jointly-held property. The IRS enjoys even broader powers. If a husband and wife, for example, own a home in joint tenancy, or as tenants-by-the-entirety, the IRS can then force the sale of the entire property even though only one spouse has the tax liability. The IRS–of course, must remit to the non-liable spouse his or her half of the net proceeds. Even when the IRS seizes a partial interest, such as the husband's interest, buyers of the husband's interest can then petition the court to partition the property and order it sold with the proceeds divided.

As a matter of policy, the IRS seldom forces the sale of jointly-owned marital property when only one spouse owes taxes. Nevertheless, your best protection is to convey jointly-held property beyond IRS reach before a lien is placed against it.

Joint bank accounts are even more perilous. The IRS levies the entire funds in a joint account and then leaves it to the non-liable joint-owner to prove they contributed equally to the account. The bottom line: Never put your money into a joint account with another person unless you are absolutely certain the individual is free of tax problems. This applies even to spouses.

Also beware of filing a joint return with your spouse. You may pay a slightly lower tax then when filing singly, but the trade-off is that the IRS cannot then collect from both spouses. When you file singly, your spouse has no danger of an IRS assessment and can safely hold the marital assets.

If you do file separate tax returns, you have no liability for your spouse's unpaid taxes. But the IRS can take your share of jointly-owned real estate, savings or checking accounts, stocks and bonds, and even automobiles and other jointly-held assets. Therefore, you will want to protect this property by taking these assets out of your spouse's name before they are levied or liened by the IRS. Should you file jointly, then the tax liability can be collected, in whole or in part, from either spouse. This is the big danger with joint returns–you cannot easily protect assets since neither spouse can provide a safe harbor. Notwithstanding possible tax-savings under a joint filing, spouses should especially file singly when:

- One spouse has on-going tax problems–continuing audits or tax liabilities.

- One spouse has tax filings that may cause serious civil or criminal problems.
- One spouse has most of the assets in his or her name, and the other spouse the greater possibility of tax exposure.

How To Work For The IRS–Whether You Want To Or Not

The wage levy is the IRS' most far-reaching power. This remedy is particularly effective because there is no limit on the amount of wages the IRS can take, except for a personal exemption of $75 per week plus $25 per week for each dependent, including your spouse. The IRS need not file successive levies to attach future wages. One levy remains in effect until your tax liability is fully paid.

Wage levies, as one of the more extreme measures in the IRS collection arsenal, is ordinarily used only when less drastic collection efforts fail. But not even the IRS can realistically expect a single wage earner with a net salary of $500 to give the IRS $425 and survive on $75 a week. Thus, the wage levy serves to prod the taxpayer into a payment plan when all other efforts fail. Work out a repayment plan with the IRS before they resort to a wage levy. The IRS is usually more lenient at that point. Two key strategies you can use to counteract an IRS wage levy:

- If you own your own business, divert your income to your spouse or adult children who may work in the business. They can then gift the funds back to you. Be prepared to prove that your spouse or children are performing services for the business so you can justify their income.
- Set up another corporation to perform certain services for your primary business. You can then take your payroll from the subsidiary corporation instead of your primary business. Eventually the IRS may discover where your wages are coming from, however, this may take as long as a year. You can then repeat the process with a new subsidiary corporation. This is a perfectly legal and workable strategy.

What if you work for a large company or an employer who insists upon honoring the levy? Of course, if you owe modest taxes that can be paid with several paychecks, then you may have to grin and bear it. However, if your tax liability is so large that it cannot be quickly liquidated, you have only two options: First, negotiate a repayment plan with the IRS that you can live with. Remember: To bring you to that point was probably Uncle Sam's objective in the first place. Second, if you cannot negotiate a reasonable deal, then consider bankruptcy. This is strong medicine so avoid it if you can. Final alternative: Quit your job. It's not the sensible move for most people, but it can be for the few with other sources of income unknown to the IRS.

Why You Must Never Extend The Statute Of Limitations

The IRS has only ten years from the date of assessment to collect back taxes from you. This was extended in 1991 from six years. Once the statute of limitations expires, the IRS must terminate further collection efforts. There are, however, several circumstances where the statute of limitations is extended:

- **Waiver:** When the taxpayer signs a waiver and voluntarily agrees to extend the time period for collection.
- **Offer in Compromise:** The period of time an offer in compromise is under IRS consideration.
- **Absence from the Country:** The period of time the taxpayer leaves the country for more than six continuous months.
- **IRS Lawsuit:** When the IRS starts a lawsuit to enforce collection.

Never extend the statute of limitations voluntarily. The IRS will try to get you to sign a Form 900 Waiver, particularly when the statute of limitation is running out. The IRS may then press its most aggressive collection effort, or offer you a "lenient" payment plan in exchange for the waiver. But it's not smart to sign. Consider: If the IRS was unsuccessful in collecting from you during all the preceding years, they probably will remain unsuccessful in the short time left to enforce collection. But once the statute of limitations expires you are finished with the IRS once and for all. Extend the statute of limitations and your IRS problem needlessly continues. Rarely does the IRS commence suit to enforce collection. They may on larger cases, but taxpayers owing less than $50,000 have little concern over a tax suit.

If you do submit offers in compromise to the IRS, carefully record the dates between submission of your offer and the IRS rejection of your offer. Add this time to the statute of limitations.

Despite the great powers of the IRS, they still allow thousands of tax claims to expire each year. Once your statute of limitations has expired, ask the IRS to abate the tax liability. This is an IRS acknowledgement that you are in the clear. Until you receive the abatement keep property out of your name. It may be just the mistake the IRS is waiting for.

When Bankruptcy Will And Will Not End Your Tax Troubles

There are essentially two types of bankruptcies and two types of taxes. The effect of bankruptcy on your tax obligations depends upon both the type bankruptcy you select and the type tax you owe.

First, you may be liable for either personal income taxes or for withholding taxes (usually due from a business that you owned or managed). Withholding taxes are never discharged through any type bankruptcy. Personal income taxes are discharged in Chapter 7 bankruptcy–but only if assessed at least three years prior to the filing.

Now consider the types of bankruptcies. Income taxes, whether more or less than three years old, are not discharged under a Chapter 13 wage-earner plan or Chapter 11 reorganization. Under Chapter 13 you agree to make monthly payments over a three to five year period to pay off either a portion or all of your debts. Because taxes are a priority claim, you generally pay the entire tax claim under a Chapter 11 or Chapter 13.

A Chapter 7 bankruptcy can be an effective way to rid yourself of old tax claims, but you must move carefully:

- Make certain that the taxes are no less than three years old, measured from date of assessment. More recent taxes are not dischargeable.
- If you negotiated a settlement or had your tax claim adjudicated, you must wait at least 240 days from that date for filing bankruptcy.
- Bankruptcy won't help you if you understated income or filed false tax information for the years you want discharged. The IRS can still come after you for any deficiency found on audit, so make certain your taxes for these years are accurate.
- Filing bankruptcy has no effect on liens already placed against your property. The IRS can, with bankruptcy court approval, sell the property under IRS seizure. Your remaining tax obligation will be discharged.

If you can fully pay your taxes over time, then a Chapter 11 or Chapter 13 may work well for you. A Chapter 13 gives you three to five years to pay your taxes and the IRS cannot bother you during this time. In a business or profession? You can elect a Chapter 11 reorganization. This gives you six years from date of assessment to fully pay the IRS. A Chapter 13 or Chapter 11 bankruptcy is recommended only if you have assets you do not want to lose. If you have relatively few assets, and a substantial tax liability, wait the three years and fully discharge the tax under a Chapter 7 bankruptcy.

As powerful as the IRS may be, the federal bankruptcy laws are considerably stronger. Once you file bankruptcy the IRS must stop all further collection action. So bankruptcy can be an effective way to save your assets and stretch out your payments to the IRS. But don't make that one fatal error: Waiting too long before filing bankruptcy.

Example: If you are in business, the IRS may have levied your cash and your accounts receivable. Perhaps they seized and closed your business as well. Under a Chapter 11 or Chapter 13 you can compel the IRS to turn these assets back to you. That, however, can take time to enforce. Your attorney must file a complaint against the IRS for turnover. The bankruptcy court may take several weeks, or even months, to act. Meanwhile your business remains closed, employees find new jobs, and customers flock to your competitors. Customers that owe you find the IRS levy a convenient excuse not to pay and take their business elsewhere. Few businesses can survive so serious a disruption.

If you cannot reach a payment agreement with the IRS, then file for bankruptcy protection before the IRS steps in and does its damage. Bankruptcy then becomes an empty remedy.

Your Taxpayer's Bill Of Rights: The Best Kept Secret Of All

You gained several important rights against the IRS in 1988 when the IRS published a Taxpayer's Bill of Rights. It's purpose: To educate taxpayers and to let them know in plain English what the IRS can-and cannot do-when dealing with taxpayers. A copy of the Taxpayer's Bill of Rights is available at your local IRS office.

Garrett Publications also has available as a special report *The Official IRS Collection Manual.* This gives you all the inside information on what the IRS will do to collect money you owe. Order your copy on the order form in the back of this book. It can be your most powerful weapon when fighting the IRS.

Who To Call When You Owe The IRS

CPA's and tax attorneys can both represent taxpayers before the IRS. There's one major difference between these professionals. What you tell your accountant is not privileged. If the IRS wanted to press for information it can subpoena the accountant at any administrative proceeding or trial. This extends also to any documents you may have given to your accountant. What you tell your attorney, on the other hand, is privileged. Neither the IRS, nor any other party, can force your attorney to disclose confidential communication without your permission. Thus, you can confide in your attorney the deepest secret, including disposition of your assets, without fear of forced disclosure.

Does this mean that you should not use an accountant, or not confide in one that may represent you? Not at all. Have your tax attorney, or family lawyer for that matter, retain the accountant to handle your case. Working under your lawyer, communication to the accountant is as protected as communication to your lawyer.

If you doubt your ability to negotiate a tax resolution on your own behalf, you can hire either a CPA or attorney experienced in such tax matters. But these professionals can be expensive. Do you want to save money? Call an enrolled agent (EA) to assist you. Enrolled agents are neither accountants nor lawyers. They are usually former IRS agents or examiners, so they have a fair idea of how to deal with the IRS. To find an enrolled agent in your area call the National Association of Enrolled Agents at (800)424-4339.

Another excellent source of good tax representation is Taxpayer's Assistance Corporation (TAC). They maintain offices in most major cities and are staffed with highly-qualified accountants who specialize in negotiating installment payments with the IRS. To reach the Taxpayer's Assistance Corporation phone (800)IRS-HELP.

Key Secrets To Remember

- The IRS can be ruthless when it comes to collecting their money. To survive you must know your rights and assert your rights.
- You cannot hide from the IRS. That means you must face up to your IRS troubles as soon as possible and before the IRS becomes uncooperative.
- Judgment proof yourself before you provide financial information to the IRS.
- Never assume the IRS won't seize your assets. The safe course is to always assume your assets are in jeopardy.
- Bankruptcy can be your most powerful ally against the IRS. But choose the right type of bankruptcy.
- Don't attempt to resolve serious tax problems yourself. Retain a qualified professional to represent you.

12

SUREFIRE STRATEGIES TO STOP FORECLOSURES AND REPOSSESSIONS

A foreclosure is not a pleasant experience. Not only does it mean the loss of your family home, a valuable investment property, or some other important asset, but in its aftermath may be a large deficiency owed to the secured lender. This can jeopardize even more assets as the lender attempts to collect whatever balance is owed.

Foreclosures can apply to any type property. However, the strategies and principles between lender and debtor are much the same whether the foreclosure involves real estate, a boat, a car, or an apartment complex. In each instance the lender is secured by specific assets as collateral. Should you default in your obligations, the lender has the right to sell the collateral and apply the proceeds to the loan. If there is a surplus, it belongs to you. If there is a deficiency, in other words, you still owe money, then you remain liable for that unpaid balance (although this is not true in all states concerning real estate).

A secured lender with specific collateral to foreclose on and sell is obviously in a considerably stronger position than an unsecured creditor. Unlike the secured lender who can sell his collateral, the unsecured creditor must first obtain a judgment. Only then can the unsecured creditor search for assets that the debtor owns, and has sufficient equity to yield a worthwhile recovery at a sheriff sale. Should the debtor file for bankruptcy during this process, the unsecured creditor can do nothing further but must wait for whatever dividends are paid to unsecured creditors. Secured creditors, in contrast, retain their rights to their collateral, even in bankruptcy, and remain in a far stronger position.

Although secured lenders are in a strong bargaining position, that doesn't mean you can't work out a reasonable solution with your lender if you're unable to pay your loan. Lenders don't want your collateral, they want payment. Few lenders enjoy the hassle of foreclosure, and excessive foreclosures on the records of a loan officer reflects poorly on his judgment. Still, no lender can remain idle while a loan continues to fall further behind. Both lender and borrower in a loan workout must appreciate the other's position and be willing to temporarily compromise until the problem can be permanently resolved. This is usually accomplished through new financing or voluntary sale of the collateral by the debtor.

Loan workouts can be quite creative. There are many steps you can take to show your lender you are working in good faith and protecting the lender to the extent possible. As you proceed through this chapter you'll see many illustrations, each easily modified to your own situation.

This does not suggest that as a borrower you must humble yourself before your secured lender. Lenders can be unreasonable and even go beyond the limits of the law. To succeed, you must know when to cooperate and when to fight. And you must know how to do both well.

The less experienced you are in resolving problem loans, the more you'll fear your problem. But avoidance is the most common and costly mistake you can make. Lenders are less forgiving of borrowers who hide from their problems, and more cooperative with those who anticipate trouble and immediately negotiate an equitable interim arrangement until a long-term solution can be found.

Why are there so many foreclosures? Newspapers in most cities are loaded with page after page of homes, investment properties, businesses, equipment, cars, boats and virtually every other asset you can name–all to be sold under the auctioneer's hammer.

The reasons for foreclosure are, of course, as varied as the reasons people and companies run into economic hardship. A poor economy, unemployment, rising interest rates, business failure and personal problems head the list. Often the best solution for a troubled loan is to find out why it became a problem in the first place.

The most common problem? You borrowed too much against your assets. Loans commonly exceed the value of the collateral. Your key objective then is to have the lender reduce the debt to correspond to the value of the collateral. Similarly, you may be so heavily indebted, or the loan so poorly structured, that you cannot pay the interest on the loan. This requires you to adjust the loan terms to payments you can afford. Either situation requires you to restructure your loan, whether by cancelling part of the debt, or extending the payment terms.

How To Negotiate New Loan Terms You Can Pay

The fair market value of the collateral determines the maximum debt you can support, but that's not how your secured lender views his bargaining position when negotiating the debt restructuring. Secured lenders consider instead the liquidation value of their collateral, plus whatever recovery is likely from any guarantors.

Expect these events in your negotiations:

- Anticipate disagreement on the liquidation value of the collateral. The nature and condition of the collateral, auction location, and even seasonal demand for the collateral are only a few of the many factors that control what a lender recoups under a forced sale. It's often only a matter of timing and whether there's an interested buyer when the collateral is sold. Many types of collateral defy accurate liquidation estimates. The costs of liquidation must also be considered. Auction and attorneys fees, and other expenses, can significantly reduce the creditor's recovery under a forced liquidation. These variables explain why there can be a substantial difference between what you and the lender anticipate as a recovery from the collateral.

- Lenders may pursue other options. For example, lenders enhance the value of their collateral by attracting buyers who may pay considerably more than auction price for the secured assets. One danger of a delayed settlement is that your lender has time to find a buyer who will pay top price. This weakens your own position when you negotiate. Delay by the lender, on the other hand, is to be welcomed if your primary objective is to completely bail-out of the loan. You then share the lender's objective to sell the collateral at top price.

- Do you want the lender to compromise and show leniency? Consider many factors. Lenders resist re-negotiating a loan for a wide variety of reasons. Example: Lenders backed by the SBA, or other financially strong guarantors, can take a hard stand as they rely more on the guarantors than on the collateral. Always consider the lenders alternatives before you negotiate.

- Lenders who hold low interest loans are the best candidates for a favorable workout. A lender will more willingly accept a fast $30,000 settlement on a $50,000 loan if the interest is well below market rates. Reason: The lender can earn more by lending the money again at a higher rate–rather than watch the loan tied up in your bankruptcy. This example also shows why it's important to view the situation through your lender's eyes.

Lenders will do almost anything to avoid cancelling part of their loan. Lenders prefer to extend payments as long as necessary to get fully paid. Lenders realize that with patience a troubled business or distressed real estate project may turn itself around to the point where the loan can be fully paid. The time to strike and force a cents-on-the-dollar compromise is when you have poverty on your side. Make the lender believe the settlement you offer is the better alternative to a forced liquidation that will only bring less.

Lenders can be coaxed to settle for slightly more than a foreclosure price. They are far more likely to accept the proposition if you offer immediate cash rather than deferred payments. Arrange alternate financing before you approach your lender with your cents-on-the-dollar deal. Wave money. Your lender will listen very carefully.

Why You Must Bullet-Proof Yourself Before You Battle Your Lender

Never battle your lender with other assets exposed. Your lender may quickly attach these assets without warning. Protect your other assets from your lender before a conflict arises. Ideally, you sheltered your assets before you accepted the loan. This provides you considerably greater protection against a fraudulent conveyance claim. If you're not judgment proof, make that last minute effort to place your other assets out of the reach of your lender before a pre-judgment attachment is attempted. Most vulnerable is money on deposit with your lender. A bank can, without notice, apply all funds in your checking or savings accounts against the loan balance. Similarly, the lender can set-off deposits of any guarantors to the loan. Don't assume the lender won't go after your other assets. It can be a costly mistake.

Once your loan becomes shaky your lender is likely to demand additional collateral for the loan. Should you give it? Usually the answer is no. When a lender questions whether the present collateral is sufficient to cover the loan, the chances are that it's not. It makes no sense to jeopardize more of your assets. This only improves the lender's position and weakens yours.

Your refusal to pledge more collateral won't prompt the lender to foreclose faster. In fact, the more secured lender is quickest to foreclose because this lender knows there is ample security to cover the loan. The lender with too little collateral hesitates to foreclose because time alone gives him the best opportunity to recover more.

Lenders make valuable concessions in return for additional collateral. They may offer moratoriums on payments, lower interest, or even more cash advances. Still, these concessions are seldom in your best long-term interest. The underlying problems that caused your loan difficulties can send you into default again. However, the heavily secured lender, not you, will now hold the trump card.

How do you gracefully refuse the lender's demand for more collateral? Best approach: Have your other property titled with your spouse. While you are willing to grant the lender's request, your spouse and you are having marital problems and your spouse (and her lawyer) refuse to encumber other property. This story is one face-saving way to politely refuse a lender–and it works!

In sum: When your loan is in trouble, your lender's first reaction is to go after additional assets to more fully secure your loan. If you have other assets exposed, your lender may attach them or pressure you to pledge them as additional collateral. Turn poverty into power. Never leave other assets exposed to your lender. Confine the lender only to the collateral he holds.

Five Lender Concessions To Bargain For

What points may you and your lender negotiate when you are unable to make payments on your loan? Here are the five most common concessions:

- Extend the loan: This is most acceptable to the lender because your loan remains both fully performing and earmarked for full payment. Faced with a potential default, lenders frequently extend loan payments well beyond their original term.
- Defer principal payments: This is another common solution for reducing stranglehold payments as a large portion of a monthly payment may be principal. This concession provides little relief on newer loans that call primarily for interest on the earliest payments.
- Defer interest payments: Lenders more actively resist this request as it produces a non-performing loan. Alternative concessions (such as extensions) that yield the same monthly payments are more readily accepted by a lender since these loans are not considered in default.
- Concession of interest payment: In more severe cases a lender may concede one year's interest. Beyond that the loan should be completely restructured.

- A freeze on all loan payments: This is the most difficult proposition to sell, but lenders dealing with borrowers with acute cash shortages frequently have no choice but to temporarily suspend all payments. Lenders more willingly suspend payments when they are adequately secured, the collateral will retain its value, and the freeze is only a short-term arrangement.

Concessions granted by a lender during a loan workout frequently change. Both you and your lender must adopt a policy of flexibility and constant reassessment of the situation to insure a workout plan that remains fair to both.

How A Little-Known Law Can Help You Avoid Foreclosure

Lenders do not always listen to reason. Here then is a little-known remedy that may work for you when you face foreclosure.

Enacted into law during World War II, the Soldiers and Sailors Relief Act prevents a creditor from taking legal action against someone on active duty in the armed forces.

This raises an interesting question if you face foreclosure: What if you transferred your property to a friend or relative in active military service? Clearly, the lender would be unable to proceed with the foreclosure until the new owner comes out of the service. Caution: Some courts find the law inapplicable to the situation.

In either event, this maneuver can turn a fast foreclosure into a protracted court case. Your case will be considerably stronger if your mortgage grants you the right to transfer your property without lender consent. You must also timely raise the Soldiers and Sailors Relief Act defense during the foreclosure proceeding. Handled properly this tactic may extend foreclosure many months. Tip: This strategy also works if you grant a partial interest in the property to someone in the armed services. You then remain in control of the property and simultaneously take advantage of your new partner's military status to hold the lender at bay.

Try The Option-To-Equity Solution

Here's a possible solution if you need more money each month to pay your mortgage. Assume your property rents for $800 a month and it costs you $1000 a month to cover your mortgage. You must either dip into your own pocket to cover the $200 deficiency or eventually lose your property.

Possibly $800 a month is all the property can be rented for. The strategy: Give a tenant more than a rental. Offer an option-to-equity. Here's how it works: Your tenant would pay $1000 a month rent, but at the end of a stated period—perhaps two or three years—your tenant would own an interest in the property. The extra $200 a month rent would be credited toward ownership. This type

arrangement may be structured in any number of ways, and may even eventually give the tenant outright ownership.

The option-to-equity works particularly well when the negative cash flow on the building is not too significant and you can locate a tenant interested in acquiring all or part of the real estate. The obvious place to start is with current tenants. They may not be ready to buy today, but may be interested in future ownership.

This strategy is not limited to real estate. It works equally well on other types of collateral. Would someone pay you each month for occasional use of your boat—particularly if this individual could eventually purchase your boat with a portion of the rent? Do you have plant equipment—a printing press, for example—that may have "downtime" someone else could utilize? Think creatively. There are a number of ways to make an asset produce more income, and that additional income may be enough to cover your note payments and prevent loss of your property.

How To Refinance Your Way Out Of Trouble

Refinancing your property can be an ideal way to save your property from foreclosure under certain circumstances. Refinancing works well if you have equity in your property that gives you additional borrowing power. You can then use the proceeds of a new second mortgage to pay arrears on your first mortgage. Alternatively, you may refinance with a new and larger first mortgage to replace your existing mortgage. Apply the surplus to cover future payments on your new loan.

Refinancing makes sense only if your negative cash flow is temporary. It also helps if interest rates are now lower. Why replace a nine percent mortgage with a new 12 percent mortgage? If you can refinance with a lower interest mortgage it helps ease your cash flow even more.

Can your second mortgagee bail you out? Remember, when you're in default on a first mortgage you're in serious trouble. But also in deep trouble are the mortgage holders behind the first mortgage. Faced with a foreclosure they must either pay off the first mortgage or risk having their mortgage wiped out entirely. Subordinate mortgage holders may prefer to assist you and themselves by loaning you the funds necessary to keep your first mortgage current.

Interim second mortgage financing is especially a solution when your negative cash flow is temporary and the second mortgage holder can foresee no further need to subsidize the first mortgage. Caution: The second mortgage holder may bargain for a bonus: Some equity? Higher interest? A shorter term on his own mortgage? Negotiate!

Exploit this bail-out strategy. Ask who besides yourself would be hurt by a foreclosure. Do you have a key business tenant whose lease would be in jeopardy under a foreclosure? If your business is under foreclosure, consider your primary suppliers, particularly your unsecured creditors. Your creditors don't want to lose your business, nor what you owe them. Even your landlord may help pay a lender on business assets rather than lose a good tenant. It's a simple strategy. When you have a problem loan, others inevitably share that problem with you. Make them a part of the solution.

SECRET #144

How To Attract Cash-Bearing Partners

Do you have a real estate project in financial trouble and heading for foreclosure? While your venture may understandably cause you headaches, it may be just the right medicine for wealthy investors looking for a tax break and long-term capital appreciation.

Many investors fit this bill. These are individuals who want real estate tax shelters but don't have the time or expertise to manage their own investment properties. If you think investors can save your property from foreclosure, you'll need the right approach:

- Advertise for investors. Physicians, attorneys, executives and successful business owners are your best candidates.
- Form a limited partnership. A limited partnership is a partnership where the investing partners have their liability limited to the loss of their investment. Limited partners do participate in profits and in tax write-offs.
- Allow your investors 100 percent of the tax write-offs. This means they would be able to deduct all the

taxes, interest, depreciation and negative cash flow. This can be a hefty sum.

- In exchange for these tax benefits your investors would advance all the funds necessary to cover the negative cash flow and keep the property out of foreclosure.
- Set up your deal so that when it comes time to sell the properties, the profits are split 50/50. This is permissible even if you own one percent of the partnership.
- You would serve as general partner and manage the properties-possibly for a fee.

This is precisely the type deal that attracts so many passive investors to real estate, and even those that are operating precariously with a negative cash flow. Ask your accountant. He or she can show you the benefits your investors may reap and the benefits you must sell. Caution: Real estate limited partnerships aren't as attractive an investment since the 1986 Tax Reform Act, but properly structured it can still dazzle investors.

SECRET #145

When To Sell Your Property For No Cash Down

Another possible solution for the negative cash flow property: Sell it to a buyer who can afford to cover the negative cash flow. Who would buy such a property? Someone who can buy the property on no cash down terms.

A buyer, for instance, may foresee a $20,000 or $30,000 negative cash flow before he can revitalize the property and increase its income to break even. This same buyer will more enthusiastically tackle the project if he can use his down payment to instead cover the negative future cash flow.

When you face foreclosure you can no longer afford to offer your property on conventional terms-a high price and healthy down payment. Your goal is to sell your property before you lose it. Therefore, you must either sacrifice price, down payment, or both. If you have a reliable buyer and can well secure yourself with a mortgage on the property, you'll sell fastest demanding only a small down payment. This is more important to most buyers than a lower price.

In sum: Set new priorities. A speedy sale is more important than a higher price or larger down payment. Your first priority is to sell quickly. Don't hold out for a high price or big down payment that only discourages buyers. Greedy sellers often end up with nothing but foreclosure because they ignored this advice.

Tip: You may inevitably lose your property. You may have swarms of creditors and be facing certain bankruptcy. This is the time to tap any equity in the property you can salvage either by refinancing or selling. You may not be able to squeeze very much from the property, but whatever you do salvage is money in your pocket. Common sense? Sure. Yet people go bankrupt or lose their property everyday having made no effort to first extract more dollars from equity remaining in their property. A second mortgage lender is your best money source. They loan up to 80 percent of appraised value. Some go as high as 90 percent. How much extra cash would that give you before you lose the property?

How To Handle Those Dangerous Balloon Mortgages

Many mortgage defaults involve "balloon" mortgages. With a balloon mortgage the borrower must pay the entire principal on a mortgage on a fixed date. Sellers, for example, often accept balloon mortgages from buyers who can only afford interest payments in the early years. This arrangement assumes that eventually the buyer will refinance the first mortgage and receive sufficient proceeds to pay the first mortgage. This may occur several years after the sale.

Balloon mortgages make sense when the parties anticipate an increase in property values and the buyer then has the opportunity to refinance and pay the balloon mortgage. Unfortunately, property values do not always increase as predicted and buyers then have no means of refinancing the property. If you're that troubled borrower don't overlook these two options:

- Offer the mortgage holder a higher interest rate in exchange for an extension. This is a reasonable proposal when there is sufficient cash flow to accommodate a slightly higher monthly payment.
- Seek an equity investor who will put in sufficient cash to pay the mortgage. It doesn't have to be an even exchange. If the numbers don't work, give the investor a part equity plus a mortgage on the property.

Plan ahead and act well in advance of the mortgage due date. Allow yourself ample time to find an investor and negotiate a sensible deal. If your property operates with a positive cash flow, shows signs of appreciation, and offers favorable tax advantages, you'll have little difficulty locating the right investors or buyers.

How To Use The Poison Pill Strategy

Lenders will do anything to avoid foreclosure on property with hazardous waste problems. A lender who forecloses and takes possession of the property becomes liable for the cleanup costs plus any damages that occur during the lender's control over the premises. The lender will, of course, find it exceptionally difficult to resell the property because no buyer wants to assume such mammoth cleanup costs. Those few buyers willing to assume the problem will certainly look to steal the property. Whatever the lender loses under such a distress sale may be substantially less than what the lender would incur as penalties under the environmental laws.

If your property has hazardous waste

problems, do everything possible to avoid and eliminate the problem, but also use the problem to your advantage. Your lender may decide that it is smarter to be very lenient with you rather than inherit the "poison pill" property.

SECRET #148

Lender Liability: How To Wave The Big Club

Lender liability lawsuits have become a major weapon in the beleaguered borrower's fight against lenders. The courts have increasingly sanctioned lenders for a wide number of violations in their dealing with borrowers. Lenders are now extremely sensitive to a possible lender liability claim. Their concern is justified. Depending upon the nature of the violation, the court can award you considerable damages and even discharge your loan obligation to an overbearing lender. Here are the seven most common violations to look out for:

- Fraudulent lender conduct or misrepresentation in either making the loan or in their handling of the loan.
- Changes in loan terms without your consent.
- Unreasonable control exercised by your lender–particularly when your lender asserts management authority over your business.
- Failing to make future advances as promised.
- Making derogatory comments about you as the borrower.

- Calling a loan into default without justifiable cause.
- Negligence in the administration of the loan to your detriment–particularly in the way they dispose of your collateral.

These are only a few infractions that can put a lender on the defensive. The point is that you must carefully review all dealings with your lender. Underscore lender actions that you believe may be questionable. An attorney knowledgeable in lender liability law can review the merits of your claim, but if you have a strong case you can very easily put your lender on the defensive. This can indeed be powerful leverage to favorably resolve your financial problems with your lender.

SECRET #149

How To Capitalize On Your Lender's Mistakes

Another self-defense tactic: Never take it for granted that your lender holds a valid mortgage against your property. You and your lender may assume the mortgage is airtight, yet there can be any number of legal defects in your mortgage. These defects may make the mortgage entirely worthless (but not necessarily the obligation), or at the very least delay foreclosure for months until the defect can be corrected.

Whether a mortgage is valid or defective requires a professional review by an attorney. Have your attorney check the five most common defects in the loan documents of a foreclosing creditor:

- Incorrect name of the mortgagor
- Mortgagor's signature is missing
- Incorrect property description
- Incorrectly filed in the public records
- Failure to file in the public records

Faulty security interests (mortgages on personal property) are even more prevalent than are errors in real estate mortgages. The errors most likely encountered with security interests are:

- The security interest lapsed because the financing statements were not re-filed after five years.
- The debtor's name is incorrect.
- The collateral is incorrectly described, or is missing major categories of assets (i.e., inventory or accounts receivable).
- The financing statements are incorrectly filed in the public records–or are not filed at all.

Some of these defects render the mortgage or security interest void as against third-parties, but not necessarily the debtor. A bankruptcy, Chapter 11, assignment for the benefit of creditors or similar insolvency proceeding constitutes a transfer to a third-party that voids the defective security interest. The mortgage holder, under these circumstances, also loses his security as against any subsequent lien holder.

Uncovering a serious defect in your mort-gage gives you enormous bargaining power over the lender. Your cooperation is usually needed to correct the problem. It may be to your advantage to cooperate if the lender can then be enlisted to help you achieve your broader asset protection objectives. This certainly should include a generous restructuring of your loan. The secured lender may even agree to conduct a friendly foreclosure to free the asset from the grasp of any other creditors after you.

SECRET #150

How A Foreclosure Can Work Miracles For You

Foreclosure of your real estate, personal property or even business assets may be the ideal way to safely transfer your property with the fewest questions raised by inquisitive creditors.

What if you plan to file bankruptcy but own property with a modest equity? If you transfer the property the transfer must be disclosed in any bankruptcy filed within the following twelve months. Even without bankruptcy, your creditors may attack the sale as a fraudulent conveyance. Moreover, a transfer wouldn't clear the property of any junior liens or attachments that remain attached to the property.

If your objective is to save the property with the least possible trouble from other creditors, then encourage your lender to conduct a friendly foreclosure. The lender can re-sell the property to a corporation you organize to accept title. A corporation is recommended rather than a limited partnership or trust, since a corporation offers greater privacy and allows you to more completely conceal your ownership. Make your lender your ally so you both come out ahead. The lender may cooperate if you offer incentives such as higher interest. Your lender, however, may happily participate if only to keep the property, and his mortgage, out of bankruptcy.

This tactic works well with a secured lender who may hold a security interest (mortgage) on a car, boat, airplane, or even business assets. The objective is to have the asset transferred to a third-party by foreclosure rather than direct sale from you. Unless your creditors can show it was not a commercially reasonable sale-or that there was open collusion between you and your lender-they cannot set the foreclosure sale aside.

SECRET #151

How To Spot A Sham Foreclosure Sale

It's painful, but also therapeutic, to attend an auction of your property. But do attend so you can be certain the auction sale is conducted in a commercially reasonable manner and likely to bring the highest possible price. This checkup is vital when you are responsible for any deficiency and want the property sold at or above the amount of the mortgage. Don't fool yourself. Lenders do conduct bad auctions. They may intentionally suppress the price so they can end up

with the property at a bargain price while you end up with a jumbo deficiency on the note. Don't be victimized. Here's what to look for:

- Rush bidding, with insufficient time for counter-bids.
- Discouraging bidders with negative remarks about the property.
- Unrealistic terms of sale, such as a high deposit or fast closing.
- Insufficient notice. Auction ads that inadequately announced the sale, or were advertised too soon before the auction.

You can protect yourself from these tricks. Hire another auctioneer-preferably from another city so that relationships with the lender's auctioneer will not be a factor. Have your auctioneer attend the auction with you. Bring a tape recorder so you can record the proceeding. Once the lender knows he cannot steal your property you can be saved from a big deficiency and may even find surplus funds from the sale returned to you.

SECRET #152

Three Pointers To Win Back Your Property After Foreclosure

All is not necessarily lost even after your lender takes your property by foreclosure. You may convince the lender to sell you back your home, auto, boat or other foreclosed asset. Why would a lender sell you back your property after your lender went to the trouble to foreclose? There are three reasons:

• The lender may have anticipated selling the property at a higher price to an outside buyer. If that buyer didn't materialize the lender may have no reasonable alternative but to sell the property back to you.

• The lender may now see you in a stronger financial condition, particularly if the foreclosure eliminated other liens and attachments against the property, or you went through bankruptcy to free yourself of burdensome debts.

• The lender may want to quickly dispose of the property to avoid storage or maintenance costs.

If you want your property back, convince the lender that you won't default again. If the collateral was your home, ask the lender to rent the house back to you for an amount equal to the mortgage payments. Prove you can make timely payments, perhaps for six or nine months, and the lender may develop sufficient confidence in you to deed you back the property. Property is never lost until you have no chance to reclaim it.

How To Avoid A Deficiency On Your Loan

If you have property foreclosed upon or repossessed you can lose far more than the property. In most states you can also be liable for a deficiency. A deficiency is the difference between what you owe your lender (including attorneys fees and costs) and what the lender sells the collateral for at foreclosure.

Your lender must usually go to court to obtain the deficiency judgment but this is easily obtained. Once the lender has the deficiency judgment he can enforce it like any other judgment. How can you avoid a deficiency judgment?

• Offer the lender the collateral, waiving all foreclosure proceedings and rights of redemption. Be a cooperative borrower and help your lender avoid hassles and legal costs. The lender will then be more inclined to accept the property and forget about deficiencies. This is certainly so if you can convince the lender you are judgment proof.

• Find a buyer for the collateral. You'll obtain a much higher price, and incur less of a deficiency, if you can sell the property privately without a distress or auction sale.

Whether you avoid a deficiency judgment or not, there's still another asset of considerable importance to protect—your credit rating. If it's futile to resist foreclosure then your objective should be to fully cooperate with the lender. However, in addition to a release from any deficiency, demand assurances from the lender that the loan default or foreclosure will not injure your credit rating. Always obtain these lender concessions in writing.

Check your timing. Negotiate these points with a lender when he most senses the danger of interference and opposition from you. That's when "cooperation" is a bargaining chip-not after the foreclosure when you no longer have leverage.

How To Get Your Car Back After Repossession

Most states allow the debtor a short time period to redeem their auto (or boat or plane) after it's repossessed. In these states you can reinstate the loan and reclaim the repossessed item by paying all missed installments, late fees and reasonable legal and repossession costs incurred by the lender. This is not, however, an absolute right. You can't reinstate the contract and take back your property if you:

- had the installment contract reinstated before.
- concealed the property to avoid repossession.
- allowed the property to become damaged or neglected.
- physically interfered with the repossession, or threatened violence.
- misrepresented facts on your credit application.

Your lender must provide you a notice of your right to reinstate in those states where it's possible. If your lender violates this notice requirement you may have the right to reclaim the property without clearing overdue payments-but you must be timely on future installments. To reinstate the contract you must notify the lender as rapidly as possible.

If you fail to reinstate the contract or loan within the time stated in the installment agreement (60-90 days is most common), the lender can then hold you liable for the entire loan balance as well as notify you of his intent to sell the repossessed property. You then have a limited time prior to the sale to reclaim the property, but only if you pay the entire obligation plus costs.

What about those personal items you may have left behind in a repossessed car, boat or plane? If your vehicle is repossessed with your personal objects in it, you can demand their return if you notify the lender (or repossessor) within the time stated in your contract or within a reasonable time if no specific time is mentioned. Play it safe: Contact the lender as soon as possible.

When To Use Bankruptcy To Stop Foreclosure Or Repossession

Bankruptcy is the one remedy that will immediately stop a foreclosure. Once bankruptcy is filed, the secured lender must immediately halt all foreclosure or repossession actions. Bankruptcy may still not be your perfect solution to foreclosure:

- You may be in good financial shape other than with this one problem property. A bankruptcy to stop a foreclosure on one property may make no sense if the property is not of great importance to you.

Tip: You may transfer your property to another entity such as a corporation. The corporation, in turn, can file the Chapter 11. This keeps you out of bankruptcy personally. Some bankruptcy courts may be disinclined to protect the property now titled to the corporation–but in many instances the strategy will work.

- The property may not have any equity or intrinsic value worth saving.
- The bankruptcy may only incur additional legal costs, etc., and even bring less for the property than could be obtained without the constraints of bankruptcy.

A bankruptcy does make sense under two conditions:

- The property has a substantial equity worth saving and with time you'll have the resources to turn-around or sell the property and "cash-out" your equity.
- You need the bankruptcy laws to cram-down the mortgages to the actual collateral value of the property. This will solve the problem of over-financed property. This is a sound strategy when you can obtain new financing to replace the crammed-down loan.

Secured lenders still have considerable rights if you file bankruptcy. Your filing a bankruptcy (Chapter 7, 11 or 13) will temporarily stop a foreclosure or repossession but may not necessarily stop it permanently. The lender may request permission from the court to foreclose. This will be granted if the lender is not adequately protected. This means that any court imposed delay in foreclosure will not hurt the lender or put the lender in a worse position. The lender, for instance, would be in a worse position if the balance owed increased (if you did not make interest payments). and/or the collateral was decreasing in value (for example, real estate prices were decreasing or the property was neglected and in disrepair).

Bankruptcy can tame a lender quick to foreclose, yet bankruptcy is not the answer in every case. Before you allow a valuable property to go to auction, discuss your situation with a bankruptcy specialist.

Key Secrets To Remember

- Never assume you can't cooperatively work out a problem loan with your lender. There are many ways a lender and borrower can restructure a loan to their mutual advantage.

- Make certain other assets are not exposed if you run into trouble with a loan. You may owe your lender money even after the collateral is sold.
- It's usually wiser to sell the property for a low, low price, or on lenient terms rather than lose it through foreclosure.
- Watch out for lender liability. It can give you considerable leverage when negotiating with lenders.
- It may be wise to voluntarily surrender property to the lender rather than have it foreclosed upon and produce a large deficiency.
- Carefully check your loan documents. You may have iron-clad defenses to a foreclosure.
- Bankruptcy can stop a foreclosure–but it's not always your best solution.

13

HOW TO KEEP YOUR WEALTH AND GET FREE NURSING HOME CARE

There's A Financial Crisis In Your Future

It may come as a nasty surprise but there's an excellent chance you'll lose your entire life savings to catastrophic illness or nursing home costs. Many people do. Unfortunately, our current Medicare and Medicaid laws are rigged so the average American family loses everything they own should one spouse require long-term nursing home care. Only when you and your spouse become virtually impoverished does Medicaid pay your nursing home costs. Until you qualify for Medicaid assistance you must spend-down and pay the nursing home whatever wealth you accumulated over the years. Think about it. Your financial security is suddenly wiped out. Your children and other loved ones inherit nothing despite your lifetime of labor. This

is certainly not how most people envision their final years, yet many Americans do end up precisely this way.

This problem discriminates most against the average family. These are the families too wealthy to qualify for Medicaid benefits and too poor to finance their long-term nursing home costs without losing all or most of their assets. These are the families, who rightfully concerned about present or future nursing home costs, must restructure their financial affairs so they can qualify for Medicaid's long-term care benefits. These are the families who will preserve at least some of the financial independence and security every family needs. If that's your situation and you want to achieve this financial security, you must understand how Medicaid works, how it decides who qualifies for Medicaid assistance, and how you must manipulate the system so you too can get free nursing home care, as so many other families do.

How To Tell If You Qualify For Free Nursing Home Care

To receive Medicaid benefits for nursing home care you must meet three eligibility tests: 1) Eligibility based on category (age or disability), 2) Eligibility based on income, and 3) Eligibility based on assets.

•Eligibility based on age or disability:

To apply for Medicaid nursing home benefits you must be in one of the categories eligible for benefits: Age 65 or older, physically or mentally disabled, or blind. An individual over 65 need not be disabled but must need long-term care and also meet the income and assets test. A disabled or blind applicant of any age qualifies.

•Eligibility based on income:

The second requirement is that your monthly income not exceed the amount set by your state. This amount varies between states and is frequently adjusted so you must check the current income limits of your state. Should your income exceed this limit you can still qualify for assistance provided your income subsidizes your nursing home costs. Medicaid then pays the difference. Once one spouse is in a nursing home, the other spouse's income is considered separately without a ceiling on his or her income. Medicaid does not require the healthy spouse to support the spouse under nursing home care. In determining which

spouse is entitled to the income, the "name on the check" rule applies. Income payable to both spouses jointly is considered equally owned. Tip: Wherever possible assign the income of both spouses to the non-institutionalized spouse. This is critical if it allows the institutionalized spouse to pass the income test. After you pass these two tests, move on to the third, and for our purposes, the most important test.

How Medicaid Measures Your Wealth

The third test–the assets test–limits the amount of assets an individual may have and still qualify for Medicaid. Two categories of assets are considered under this test:

- •Countable assets: Assets that determine whether an individual is too wealthy for Medicaid.
- •Non-countable assets: Assets not considered when determining eligibility. Under this category is the subcategory called inaccessible assets. An inaccessible asset is an asset that is ordinarily countable, but is now held under such circumstances that it is considered inaccessible to the Medicaid applicant (for instance, held in an irrevocable trust).

The general rule: All assets are countable, except exempt non-countable assets or those the applicant has no access to. For Medicaid eligibility you cannot have more than $2000 of countable assets. If you do have more than $2000, you must spend-down the excess before you are eligible.

SECRET #159

Assets You Can Own And Still Qualify For Medicaid

Non-countable assets you can own, without affecting Medicaid eligibility, are largely prescribed by federal Medicaid law. The states may also exempt certain assets which generally include:

- The principal residence. Ordinarily the most significant asset a family owns, the home is always exempt no matter what its value. This exemption applies only to the principal residence and not vacation homes or investment properties. This creates questions: Is a two-family home protected when you only occupy one unit and rent the other? Do cooperative apartments qualify? A movable trailer? These issues are decided differently between states.
- Household items. May or may not be fully exempt. Some states limit the value of owned household items.
- Segregated burial account. Limited to $2500 and designated for burial purposes only. Prepaid, non-cancellable burial contracts are also exempt.
- Cash value life insurance contracts

under $1500. If the total face value of all life insurance contracts exceed $1500, then the total cash value of these policies is countable.
- Term life insurance of any face value, since such policies have no present value.
- One automobile of any value. Tip: If you own two or more vehicles, select for exemption the more expensive auto.

Caution: Carefully check the specific exemptions in your state. They may differ from the above list.

SECRET #160

How To Take Advantage Of The Inaccessible Asset Loophole

An inaccessible asset is one that is not countable and therefore counted as an exempt asset. What assets are considered inaccessible?

An inaccessible asset is one that the applicant has no access to now or at some future date. An asset is accessible, if at any time the applicant owns a legal share in the asset or the right to use or dispose of that interest. If the goal is to make an asset inaccessible, then make it permanently inaccessible to the applicant, but it may be owned or accessible by a relative or a trusted friend. In this way the asset is still preserved for the applicant's benefit.

IRA or Keogh accounts are considered accessible unless you also set up Keoghs for the benefit of other employees. Funds in a pension plan established by your employer are not considered accessible. Assets subject to present or future court order, such as in a divorce or litigation, are also inaccessible.

From the standpoint of asset protection, the inaccessibility issue most often arises with assets held in trust. Although discussed later in this chapter, the prevailing rule for purposes of Medicaid eligibility is that trust assets are countable only when the trustee can legally transfer assets from the trust to the applicant.

Jointly-owned property presents comparable problems. First, jointly-owned bank accounts are distinguished from all other jointly-held assets. Joint bank accounts are presumed to be owned entirely by the applicant, unless the other spouse or joint tenant can prove her contribution to the account. If successful, that share will not be considered part of the applicant's assets.

All other jointly-held assets, including real estate, stocks and bonds, promissory notes receivable, money-market accounts, and all other jointly-titled properties (except bank accounts), are treated as if each joint owner owns the asset equally. As with joint bank accounts, this presumption of equal ownership can be overcome by proof that the non-institutionalized co-owner contributed more than half to the jointly-owned assets.

How To Safely Own Assets With Your Spouse

Under earlier Medicaid law, each spouse could keep his or her own individual assets without affecting the Medicaid eligibility of the other. This is no longer true. Now all property between spouses is pooled. Therefore, it no longer matters which spouse owns the assets.

For a spouse placed in a nursing home after September 30, 1989, Medicaid requires a determination of the countable assets of both spouses. From this total, each state allows a "spousal resource allowance" for the non-institutionalized spouse. Assets above this spousal resource allowance are counted for determining eligibility for Medicaid by the spouse requiring nursing home care. After the assets are pooled, a spousal resource allowance equal to one-half the total countable assets is allowed for the non-institutionalized spouse. This allowance has a maximum and minimum range as set by each state. Massachusetts, for example, presently allows no more than $62,500, nor less than $12,000.

To determine the spousal resource allowance, the state "snapshots your assets" as of the date of institutionalization - although the application for Medicaid may come later. This snapshot, however, is not automatic. If no request is made, then the determination of spousal allowance is calculated by the state when you apply for Medicaid. Once this determination is made, the institutionalized spouse must transfer the assets comprising the designated allowance to the non-institutionalized spouse within 90 days of Medicaid qualification. Unless done punctually, the non-institutionalized spouse could lose the allowance, since those assets remaining in the name of the institutionalized spouse after 90 days would be fully countable. Once benefits are determined, the non-institutionalized spouse may accumulate assets without disqualifying the institutionalized spouse.

How And When To Transfer Assets So You Can Collect Medicaid

Medicaid is a financial need program. Its purpose is to provide for those who genuinely cannot care for themselves. To stop families from intentionally impoverishing themselves by transferring assets, Medicaid provides that asset transfers for less than fair consideration, or below market value, must be counted as part of the applicant's assets. This is unless the transfer came well before the Medicaid application. Thus, a waiting period must elapse between the time of the transfer and the application for Medicaid.

Don't misunderstand the effect of this rule. A gift of $50,000, for example, just prior to application for Medicaid, does not invalidate the transfer or require the $50,000 to be repaid. Medicaid instead ignores the transfer and counts the $50,000 among the applicant's countable assets–even though the applicant no longer owns it.

Thirty months is the present waiting period for the disqualification of assets. You must, therefore, wait thirty months from the date you transfer assets to the date you apply for Medicaid. Apply sooner and Medicaid will count the assets transferred.

There are two exceptions: First, if the amount representing the value of the asset transferred is subsequently spent on nursing home care within the period, then to that extent the transfer does not effect eligibility.

A second–and even more important exception–is the transfer of countable assets from the applicant to their spouse. This is because under the pooling of interest provision, Medicaid bases eligibility on the assets of both spouses. Obviously, the spouse receiving assets cannot, gift the assets to a third-party to avoid it being counted in the eligibility test. Other spouse-to-spouse transfers to protect family assets ordinarily do not impact upon Medicaid eligibility. Given the many obstacles of the current Medicaid laws, how can you protect your assets and at the same time qualify for Medicaid?

Before you learn specific asset protection strategies, understand first what assets can be transferred–and under what circumstances–without affecting eligibility:

- Your first step is to distinguish between exempt assets (including inaccessible assets) and countable assets (including jointly-owned assets). It is important to check current state law so you work with an accurate list of exempt assets.
- Second, calculate the value of the countable assets owned by both spouses.

- Third, subtract from the countable assets the spousal resource allowance (usually one-half the total countable assets, but subject to the minimum and maximum limits set by state law).
- Fourth, calculate the difference between the countable assets and the spousal resource allowance. This is the amount at risk, or the amount of countable assets that must be spent before Medicaid eligibility is achieved.
- Fifth, once you know how much you must reduce your countable assets, you must dispose of them no less than thirty months before you apply for Medicaid.
- Sixth, the assets transferred must be transferred in such a manner that they no longer are considered part of the property owned by either spouse. You probably share the goal of most people who want assets transferred within the family in a manner that allows you some continued control. This is usually accomplished through: 1) Gifts, 2) Outright sales, and 3) Trusts.

How To Intelligently Gift Countable Assets

Any gift of countable assets starts the thirty month disqualification period unless it can be conclusively proven that the gifts were for purposes unconnected to Medicaid. A common error is to believe that it's safe to make gifts under $10,000 without affecting Medicaid eligibility. Don't confuse tax law with Medicaid. You can make an unlimited number of gifts under $10,000 without tax liability, but any gift can trigger the disqualification period under Medicaid.

Any gift that does not fall within one of the allowed exceptions causes disqualification of benefits for up to thirty months following the gift. Therefore, if you make gifts, they must either fall under one of the exceptions (gifts to a spouse or gifts unconnected to Medicaid), or else you must wait thirty months to apply for benefits. For example, you may transfer a major asset to your spouse, but this spouse cannot later gift those assets to another individual without starting the thirty month disqualification period.

A gift of an exempt asset can be made at any time and to anyone, without affecting eligibility. This is because the exempt asset is not counted in determining eligibility. The marital home, even where exempt, does not always fall within this rule, and therefore is discussed separately.

The big danger is that in making a gift of exempt assets you inadvertently convert it to a non-exempt asset. Example: You sell your car (an exempt asset) to your child and accept a $20,000 promissory note in payment. Your strategy is to forgive $10,000 in payments each year as a non-taxable gift. Your now in a position where you traded an exempt asset (the car) for a non-exempt asset (the note) that counts against eligibility.

A second problem: Once you make a gift you lose control over it. Parents frequently gift a home or ownership of a business to children with the understanding their children will in return support their parents. But for this to be a sensible plan you must have the utmost confidence in the honesty, capability and stability of your children. Some children do recant on parental support agreements. Others, despite their best intentions, lose the property through divorce or their own financial problems. Safety is a vital consideration in asset protection–and all too often a gift to a family member or close friend is anything but safe.

How To Be Rich And Look Poor To Medicaid

Your overall objective in this grand plan is to dispose of countable assets in a way that does not jeopardize Medicaid benefits. Sometimes this is most easily accomplished by changing the character of assets from countable to non-countable (or exempt). Bear in mind, the rule forbidding transfers within the thirty months only challenges transfers without adequate consideration. If you receive property of equivalent value, you did not make a gift and the transaction doesn't count against you. This is true even if it was an exempt asset received in exchange for a countable asset.

Example: You may safely use savings to pay down a mortgage on your home. This is because you have received an equivalent value for the payment–forgiveness of the

debt and an increase in home equity. In sum, you end with the same net worth, although the assets that comprise that net worth changed to less countable assets (savings) and more exempt assets (home equity).

Consider all possibilities. If you have no home mortgage to reduce, can you use savings for a new addition to your home, or to make major renovations or improvements? How about buying a new car? On a larger scale you may, for example, have $400,000 in countable liquid assets. Faced with the need for nursing home care, you may buy a home for $325,000 leaving $75,000 for support. Since the home is exempt, only $75,000 will be counted, and all, or nearly all this amount, will be left for the healthy spouse. This one tactic would save you approximately $325,000 otherwise earmarked for nursing home costs before Medicaid would pay. Intelligent planning is essential if you are to safeguard your wealth.

How Trusts Protect Assets From Nursing Home Costs

Trusts are a valuable device for protecting assets from nursing home costs. Tens of thousands of American families have assets safely sheltered in trust so one or more family members can collect Medicaid nursing home benefits.

Typically, a husband and/or wife set up an irrevocable, discretionary trust. Most or all of their savings, securities and other liquid assets are transferred to the trust. A child, other close relative or trusted friend is appointed trustee. Under the trust terms, the trustee can give to the beneficiaries (usually the husband and/or wife who are also grantors of the trust) any amount of principal or interest the trustee deems proper. But because the husband and/or wife transferred legal ownership and control of the property to the trustee, the assets now in trust are considered inaccessible to the couple. As a consequence, individuals with even millions of dollars in trust can, as trust beneficiaries, be eligible for Medicaid, provided their other countable assets remain below $2000.

Discretionary trusts, popular at one time, are no longer permitted Medicaid shelters. In 1986 the federal government passed the COBRA law that fully counts the assets in these trusts to the extent the trustee has the discretion to distribute them. Tip: One exception is when a trust is funded under a will. A common example: A husband's will leaves assets to a wife through a trust for her benefit. These assets are not countable, notwithstanding the fact that had this same trust been funded during the husband's lifetime, it would have been countable. This particular strategy is recommended when one spouse is terminally ill and the other anticipates nursing home care.

With this background of trusts three questions arise: 1) What type trusts should you consider? 2) What are the advantages and disadvantages of each? and 3) How should trusts be designed so they can best insulate assets from Medicaid? Several different trusts may be considered:

• Revocable Trusts: The revocable trust, which can be terminated by the grantor who establishes it, offers no advantage toward qualifying for Medicaid. Since the grantor has the right to revoke and modify the trust, he also has full access to the trust assets.

The living trust, or "loving trust" as it is often called, is the most common example of a revocable trust. There are two situations when a living trust can be useful in Medicaid planning, and they will be covered later in this chapter. The general rule to follow now is that the revocable trust, or any trust that allows the grantor the right to revoke or modify the trust, or directly or indirectly control the management or expenditure of trust assets, is not acceptable for Medicaid eligibility purposes.

• Irrevocable Trusts: An irrevocable trust is the only trust that can effectively shelter family wealth against nursing home costs. Medicaid counts assets only to the extent the trustee has sole discretion to pay trust assets over to the trust grantor who is now the Medicaid applicant. Therefore, it is obviously necessary to limit the trustee's discretion. The irrevocable trust is the answer if the irrevocable trust: a) Is not subject to a right of revocation, b) Does not give the grantor authority to modify or amend the trust, and c) Only gives the beneficiary (as a Medicaid applicant, or his spouse) income without the right to invade principal.

Typically, the husband and wife transfer title to most of their assets to a trustee of an irrevocable trust and name themselves as beneficiary. A child or trusted friend is usually appointed trustee. The trust provides that income only be paid to the beneficiaries. The trust also provides that should a spouse enter a nursing home, then all income goes to the non-institutionalized spouse with nothing for the spouse in the nursing home. Upon the death of both spouses the trust ends and its assets distributed as designated in the trust. Notice the important provision terminating income to the nursing home spouse. Without this provision the continued income to the institutionalized spouse would disqualify that spouse from Medicaid assistance. This provision is perfectly legal and one of the most important clauses for your trust.

It's equally important to remember that a transfer of assets to an irrevocable trust also triggers the thirty month waiting period. Upon the transfer of assets into the trust, you must wait thirty months before becoming eligible for Medicaid. Once the thirty months expires, the assets in trust are safe and cannot be counted by Medicaid. Moreover, only one-half the income can be counted for each spouse, but this also ends when one spouse enters a nursing home. The healthy spouse then receives all the income. The disadvantage: The spouses as grantors lose access to and control over the trust assets.

There are two often-overlooked ways to build some flexibility into an irrevocable trust. First, give the trustee the authority to make periodic lump sum payments from principal to children or grandchildren. Nothing prevents the children, in turn, from gifting funds back to the parents, or subsidizing their expenses. Second, you can also provide that upon a substantial change in circumstances, the trustee can dissolve the trust and distribute its assets to the beneficiaries–if this is in the best interests of the family.

Another significant difficulty with the irrevocable interest-only trust is that if one spouse enters a nursing home within the thirty month waiting period, there may not be sufficient interest to cover all nursing home costs. This problem is compounded because Medicaid assistance remains unavailable. You can solve this by granting the trustee the right to make payments to each spouse from the date of transfer to the trust and ending with the expiration of the thirty months. This protects the principal after the waiting period but provides one or both spouses some access to the principal if nursing home care is required in the interim period.

The rigid rules concerning discretionary trusts applies only to trusts set up by you and/or your spouse. These rules do not apply to a trust set up on your behalf by a third-party, such as a child or other relative or friend. Should someone else establish a trust for you, that trust is not counted when determining your Medicaid eligibility. Committing your assets to an irrevocable trust that puts your assets beyond your control is a serious step. Before you make that decision review your options with your financial planner and attorney.

A third possible alternative is the:

- Convertible Trust: The advantage of the convertible trust is that it features flexibility and can thus be shaped to the specific needs of the grantor. The convertible trust is designed to be fully controlled and revocable by the grantor while healthy, but upon entry into a nursing home the trust becomes irrevocable.

The convertible trust begins as a standard revocable trust that usually contains the grantor's investments and savings. If the grantor and his spouse never require catastrophic or extended nursing home care, then the trust remains revocable during their lifetime. The trust also provides that if the grantor or his spouse enter a long-term care facility on a permanent basis (usually based on a physician's written opinion), then the trust becomes irrevocable.

Once the trust becomes irrevocable, the grantor and his spouse receive only income from the trust. But this cannot occur until the thirty month waiting period expires, and this waiting period does not commence until the trust became irrevocable. During this waiting period the grantor and his spouse remain entitled to distributions of principal as well as interest from the trust. With adequate interest from the trust there's no need to invade principal.

Four Key Provisions For Medicaid Trusts

Trusts used for Medicaid planning must be carefully drafted. It is remarkably easy to incorporate provisions into the trust that disqualify the trust as a way to make assets inaccessible–and thereby lose Medicaid. While trusts used in Medicaid planning are quite similar to other trusts, a well-designed Medicaid trust contains features not found in other trusts. Here are four essential drafting pointers:

- Selection of trustee. Before the 1986 COBRA law, a husband and wife could not be trustees for themselves as beneficiaries. This has changed with COBRA because Medicaid essentially allows only an income trust. Therefore the trustee no longer has wide discretion in what can be done with trust assets. Since the trustee is restricted, Medicaid no longer objects to spouses serving as trustees for themselves as beneficiary. This still is not suggested for purposes of general asset protection. Courts do not recognize a trust as creditor-proof when the trustees and beneficiary are the same.

Typically, with a Medicaid trust, the spouses serve as their own trustee until neither spouse can serve. Then a child or other relative becomes successor trustee. Large estates may be managed by a professional trustee, such as a bank. Professional advisors are often appointed trustee, but they are not always your best choice, particularly if they are too busy for the job. You can remove a poorly-performing trustee. Should someone other than your spouse or yourself serve as trustee, have the trust empower you or your spouse to remove the trustee and appoint a successor at your discretion.

- Selection of beneficiaries. You and your spouse may be the named beneficiaries while you are both alive. Upon the death of the surviving spouse, your children, if any, would inherit the trust assets. Of course, your contingent beneficiaries can be anyone you choose, and you may even name charities as beneficiaries, as well as sprinkle legacies to grandchildren. Caution: Never name your estate as beneficiary of your trust. This disqualifies your trust as a safe harbor under Medicaid.
- No invasion of principal. Remember that the Medicaid trust eliminates your right to receive principal from the trust. Instead, provide a "safety valve" whereby the trustee can distribute principal to children, grandchildren or any beneficiary other than you and your spouse.
- Specifically prohibit use of trust assets for long-term medical care. The trust should provide that neither trust principal nor interest can be used for the medical or long-term nursing home care of either spouse. This avoids dispute whether the

powers of the trustee preclude this use of funds, which would, of course, disqualify the Medicaid trust.

How Divorce Can Qualify You For Medicaid

As we commonly see, individuals and families do unusual things to protect their wealth. Divorce and separation are examples, and these measures are sometimes resorted to when one spouse must enter a nursing home.

The strategy of going through a divorce makes financial sense when you consider the Medicaid rules. This is because divorce decrees ordering the transfer of assets or payment of income from the institutionalized spouse to the healthy spouse do not come under the spousal allowance limits under Medicaid.

Under a divorce, for example, the ill spouse can transfer any asset to the healthy spouse, or assign any income, and none of it will come under the spousal allowance rule. A couple could go through a divorce for purposes of Medicaid, and once the institutionalized patient qualifies for Medicaid, the couple could re-marry. Tip: This strategy can be further strengthened by a pre-marriage agreement between spouses that disclaim any future interest in the assets on the part of the institutionalized spouse.

Obviously, this strategy is not for everyone. Nor will many couples who have been married for many years go through the ritual of divorce, even when there are important economic benefits. Nevertheless, the loophole is there for couples who want to take advantage of it.

SECRET #168

Six Pitfalls To Look For In Nursing Home Insurance

The economic problems of nursing home care disappear if you have good insurance to cover its enormous costs. Unfortunately, you can't simply buy a policy. Too many policies offer inadequate protection. You must know the key features to look for–those provisions that will give you financial security and the confidence that your personal assets will be forever safe. While it's difficult to find such a policy, here are several major points to examine in long-term care insurance:

•*How fixed is the fixed rate?*

Many policies claim a fixed rate but may in small print reserve the right to increase premiums. Caution: Rates under some policies have skyrocketed in recent years, making insurance costs prohibitive.

•*What diseases are excluded?*

Many policies, for example, exclude nursing home care when prompted by Alzheimer's disease or Parkinson's, yet these are the two most common reasons for institutionalization.

•*Can you go directly into the nursing home?*

Many policies only cover you if you go into a nursing home directly from a hospital. However, this happens in the fewest number of cases. Most nursing home patients are admitted directly from their home, and thus are not covered under their policies.

•*Can the policy be cancelled by the insurer?*

Older policies do give insurers this right, however, newer policies usually provide that the policy is "guaranteed renewable".

•*What about a waiver of premium?*

Some policies waive further premiums once the policyholder is institutionalized. This can be an important feature–particularly if you cannot afford to continue premiums once you're in a nursing home.

•*What is the benefit limitation?*

Benefits are nearly always limited, either in dollar amounts or coverage periods. Policies may also state limits as a percentage of the total nursing home bill. You can buy policies with varying limitations, but buy a policy that gives you the greatest coverage per premium dollar. You also want a ceiling that provides realistic coverage. On the other hand, don't over-buy. Most patients remain in a nursing home for less than thirty months–which is precisely why Medicaid imposes a thirty month wait. Buying insurance for a longer period of time may waste your money.

Three Ways To Protect The Family Home From A Medicaid Lien

You're probably most concerned about protecting the family home while gaining Medicaid coverage. Remember, in some states the home is not an exempt asset. In other states the healthy spouse can continue to reside in the marital home while Medicaid covers the ill spouse's nursing home costs. Medicaid then places a lien against the home to recover the covered nursing home costs. Check with your state Medicaid office to determine if your home is vulnerable to a state lien for payments made to a spouse.

If your state doesn't exempt your home, then you need a strategy to protect it from a Medicaid lien. You have four options: 1) Sell your home to your children, 2) Gift your home to your children, 3) Make a gift of your home to your children, but reserve a life estate, or 4) Transfer your home to a trust.

- Selling the home to your children is usually unwise when the objective is to preserve assets. If the home is non-countable you would simply be exchanging it for cash which is countable. Moreover, the transaction may create a tax problem. Where the home is countable you are still swapping two countable assets.
- Making a gift of the home to children is preferable to a sale of the home, but it is still not an ideal solution. Once you gift the home you lose the legal right to live in the home. Further, the home may be lost if your child goes bankrupt or falls into other financial misfortunes.
- Gift the house but retain a life estate. A life estate grants the donor the right to occupy the premises for the balance of his or her life. This option at least gives you the security of a future tenancy that cannot be defeated by your children's financial difficulties. If you and your spouse reserve a joint and several life estate, then the life estate continues until the death of both spouses.

Under the terms of your life estate you can reside rent-free, but you and your children may decide that you will pay maintenance and possibly even real estate taxes. The goal should be to apportion costs in a way that is financially advantageous to yourself and your children.

If one spouse enters a nursing home, the other spouse still has the right to occupy the home. Should both spouses enter a nursing home, the life tenancy still continues until both you and your spouse die or waive further interest in the life estate. This occurs when you are certain you are not leaving the nursing home.

The advantages of a gift/life estate arrangement are: 1) For purposes of Medicaid eligibility the home is protected from countability, at least after the thirty month post-transfer period. 2) You and your spouse are protected in your right to live in the property until the death of both. 3) Upon your death as life tenant, the home avoids probate since it was earlier transferred. This may save legal fees. Of greater importance–the state could not place a Medicaid lien against the home to recover Medicaid payments on behalf of one or both spouses. 4) The transaction avoids gift taxes. 5) Your children may later save on taxes. Since they receive the home with a "stepped-up" basis they will have a smaller capital gains tax when they sell. The disadvantage? As in most transfers there is a loss of control. While you and your spouse can live in the home, it is no longer yours to sell, mortgage or gift.

> •Transfer to a revocable trust may, in many situations, offer the greatest array of advantages.

The threshold question is whether to convey to a revocable trust or irrevocable trust. Certainly, the irrevocable trust causes total loss of control and this is its major disadvantage. It's important to remember that other assets must necessarily be placed in an irrevocable trust (or otherwise disposed of) to reduce the countable assets to the eligibility level. The home, on the other hand, may not be a countable asset. The primary purpose here for transferring the home is to prevent a Medicaid

lien against the property in states that follow that practice.

One danger of transferring the home to a trust is that the transfer of the home may inadvertently convert a non-countable asset (your home) into a countable asset (your ownership of the beneficial interest of the trust). Some attorneys reserve, for the grantors, a life estate and even prohibit a sale or re-mortgaging of the property without consent of the grantor. These reserved rights strengthen the argument that the grantors still have an interest in non-countable real estate rather than countable beneficial interests in a trust.

Many attorneys place the home in a revocable trust rather than an irrevocable trust. This is chiefly because there is no legal necessity for having the home in an irrevocable trust where it is non-countable. On the other hand, the revocable trust keeps the grantor in control because he can take the property back. Moreover, a transfer of the home to a revocable trust does not trigger the Medicaid waiting period. Either type trust allows you to bypass probate and pass the property on to your heirs with a minimum of cost or delay. Most importantly, because the home is no longer titled in your name, Medicaid cannot lay claim to it with estate liens to recover Medicaid benefits paid on your behalf. Of all the possibilities, the transfer of the marital home into a revocable trust is the one with the fewest disadvantages and most advantages.

Key Secrets To Remember

- Nursing home costs can be the most devastating threat to your family wealth and financial security.
- Start planning–if you and your spouse are approaching an age where nursing home care may be needed in the foreseeable future. You can't afford to wait. It may then be too late to protect your assets.
- Design your asset deployment strategy to best protect you under your state Medicaid laws–as well as best satisfy your personal needs and objectives.
- Draft your Medicaid trusts with the protective provisions you need.
- Nursing home insurance can be costly and still give you poor protection. Check your policies carefully and preferably with an independent advisor.
- You may be allowed to keep your home and it still may be liened upon by Medicaid. Check whether your state liens homes to recoup what it paid under Medicaid. If it does, then transfer the home to a revocable trust.

14

ASSET PROTECTION FOR THE DIVORCED AND ABOUT-TO-BE DIVORCED

Separating from your spouse shouldn't mean separating yourself from all your hard-earned property.

Divorce is an emotionally and economically devastating experience and perhaps the greatest financial catastrophe of your life. Nor is it always avoidable. For many, marriage is no longer a lifelong commitment. One out of two marriages do end in divorce. Asset protection planning for those who are married–or about to be married–is essential.

Divorce is also adversarial. Each spouse, guided by counsel, fights to win as much marital property as possible. The battle tactics are often trickier and nastier than in other courtroom feuds. What can you do to best prepare yourself? Proceed through this chapter and you'll see the three basic strategies: 1) pre-marriage and post-nuptial agreements, 2) financial privacy, and 3) street smart tactics.

Why An Ironclad Pre-Marriage Agreement Spells Protection

A solid pre-marriage agreement is the foundation of your asset protection plan in a divorce. A pre-marriage agreement is a written contract between intended spouses which specifies the division of property and income, as well as the responsibilities to each other and their children upon divorce. Pre-marriage agreements are also called pre-marital agreements, pre-nuptial or ante-nuptial agreements (from the Latin prefix "ante" which means before and "nuptial" which means marriage).

You may think of pre-marriage agreements only in connection with the wealthy or famous. But people of ordinary means increasingly find pre-marriage agreements an efficient and equitable way to settle matters should they later divorce. And the likelihood of a divorce has never been higher and is steadily climbing.

Pre-marriage agreements gained popularity because they so effectively resolve the many complex issues not easily reconciled by divorce courts. Example: One spouse has accumulated substantial assets before marriage and children targeted to inherit the wealth. A pre-marriage agreement can make this wish secure. A pre-marriage agreement can also guarantee a spouse a pre-determined amount of money or property upon separation, divorce or death. Both parties can then be confident their respective needs will be met should the marriage end.

Pre-marriage agreements are particularly helpful to spouses who are both wealthy and need not rely upon each other for financial support. These couples often marry for companionship. If one or both spouses has significant wealth, or has children from a prior marriage, a pre-marriage agreement is vital. Here, the couple may agree to share assets accumulated during the marriage, but keep separate and apart those assets accumulated prior to the marriage.

There are, of course, many other situations where a pre-marriage agreement is advisable. Example: A couple in an interfaith marriage may want a clear understanding beforehand concerning the religion to be followed in the upbringing of their children. Contemplating marriage? Consider the many ways a pre-marriage agreement can help you:

• Avoid Hostility: Divorces are usually hostile because spouses fight over property and their children at the worst possible time–when angry emotions are at their peak. A pre-marriage agreement allows you to resolve these matters in advance when both parties are friendly, rational and obliging. With a comprehensive pre-marriage agreement the dissolution of your marriage involves little more than filing the necessary papers in court. Costly, time consuming and emotionally turbulent legal battles are avoided.

• Promote Fairness: You can't always rely upon the divorce courts to divide your property equitably. Courts are often unfair because they don't always hear all the relevant facts. Nevertheless, without a pre-marriage agreement the court decides how your property is to be divided. The judgment of a court is necessarily substituted for what the parties themselves may have considered equitable and fair. Seldom are both parties satisfied with a court decree.

• Save Money: Contested divorces are costly. Divorce lawyers charge $150 to $250 an hour. A couple with modest assets may easily pay their attorneys many thousands of dollars to do battle for them. Lawyers often end up with one-third of the family assets, or even more. This costly conflict is avoided with a pre-marriage agreement. Your attorney need only file the appropriate divorce papers in court and obtain court confirmation of your pre-marriage agreement so it becomes a part of your divorce decree.

- Divorce Faster: A contested divorce is nearly always a long drawn out matter. In many states a two or three year wait for a divorce is not unusual. This delay is because the court must decide disputes that could have been effectively resolved before marriage through a pre-marriage agreement.
- Plan Properly: Perhaps the greatest value of a pre-marriage agreement is that it encourages both parties to consider what they really desire from the marriage. The agreement has you express what you want from the relationship, both in terms of what you expect to give and what you expect in return from your partner. Example: A couple planning marriage are wise to discover that she plans on a large family while he wants no children. Similarly, she anticipates a lifelong career while he assumes his wife will stop working to raise a family. An agreement brings these issues to the forefront. Remember—if you cannot agree on such basic issues before you marry, it's unlikely you'll reach amicable agreement afterwards.

Seriously consider these important benefits of a pre-marriage agreement. You'll better appreciate why a pre-marriage agreement is one of your most important asset protection documents.

How Courts Divide Property—Without A Pre-Marriage Agreement

Without a pre-marriage agreement, the divorce courts decide all issues for you and your spouse:

- How your property will be divided (including property of both spouses owned before marriage as well as property since acquired).
- Child support.
- Alimony.
- Custody and visitation arrangements.

How do courts divide property without a pre-marriage agreement? They basically follow one of two approaches:

- **Equitable Distribution States**

In an equitable distribution state, the court "equitably divides" the marital property. The court normally considers the length of the marriage, age, health, conduct of the parties, occupation, skills and employment of the parties. Equitable division does not mean equal division, and seldom is property equally divided.

With equitable distribution, all property acquired during the marriage is "marital property" and all property owned before the marriage is "non-marital property". Gifts or inheritances to either spouse during the marriage is non-marital property. This doesn't mean non-marital property is safe in a divorce. The court may leave this property with the respective spouses, but courts in most equitable distribution states apportion these assets between spouses as they do with marital property. In fact, one purpose of a pre-marriage agreement is to keep separate the couple's pre-marriage assets.

The following are equitable distribution states, by either statute or common law: Alabama, Alaska, Arkansas, Colorado, Connecticut, Delaware, District of Columbia, Florida, Hawaii, Illinois, Indiana, Iowa, Kansas, Kentucky, Maine, Massachusetts, Michigan, Minnesota, Missouri, Montana, Nebraska, New Hampshire, New Jersey, New York, North Carolina, North Dakota, Oklahoma, Oregon, Pennsylvania, Rhode Island, South Dakota, Tennessee, Utah, Vermont, Wisconsin and Wyoming.

•Community Property States

Community property states, in contrast, require equal division of the community property in the event of divorce. This includes property acquired by each spouse prior to the marriage, as well as property acquired thereafter.

There are eight community property states: Arizona California, Idaho, Louisiana, Nevada, New Mexico, Texas and Washington.

Whether a state follows equitable distribution laws or is governed by community property statutes, upon marital dissolution the assets may be unfairly divided by the courts.

Mississippi stands alone as a title state. Property is awarded to each spouse based upon who holds title to it. In no other state is "title" a conclusive factor in who receives property. Asset protection in Mississippi obviously means holding title to as much spousal property as possible.

Four Objections To A Pre-Marriage Agreement And How To Overcome Them

The one great barrier to a pre-marriage agreement is the hesitancy of future spouses to raise the delicate subject with their intended. You too may believe:

- •Discussion about pre-marital agreements communicate distrust and lack of commitment to the marriage.
- •Discussion about such matters is unromantic and too "business-like".
- •A pre-marriage agreement contemplates only the marriage ending in divorce.
- •A pre-marriage agreement is too costly to prepare, and it's preferable–and cheaper–to avoid lawyers.

Other reasons for avoiding a pre-marriage agreement? Many people optimistically believe their marriage cannot fail. Others are too unassertive or overly trusting. Still others are poorly organized and improperly plan in all areas of their lives. Finally, many people simply don't realize that a pre-marriage agreement can protect them so effectively should their marriage fail.

A pre-marriage agreement is understandably a sensitive subject to raise. You can begin the discussion by voicing concern for your children from a prior marriage. You may say that you place great trust in your lawyers and always follow their advice. Your lawyer now insists upon it. Why not bring the subject out in the open by suggesting that you came across information on the subject in this book, and that you want to discuss the ideas and issues raised?

Onc discussion opener which appeals to many people, is to call a pre-marriage agreement "an estate plan". For example: "Mary, I think we should prepare a complete estate plan before we get married." Obviously, the term "complete estate plan" includes a pre-marriage agreement. But why disclose this at first? Your future spouse will certainly be less disturbed with this approach.

It's never too soon to tell a prospective spouse that you would want a pre-marriage agreement should you ever marry (or marry again). The earlier your wishes are known the sooner you can plan both your wedding and the financial aspects of your marriage. Also, the longer your intended knows your position, the more he or she will accept your wishes.

How To Draft An Airtight Pre-Marriage Agreement

Your pre-marriage agreement need not be long or complicated to be effective. A simple agreement that adequately covers the basic points may do. Yet, couples often prefer to incorporate as much detail into the agreement as possible. It's certainly desirable to resolve as many issues in advance as you possibly can, yet it's impossible to foresee all contingencies in your marriage. A well-designed pre-marriage agreement will, however, answer:

- What are the respective rights of the spouses to the property each brought into the marriage?
- What are their respective rights to property acquired during the marriage?
- What are their respective rights to income earned during the marriage?
- What disposition shall be made of property upon death of either spouse? Does this disposition change in the event of a prior divorce?
- What insurance is to be maintained by the respective spouses, and who shall the beneficiaries be, both during the marriage and upon divorce?
- What are the work or career expectations of each spouse?

- Who's responsible for pre-existing debts and debts incurred after the marriage?
- What religion will the children follow, if it is an inter-faith marriage?
- What surname shall the children have?
- What child support shall be provided upon divorce?
- Who shall be responsible for the child's education? Medical care? Other special needs?
- Who shall have custody of the child?
- What visitation rights will the non-custodial parent have?
- What alimony is payable throughout the divorce, and when does it end?
- What surname shall the wife use? Can the wife regain her maiden name upon divorce?
- What mandatory counselling is required in the event of marital difficulties?
- Who pays attorneys fees to enforce the pre-marital agreement or handle the divorce?

You can consider many more provisions, but these points are generally sufficient. Pre-marital agreements are best negotiated directly by the parties. Attorneys can be used for guidance, but should not take an adversarial role in negotiating the agreement.

Why Your Pre-Marriage Agreement May Not Be Enforceable

Every state recognizes the validity of pre-marriage agreements. Your right to enter into binding contracts is guaranteed by both the United States constitution and common law. But there are limitations on what future spouses may agree upon.

Example: The rights and duties of the spouses toward their children can always be modified by the court. Proper parental support of minor children is essential, and a court will modify an agreement if it determines a child will be inadequately supported. Courts are similarly concerned with the minor children's relationships with other family members, as well as the general quality of their upbringing. Courts closely scrutinize terms concerning custody, visitation and child support, and freely change provisions found to be not in the best interest of the children. A pre-marriage agreement, in this instance, serves only as an expression of what each party believes to be fair and equitable for their children. Still, unless the agreement clearly violates the best interests of the child, it will most likely be enforced. An agreement, in any event, serves as a useful guideline to the court revealing what the couple considered a reasonable agreement.

Caution: Both parties to the agreement must honestly disclose all relevant information for a pre-marriage agreement to be valid. This disclosure does not exist to the same degree in ordinary business contracts. Since pre-marriage agreements are personal in nature, the law requires each party to deal honestly, openly and fairly with the other, particularly in disclosing all assets and debts.

If your goal with a pre-marriage agreement is to avoid sharing assets by concealing these assets from your future spouse, then a pre-marriage agreement is not for you. This doesn't mean that you cannot contractually prevent your spouse from gaining certain property in a divorce. It does mean that if you choose to keep assets separate and apart, you must tell your spouse what those assets are. Failure here is fatal to the validity of the entire agreement.

A pre-marriage agreement also doesn't allow you to terminate your spouse's rightful share of marital property unfairly or inappropriately. Courts look carefully to be certain both spouses are treated properly and fairly. When the court finds otherwise, the agreement is voided, and state law governs the disposition of property as if no agreement had been reached.

You can help insure the validity of your pre-marriage agreement if you prepare it under the laws of the state where you'll reside after you are married. State law, not federal law, governs pre-marriage agreements. The laws of each state do slightly vary, but there are efforts to achieve uniformity. According to the Uniform Premarital Agreement Act, in effect in several states, and closely followed in most others, a pre-marriage agreement is not enforceable under the following circumstances:

- If the party against whom enforcement is sought proves:

1. That the party did not execute the agreement; or

2. The agreement was unconscionable when it was executed, and before execution of the agreement that party:

   (i) was not provided a fair and reasonable disclosureof the property or financial obligations of the other party;

   (ii) did not voluntarily and expressly waive, in writing, any right to disclosure of the property or financial obligations of the other party beyond the disclosure provided; and

   (iii) did not have, or reasonably could not have had, an adequate knowledge of the property or financial obligations of the other party.

- If a provision of a pre-marriage agreement modifies or eliminates spousal support and that modification or elimination causes one party to the agreement to be eligible for support under a program of public assistance at the time of separation or marital dissolution–a court, notwithstanding the terms of the agreement, may require the other party to provide support to the extent necessary to avoid that eligibility.

- An issue of unconscionability of a pre-marriage agreement shall be decided by the court as a matter of law.

In sum, there are six points to rigidly observe if you expect your pre-marital agreement to be enforced:

- *Have the agreement in writing.* As obvious as this is, couples planning marriage often make only verbal agreements. These sweeping verbal promises can later be used in a divorce proceeding, but they are never as binding as what is agreed to in writing.

- *Attorneys for both spouses should review the agreement.* Pre-marital agreements are often contested on the basis that the contesting spouse did not fully understand it. Separate lawyers eliminate that possibility.

- *Check state laws.* Language in a pre-marital agreement must comply with how property is divided in your state. Your attorney can of course, ascertain that it does.

- *Negotiate equitable terms for you and your spouse.* If the agreement is lopsided or grossly unfair the courts may refuse to honor it, or your spouse may contest its validity. An agreement doesn't require an even split, but it should provide a certain fairness or balance.

- *Sign the agreement well before the wedding.* A pre-marital agreement should not be signed under pressure or without the opportunity to fairly contemplate what it means to you. Sign the agreement well in advance of the wedding–when you and your spouse are both relaxed and can pay proper attention to its importance.

- *Regularly update your agreement.* Circumstances change and so do assets and financial conditions. Have your pre-marriage agreement updated every few years, or whenever new business interests, higher income, financial windfalls or other significant circumstances change.

Why Property Agreements For The Already Married Are Smart

A post-nuptial agreement is similar to a pre-marriage agreement, except that it is prepared and signed after marriage, rather than before marriage.

A married couple can legally contract, however, spouses have specific rights that cannot then be bargained away as they can under a pre-marriage agreement. Some courts do not recognize post-nuptial contracts on the theory there is no consideration to support them. Since laws concerning post-nuptial contracts vary from state-to-state, obtain counsel, particularly if substantial assets are involved.

As with a pre-marital agreement, enforceability of these agreements also depends upon the court finding the agreement fair, and that both spouses fully understood it without one party taking advantage of the other. To prevent such a finding, each party should be represented by independent legal counsel.

Generally, a post-nuptial property agreement covers four important points:

- What property the wife shall keep as her separate property.
- The marital property the wife shall receive.
- What property the husband shall keep as his separate property.
- The marital property the husband shall receive.

Defining separate and marital property (or community property) is not always easy and depends largely upon state law. That's why separate attorneys are as necessary in post-nuptial agreements as with pre-marriage agreements.

A post-nuptial agreement is an ideal way to resolve the always thorny issue of business ownership. Absent a clear, written agreement, a husband-wife business will be considered marital or community property and subject to division as marital property. A post-marriage agreement clarifies the proportionate ownership owned by each. This is a simple way to prevent the business from becoming a pawn in settlement negotiations.

Inside Facts On Cohabitation Agreements

Many more couples are simply living together today without marriage. Young people want to cohabit first before committing to marriage. This tests the relationship. Senior citizens often prefer to just live together because marriage may disqualify them from certain social security or pension benefits. Others want to avoid legal responsibility for the care of an ill partner, or bypass the legal and financial complications of marriage. This is particularly true when one party is substantially wealthier than the other.

Cohabitation, even between consenting adults, is not legal in all states and where it is illegal, cohabitation agreements are unenforceable. Cohabitation is legal in Canada. Where cohabitation contracts are valid, it cannot be construed as a contract for sexual services. Such contracts are obviously illegal and unenforceable in all states.

Cohabitation agreements center on the question of property. They attempt to keep property separate and resolve the distribution of assets acquired through joint funds during the cohabitation. The cohabitation agreement also resolves the handling of joint obligations–such as leases, utilities or insurance. As seen with several of the more notorious "palimony" cases, the agreement may be as vital when the cohabitation involves individuals of the same sex. Cohabitation agreements are a necessity when one partner is considerably wealthier than the other. Without it the less wealthy partner may claim the cohabitation involved personal care and services on the promise of substantial compensation. A cohabitation agreement dispels these claims. It precisely defines the nature of the relationship and whether compensation or services has, in fact, been agreed upon. This is critical when you have property to protect and someone less wealthy sharing your quarters.

SECRET #177

How To Protect Community Property

To understand the theory of asset division in community property states, you must first understand that community property states view marriage as an equal business partnership. The law then divides property into two categories: Community property and separate property. Community property is anything acquired jointly, or by either spouse, during the marriage. Separate property is from one of two sources:

- Property that each spouse owned individually before the marriage and retained in his or her name after the marriage.
- Property that each spouse received as a gift or inheritance either before or during the marriage.

Each spouse's separate property remains separate property and is not subject to division upon divorce. If you exchange one item of separate property for another, the new

property continues as separate property. So too if the proceeds of sale of separate property are used to acquire new property. Caution: If you commingle separate property with joint property, the separate property becomes joint property subject to division. Separate property must always remain separate so it can always be distinguished from joint property.

As with assets, liabilities which either spouse has incurred prior to the marriage remain a separate obligation. While the parties may agree to keep separate debts incurred during the marriage, these provisions do not bind creditors. Be certain that marital bills are discharged or indemnified against should you go through a divorce.

How do you best protect your property in a community property state? Start by listing your property when you marry. Clearly stipulate that it is to remain separate property thereafter. Similarly, keep separate any gifts or inheritances you receive during your marriage. These assets will then always remain yours.

SECRET #178

How To Safeguard Your Assets Before Divorce

With approaching dissolution of the marriage, one or both spouses may try to hide assets from the other. One spouse, for instance, may sell stocks or bonds, or withdraw savings and claim the proceeds were spent or lost. Divorce courts, of course, see such tactics daily and severely penalize the spouse suspected of such conduct. Don't let that be you. Play fair and you'll come out further ahead. That doesn't necessarily mean your spouse will be as honest. Your goal must be to protect marital assets until they can be equitably divided by the court:

- Remove all jewelry, artworks and other valuable but movable objects to a secure place beyond the reach of your spouse. But give your spouse a complete inventory of what was taken so you can't be accused of concealing marital assets.
- Place all cash, securities, stocks, bonds and notes or mortgages due you in a secure place. If these assets are in your joint names, notify your stock broker or transfer agent not to put through any transfers without your written consent.
- If you and your spouse hold joint insurance policies, then draw down any cash value for safekeeping.
- Does your spouse own real estate in his or her name only? You'll need your lawyer to file in court for a restraining order preventing transfer of the property. You may instead file a lis pendens against the property. This puts any prospective buyer on notice of your claim to the property. This effectively encumbers the property so you don't lose your rights to it even if it is sold.
- Business interests are best protected by a restraining order preventing your spouse from transferring his or her interest. You may also seek a

restraining order against the corporate entity itself, thus preventing actions out of the ordinary course of business that may dissipate the value of the business.
- Empty checking accounts and savings accounts that your spouse can sign on. Escrow these funds pending the divorce.

Prepare a list of every asset you and your spouse own as far in advance of the divorce as possible. Record serial numbers and other means of identification. The list should include your own assets, assets of your spouse and jointly-held assets. Your attorney will want to see how property is titled to determine how it can best be protected.

Timing is the key to asset protection when a divorce looms on the horizon. Wait for your spouse to act first and there may be very few assets left to protect. There are several ways one or both spouses can play "hide and seek" with property in a divorce:

- Relocate property to a safer locale. This may mean transferring assets to offshore havens where privacy is assured, or even to an adjacent state where detection is also difficult.
- Camouflage ownership. Did you "sell" your interest in a business for cash or other consideration of little value? Fraudulent transfers of assets-particularly business interests-are notoriously common in a divorce. The defrauded spouse can attempt to prove it a fraudulent transfer, but such an effort can be quite difficult and expensive.

- Delay receiving income, inheritances or assets from other sources until the divorce is final. An accommodating employer may assist by deferring salary increases, bonuses or commissions until the divorce is over. Substantial income can also be secreted in defined-benefit pension plans. These hidden payments may be as much as 100 percent of your income.

Endless possibilities abound in a divorce for one or both parties to hide assets or income. Such actions may seem smart, but in practice you'll discover yourself to be in an even better position by remaining honest. Divorce courts award a disproportionately large share of assets to the innocent spouse when the other spouse is believed to have secreted assets. For example, if your spouse can prove that you transferred cash to an offshore bank, the court may well award your spouse equal or greater amounts of other marital assets. As you can see, it matters little that courts can't attach some assets when they can divide others.

SECRET #179

Divorce Can Be Your Best Asset Protector

Did you know that divorce can sometimes be the best way to protect your assets?

What if you are hounded by creditors and the same time divorce your spouse. Being generous you leave your spouse nearly all the marital assets as a divorce settlement.

Can your creditors then reach the assets transferred to your spouse? Not if handled properly. The reason: Your spouse gave good consideration for the assets–a final agreement on the division of assets under a divorce. Moreover, the transfer arguably was not undertaken to defraud creditors since there was a genuine reason for giving the assets to your spouse–the divorce. Tip: The transfer is far more defensible if you are left a reasonable share of the assets. Ideally, these are exempt assets or assets with only intrinsic value (such as your professional licensure or an interest in a professional practice), but without actual value to your creditors.

Many people in serious financial straits also find themselves in marital difficulty. It's not unusual to encounter this twin problem. But are there really people willing to undergo a sham divorce only to keep assets from creditors? Absolutely! The couple may continue to live together and will likely remarry once the creditor threat vanishes, but in the meantime they find a friendly divorce a practical way to protect assets. This phony divorce strategy is not for most people, but those who relish the idea have greater success if they follow three important pointers:

- Divorce as early as possible. Don't wait until creditors are at your door or assets are already seized. Don't file bankruptcy too soon after your divorce. Wait at least a year.
- Make your divorce appear legitimate. You and your spouse, for instance, should each have your own attorneys. While the divorce can be civilized, it shouldn't be too

friendly. Courts closely examine what appears to be a collusive affair. Be prepared to show the hard bargaining that produced the settlement agreement.

- Establish separate residences following the divorce. Nobody is likely to investigate how often you and your ex-spouse visit each other, but neither courts nor creditors expect to find a recently divorced couple living together.

Be practical. The phony divorce gambit only makes sense if you have substantial assets at risk to make the exercise worthwhile. Factor in the emotional turmoil. While a "temporary" divorce is just that, the mere exercise tends to weaken the sanctity of a marriage. It can be particularly devastating to children and other family members who may not really understand the events.

SECRET #180

How To Divide Pension And Profit-Sharing Plans In Divorce

What happens in divorce to all the retirement funds you or your spouse accumulated? These include social security, IRA's, Keogh's, IRS 401 K Plans, Tax Sheltered Annuities, Employee Stock Options (ESOP's) and Self-Employed Person's Individual Retirement Accounts.

There are some general guidelines to fol-

low in determining which of these assets are subject to division in a divorce:

- Social Security Benefits are never considered marital property or community property and are not subject to division in divorce. Since these are federal requirements, the states cannot change this. If you have been married for ten years or more, you have a right to Social Security benefits that accrued while you were married, even though you later became divorced. You are also entitled to Social Security survivor benefits if your marriage lasted at least ten years. Caution: If you are approaching your tenth anniversary, then have your divorce come after your anniversary date or you will needlessly lose substantial Social Security benefits.
- Stock Option or Profit-Sharing Plans are normally considered marital property and are subject to division no matter which spouse accrued the benefits. The challenge is in determining the present value of these assets. This can best be accomplished with the aid of the plan administrator.
- Military and Federal Pensions and Benefits. Like Social Security, Military and Federal Pensions are federally sponsored and administered, and they are usually divided upon divorce. Military disability benefits are not considered marital property subject to division. There is a requirement that the parties be mar-

ried for at least ten years for you to share in any military retirement benefits that have accrued during the marriage.

It is a general principle that all property owned by spouses–whether singly or jointly–can be divided by the divorce courts. This, however, does not extend to veteran's pensions and other veteran's benefits. While veteran's benefits cannot be given to the other spouse, a divorce court can take these benefits into account for purposes of making a fair and equitable division of other property or for establishing alimony.

SECRET #181

The One Asset That Can Be Your Biggest Liability

Academic diplomas and professional licenses are now commonly considered marital assets. This is particularly true when one spouse helped put the other through school to become a professional. Most valuable: Licenses to practice the high income professions–medicine, dentistry and law. The Ph.D. is also an asset the courts are likely to attach a value to.

A divorce court may easily determine professional status is a marital asset worth $1 million or more. To balance outcomes, the court may leave the spouse with professional status very little in other marital assets.

There's only one way to protect against this: Include the professional licensure and its earning power potential as an asset accounted for in a pre-marriage agreement. Specify its value and have both parties agree to it. Courts will then hesitate to disturb the agreement since this valuable asset has been fairly considered by both parties.

SECRET #182

How To Protect Your Good Credit During A Divorce

Good credit is also an asset and one certainly worth protecting during a divorce. Unfortunately, you can easily lose your good credit either because your spouse ran up big bills on your charge accounts and credit cards, or through your own inability to cope with finances amidst the turmoil and expense of divorce. Three timely steps can protect you from whatever your spouse may do to injure your credit.

- Immediately notify everyone you have charge privileges with that you will no longer be responsible for debts incurred by your spouse. Send the notice by certified mail so there can be no question of its receipt.
- Destroy all credit cards where you and your spouse share liability. Never assume you have no liability on credit cards that stand only in your spouse's name. You may have unwarily signed and guaranteed the credit application years earlier.

• Publish your disclaimer of liability for your spouse's debts incurred after the notice. In many states publication is sufficient notice to third-parties of your refusal to accept liability for debts incurred by your spouse after publication. Check the laws in your state and follow their procedures carefully.

Next, turn your attention to your own credit responsibilities. If you cannot meet your credit obligations on a timely basis during the divorce, then communicate this to your creditors before they press for payment. Let creditors know why you are having financial problems, and explain that it is a temporary situation. Offer reasonable installment payments to show good faith. Most importantly, ask your creditors not to issue a negative credit report to the credit bureau. Creditors usually will work with you if you cooperate with them. Finally, make certain you receive all bills that you may be liable for. If your spouse receives these bills it may be many, many months before you become aware of long overdue bills–only to also discover your now-ruined credit rating.

How To Keep Your Wealth From Your Lawyer

You may fight to keep as many of your assets as possible from your spouse but lose them instead to your lawyer through outrageous legal fees.

Divorce, like any other long, drawn out legal battle, can be unbelievably costly. You must learn how to contain those costs before you begin the battle or you'll end up a loser even if you win a generous divorce agreement. How can you cut costly legal fees down to size?

• *Don't hire a "name" lawyer:* Every community has one or two lawyers reputed to be the best hired guns in town. But they're probably not worth their price. Unless you are super-rich it will be junior associates handling much of your case. But you'll still be charged fancy fees. Go with an attorney who is well-experienced and well-respected yet docsn't charge for his or her reputation.

• *Foil prolonged litigation:* The best way to save a fortune in legal fees? Get the divorce over with as quickly as possible. It's obviously in your lawyer's financial interest to drag matters out with endless depositions and court appearances that mean horrendous legal bills. But this is usually without a corresponding benefit to you. Your lawyer should know up front that you want a fast resolution with a minimum of legal fanfare–and even less legal cost.

• *Consider arbitration:* Arbitration or mediation are quickly gaining ground as cost-effective alternatives to court trials. Chances are that your spouse is as anxious as you are to put the divorce behind you and save on legal fees. Arbitration can be the ideal solution for you both–particularly when there are no children involved.

•*Settle what you can yourself:* Negotiate directly with your spouse, if you are on speaking terms. Resolve between you as much as you possibly can. Once you see how few issues remain unresolved, you may quickly come to agreement on those as well.

•*Don't run up the bill needlessly:* Always remember that you largely control legal costs by what you demand of your attorney. If you call ten times a day, you'll be billed for ten calls–and at $50 to $100 a phone call, those can be expensive conversations.

•*Don't be afraid to change lawyers:* Some attorney bills can appear unreasonable, but in actuality be reasonable. Others can be rip-offs either because the lawyer padded the bill or because the lawyer "churned up" needless work to build the billable hours. Unfortunately, few laypeople can tell a rip-off from a reasonable fee. Why not have another lawyer review both the services performed and the bill rendered? Don't ask a lawyer who may serve as a potential replacement because he or she cannot be

impartial. Seek the opinion of one who can give you a candid evaluation without a stake in what you will do as a result of that advice.

Finally, if you feel your lawyer took advantage of you, then confront him with the fact. If you are still unsatisfied with his explanation, refuse to pay and offer to have the fee arbitrated before a fee arbitration committee set up by the state bar association. Confronted in this manner, most lawyers will make a reasonable adjustment to their bill.

<hr>

SECRET #184

When You Should File Your Own Divorce

You can, and probably should file your own divorce, if your divorce is uncontested, you have no minor children, and you and your spouse agree on the division of property and alimony. It's not difficult to process the paperwork necessary to get a divorce. You and your spouse can together easily prepare the few essential documents:

•Petition or complaint
•Appearance, consent, and waiver form
•Proposed final judgment or decree
•Certificate of divorce or dissolution of marriage
•Marital settlement agreement
•Financial statements for each spouse

Several states may require one or two incidental forms, and you will most likely need child support/visitation orders if a minor child is involved.

Why should you handle your own simple divorce? The most obvious reason is that lawyers are expensive. An attorney can easily charge up to several thousand dollars for even the most routine divorce. Unless you have substantial assets to spar over, a lawyer is seldom cost-justified. But there is an even more important reason for handling your divorce on your own: Lawyers bring a conflict or adversarial atmosphere to the situation. This may be counterproductive to your primary objective to get the divorce over with as quickly, equitably, pleasantly and inexpensively as possible. When you and your spouse are forced to go through the divorce process together, you usually develop a more cooperative relationship with your soon-to-be ex-spouse. This may set a healthier tone for your future relationship. While it may not be a vital consideration when there are only the two of you, a supportive and cooperative relationship is critical when you have children. How can you most easily handle your own divorce?

- Buy one or two good do-it-yourself divorce books at your local bookstore. Try to find one specific to your state so you'll have the precise forms you need. *E-Z Legal Kits* publishes excellent do-it-yourself divorce kits usable in all states. See *E-Z Legal Divorce Kits* listed in the Appendix.
- Independent para-legals or "document preparation centers" are becoming quite popular. They can be found in nearly every state if you look through the yellow pages or "legal services" section of your local paper. Most of these services will prepare your papers for under $150. Caution: These services can prepare legal documents but they cannot give legal advice. For that you still need an attorney.
- If you do hire a lawyer, then hire one who agrees to simply prepare the papers reflecting what you and your spouse agreed upon. In sum–you want a non-adversarial divorce. Some lawyers, particularly those that advertise in the newspapers, depend on volume and may happily provide the inexpensive and quick divorce you want.

Ten Steps To Protect Your Property After The Divorce

Asset protection can't stop with the divorce. There are many protective steps you must take immediately after the divorce is granted:

- Obtain from the court certified copies of your final divorce decree. You'll need this to transfer property, divide bank accounts, etc.
- Exchange personal and household property as soon as possible after the divorce. Jewelry, tools, furnishings, etc. that are due you may oth-

erwise disappear no matter what your agreement says.

- Close any remaining joint checking accounts and savings accounts, but first verify balances and insist upon bank checks so you are certain the check representing your share is, in fact, a good check.

- Joint credit accounts should be formally closed, however, this action should have been taken far earlier when you first decided upon the divorce. Estimate and pro-rate utility bills if you don't have a final balance. Destroy all joint charge cards or surrender them to the credit company. Also notify them that you no longer have responsibility for your ex-spouse's debts. Finally, establish a new account solely in your name, and with a change of address, if applicable.

- Similarly, notify lenders owed joint loans. If your spouse is responsible for paying the entire loan under the divorce agreement, then request a release from the obligation. This is generally not granted unless the lender is comfortable with the collateral or your spouse's creditworthiness alone. If you do remain bound on the loan, and your spouse indemnified you for losses under the loan, then ask the lender for *immediate* notice should your spouse default in payments. You can then take timely legal action against your spouse, as well as intervene with the lender, before the lender looks to your assets for satisfaction of the debt.

- Will you and your spouse change title on any cars, boats, airplanes or recreational vehicles? Change their registration, license plates and insurance, and transfer title with a bill of sale.

- Review your insurance policies. Direct changes of beneficiary to your insurance company or agent who administers your policies. Review all policies including accident and health, disability, homeowners, and insurance on children.

- If real estate is to change hands, you'll need your attorney to convey the property. If the real estate has a mortgage against it, you may need to notify the mortgage holder. But where the property is simply being transferred from you and your spouse as joint owners to one of you singly, no consent by the bank is normally required.

- Will you and your spouse file a joint tax return for the year or will you file separately? If you do file jointly, decide beforehand who will pay the taxes due or be entitled to the refund. Caution: To file jointly, you must be married on the last day of the tax year. For liability reasons, it's best to file separately.

- Check what needs to be done with your last will and testament. Some states automatically revoke wills upon divorce, others only upon remarriage, and in still other states neither divorce nor remarriage have an effect upon a prior will. It's safest to prepare a new will. Preparing your own will is not difficult. The *E-Z Legal Last Will and Testament Kit* is ideal for that purpose.

Five Ways Assets Can Be Seized For Child Support

There are many ways for a spouse, or even a state, to compel payments for child support. The number of remedies for non-payment have substantially increased in recent years as the states have attempted to shift the burden of support from taxpayers to the non-custodial parent. This is almost always the father, who may, for a variety of reasons, have stopped support. The five most prevalent ways of enforcing support include:

- *Levy of income tax refunds:* If you owe more than $150 in arrears, and your spouse collects welfare, she can request the state prosecutor charged with enforcing child support payments to notify the IRS and issue an "intercept" on any refunds due you. You would receive a notice of the intercept, and you do have the opportunity to challenge it, but you will be successful only if you can establish you don't owe the amount claimed. Other reasons for non-payment are not considered, no matter how compelling they may be.

Caution: If you are re-married and have filed a joint return claiming a refund due, then your ex-spouse can only intercept your 50% of the refund. Your new spouse must insure that the entire amount of the refund is not intercepted, so she doesn't lose her share of the refund as well.

- *Posting bond to insure payment:* Courts in certain states require parents under support order default to guarantee future payments by posting bond. This may, for example, take the form of a pledge of stock or bonds, or even delivery in escrow of a deed to real estate. California, Michigan, Mississippi, New York, Oklahoma, Rhode Island, Tennessee, Vermont and Wyoming provide for bonds by statute. It may be discretionary with courts in other states.

- *Property liens:* Property liens can be placed on real or personal property of an ex-spouse who has fallen behind on child support payments. The custodial parent can then foreclose on the lien to collect the arrears.

Most states require that the past due support be reduced to judgment before the lien can be imposed. In any case, you will have ample opportunity to defend yourself and explain why support payments had not been made.

- *Contempt of court proceedings:* Since child support orders are court orders, failure to support technically constitutes contempt of court.

Your ex-spouse can petition the court to schedule a contempt hearing, at which time you would be given the opportunity to explain why payments had not been made and why you should not be held in contempt.

Unless you offer a reasonable explanation for non-payment, the court can find you in contempt. You may then be jailed, and/or fined. As a practical matter the court's objective is to throw its weight behind the child support obligation so that the errant parent will choose to pay rather than incur criminal sanctions.

- *Wage garnishment:* A child support judgment is enforced the same way as are other judgments. One popular method is wage garnishment. The court authorizes garnishment once a judgment is issued. The sheriff serves this upon your employer who must then send a portion of your net wages each payroll period to satisfy the judgment. An important point: In most states a creditor garnishment cannot attach more than 25 percent of your net wages. This is not true of child support garnishments. Courts can set the garnishment for any amount, and frequently compel garnishment for 50 percent or more of the paycheck.

If your spouse cannot satisfy the judgment from a wage garnishment, your spouse may attach and sell any other property you have in the same manner as can any other judgment creditor. Seizure of a car, boat, savings or checking account, or even your home or business interests are all possibilities.

Three More Little-Known Child Support Collection Tactics

In addition to the more direct path to your assets to enforce child support, your spouse can also indirectly pressure you for payments in three lesser-known ways:

- *Reporting you to the credit bureau:* Did you know your ex-spouse can ruin your credit if you fall behind on your support payments? If you owe $1000 or more in child support, the support enforcement agencies must report it to the credit bureaus in accordance with the Child Support Enforcement Amendments of 1984. But the credit bureau can reflect your default on child support even if you owe less than $1000, if it is reported by anyone–including your ex-spouse.
- *"Most Wanted" lists:* A recent and more embarrassing tactic is for certain states to publish in the newspaper the names of parents who have defaulted on their child support payments. Delaware,

Florida, Virginia, Maryland and Pennsylvania are five such states. Other states are strongly considering this procedure as the child support default rate continues to climb. While the other states simply use newspapers to list the defaulting fathers, Pennsylvania also publicizes them on cable TV. Controversial as it is, the strategy nevertheless encourages many more fathers to pay child support after all other efforts fail.

• *Criminal Prosecution:* Your spouse may seek criminal prosecution or a District Attorney may independently commence criminal proceedings if you default on child support. This seldom happens unless your default is continual and flagrant. Criminal prosecution results in court-ordered support restitution, plus possible fines, court costs and even incarceration-particularly if you are a chronic repeater.

SECRET #188

How To Use Bankruptcy As A Shield Against Child Support And Alimony Claims

Child support and alimony obligations cannot be discharged in either Chapter 7, or Chapter 13 bankruptcy. Chapter 13, however, can protect you from collection efforts on past due alimony or child support. Under a Chapter 13, you can arrange to pay arrears over a three to five year period as part of your repayment plan. Your spouse cannot coerce faster collection during this three to five year period. She would have the right, however, to proceed against you for late support or alimony payments due *after* you file Chapter 13.

There are three exceptions to the rule that bankruptcy-whether a Chapter 7 or Chapter 13-does not discharge child support or alimony obligations:

• *Support between unmarried persons:* If there's merely an agreement to provide for support, but no court order, the obligation is dischargeable in bankruptcy as between parties who never married.

• *Support assigned to a third-party:* If your spouse assigns and transfers her right to receive income support to a third-party, that obligation is no longer enforceable in a bankruptcy. Exception: Support payments assigned to a state welfare agency are not discharged.

• *Support payments not pursuant to a court order:* Support and alimony are dischargeable-unless there is actually a court order in effect. Stated another way-only court-ordered support and alimony obligations are not dischargeable.

How The State Enforces Child Support

Because there are more divorces, and a corresponding increase in child support defaults, many states have implemented a variety of techniques to enforce child support. More common procedures to collect from a divorced dad:

- Automatic wage withholding: When your ex-spouse, or the court, forwards the child support order to your employer. Thereafter, with each payroll, your employer must withhold for your ex-spouse the proper amount from your paycheck.

The automatic wage withholding program, under the federal Family Support Act of 1988, now applies if your ex-spouse is collecting Aid to Dependent Children. Each state must include automatic wage withholding procedures in all new or modified child support orders by 1994. If you are not a wage-earner but still have regular income from social security, pensions, unemployment compensation or annuities, the court can direct the withholding order to your source of funds. An alternative: If you and your ex-spouse agree, payments can be made through a third-party escrow that you both select as intermediary. In Arizona, Kansas and Idaho, payments must go through the court clerks. This is only one of several actions states use to enforce custody payments. Others include:

- Widespread use of computers to continuously monitor payments as well as job movement by the spouse ordered to pay support.
- Automatically collecting the social security numbers of both parents upon child birth. This information is available to the state agency enforcing child support.
- Compelling the parent obligated to pay support, but cannot pay due to chronic underemployment or unemployment, to undergo training under the JOBS training program under the Family Support Act.

Key Secrets To Remember

- A pre-marriage agreement is your one best asset protector in a divorce–particularly if you are the intended spouse with the most assets.
- If you are already married it is still possible to contractually agree upon a division of property in the event of a later divorce.
- Cohabitation agreements are essential in today's society where more and more people live together–and have more opportunity to make claim to their companion's property.
- Before you split, take possession of as many assets as possible–so they can be safeguarded until the court divides them.
- A divorce provides a good reason to transfer assets to your spouse–and away from your creditors.

- Watch your credit during the divorce. It's not difficult to keep a good rating, but it's very easy to lose one.
- You may not lose your assets to your spouse because they may have been lost to your lawyer first. Watch legal costs in a divorce and consider handling your own divorce.
- Except for the IRS, no creditor has as many ways of seizing your assets as an ex-spouse after child support payments.

15

HOW TO TRANSFORM YOUR BUSINESS INTO AN IRON FORTRESS

Asset protection is not only for individuals. Businesses are also vulnerable and need their own brand of financial protection. In fact, without its own solid asset protection program, your business may be even more vulnerable to financial attack.

Surprisingly, few businesses go through the rigid drill to take the high-ground should they need to fend-off creditors and other financial threats. Why? Business start-ups are the product of entrepreneurs, and entrepreneurs are fueled by an overload of optimism, not realism. Those who journey into business happily see the upside benefits, but seldom the downside risks. With an eye only on success, they overlook the possibility of failure and ignore those precautionary steps to protect themselves should their rosy future turn bleak. Realists, on the other hand, shun rose-colored glasses. They act early and decisively to reduce risk and safeguard their enterprise. Realists prepare themselves and their business for battle long before war erupts so they gain a strong defensive position.

You too can transform your business into an iron fortress. You must believe that action now will make a vital difference in outcome should serious problems arise. Examine businesses that fail to pull out of their tailspin. You'll quickly realize how good defensive planning can be decisive in whether your business survives the hard times.

Timing is also as critical to your business as it is to your own personal situation. Don't delay. When you properly position your business:

- you–not your creditors–stay in control.
- you–not your creditors–are in the best position to negotiate business-saving terms.
- you–not your creditors–are in position to gain more if your business does fail.

Judgment proofing your business is not a complicated task. Common sense, the sense of urgency to turn your business into that impregnable iron fortress and the strategies you'll learn here are all you need.

SECRET #190

Why Corporate Protection Is Essential Today

To turn your business into an iron fortress you must first choose the correct form of business organization. The corporation is always that one best choice because only a corporation protects your personal assets from business obligations. Why venture into business without corporate protection? Why foolishly gamble your personal wealth on the success of the enterprise? Since small companies routinely fail, this gamble gives you extremely poor odds.

Surprisingly, there are still over three million unincorporated businesses in America. One explanation: Small business owners are unsophisticated in business and legal matters and don't appreciate the importance of personal protection only a corporation offers. Attorneys also fail to appreciate the hazards of business. Many do not incorporate their clients. Accountants, often more in tune with the extra paperwork of a corporation than its liability protection, also may discourage incorporation. Don't let your advisors dissuade you. Incorporating your business is the most

valuable insurance you can buy. With a corporation you limit your potential losses only to what you invest in your business. Operate as a sole proprietorship and you and your business are considered one and the same. If your business fails, your business creditors have full recourse against your personal assets.

A partnership form of organization is even more dangerous. With a partnership you can lose your personal wealth not only for your own misdeeds, but also for your partners. Nor are there tax advantages with a proprietorship or partnership. An "S" corporation offers the same legal protection as a regular corporation but with the tax benefits of a proprietorship or partnership.

SECRET #191

How To Protect Your Profit-Makers From Your Problem-Makers

Never put all your eggs in one basket. If one corporation makes sense, two make more sense. If you operate several businesses, incorporate each separately. Follow this advice and the failure of any one business will not endanger the others. It's the smart way to limit losses and defensively organize your growing conglomerate.

Many once-thriving companies disappeared only because all their eggs were in one corporate basket. Example: A restaurant owner starts with one successful restaurant and soon expands into three successful restaurants, all owned by the one original corporation. Its fourth restaurant is a disaster and quickly bankrupts with it the three healthy restaurants. It happens to the smartest business people. Consider the law of probability. No matter how smart you may be, your growing company will inevitably make mistakes and become saddled with one or two losers. Accept that reality and you'll understand why it makes considerable sense to isolate your potential losers from your present winners. This, of course, can happen only when you operate with separate corporations. As you grow, you can safely shed your losers and continue to build on the strength of the winners.

Don't organize your business based on tax factors alone. Asset protection objectives are even more important while you are still small and vulnerable. Once you become larger you cannot walk away from your losers quite as easily as when you were small. Tax, financing, creditor relations, and operational factors then begin to override liability protection.

Once you effectively insulate liabilities through multi-corporations, you can set up a holding company to own each operating corporation as a subsidiary. You can then substitute parent company guarantees for your own and really begin to look and operate like a major corporation.

Do you now own a troubled-company that can be separated into distinct corporations? It may not be too late. Isolated as separate corporations, you can either liquidate or attempt rehabilitation of the sick business while leaving your healthy operations intact. To accomplish this, you must act early so your failing corporation is accepted by creditors as a separate entity and not entangle the healthy businesses in its financial difficulties.

You may face the opposite dilemma: Your company may now be properly organized as separate corporations, but you may lose this protection because you failed to operate each as a separate corporation. Your companies, for instance, may operate with one bank account or commingle cash, inventory or other assets. It may operate with one payroll, combine corporate meetings or generally operate as one large corporation rather than several separate corporations. Should one corporation file bankruptcy, its creditors can justifiably throw your other corporations into bankruptcy as well. This is the hefty price you pay when your businesses do not properly function independently.

It takes more effort to operate your business through separate corporations, however, it's well worth the effort. You'll enjoy a greater sense of security knowing the failure of any one venture cannot jeopardize those that are successful.

Consider your own business. How can you identify and isolate the more risk-prone aspects of your business under the protective umbrella of a separate corporation? How can you restructure your organization so that failure of any one part will not jeopardize your remaining organization? Take that drill. It's survival training!

Assets Your Business Should Never Own And Never Lose

Are you an unthinking business owner with valuable assets owned by your operating company? It's a mistake. Why needlessly lose these valuable assets if your business fails? Valuable assets should be owned by another entity where they'll be safe from the business creditors. They may be owned by a corporation established for that sole purpose. These assets can then be leased or licensed to your operating company. From a tax viewpoint it may be advantageous to have them personally owned. Check this with your accountant.

Real estate is one asset that should always be owned by an entity apart from the operating company. Example: You own and operate a restaurant located in a valuable building owned by your same restaurant corporation. When the restaurant fails–as so many do–the restaurant's creditors claim the building since it is an asset of the same corporation. Why expose the real estate? It's smarter to own the real estate personally, through another corporation, a trust or even a limited partnership. The real estate then remains safe no matter what happens to the restaurant.

Valuable equipment? Ownership through another entity can again make sense. It may also be wise to title important trademarks, copyrights and patents in still another entity, and license their use to the operating company.

The objective is obvious: Limit creditors to the fewest assets possible should your business fail. With your assets sheltered, you can then either use these same assets to start another business, or sell or lease the assets for personal profit. Either way you come out the winner. If your corporation owns real estate, high-cost equipment or valuable intangible assets, then separate ownership of these assets is not only smart from the viewpoint of asset protection, but you may even gain some tax advantages in the process.

Caution: If you personally guarantee business debts, don't title these assets in your own name. Should your business fail, creditors holding your personal guarantee would then have recourse to these assets. Instead, title these assets in a limited partnership, trust or corporation.

How To Shield Your Business With A Friendly Mortgage

A "friendly" mortgage against the assets of your business is the next vital step in shielding your business.

A friendly mortgage is absolutely your very best friend when you need an ally to save your business from creditors. It's a simple strategy: Mortgage your business to the hilt to a friendly lender. If you run into creditor problems your lender can foreclose and give you back a debt-free business. Executed properly it's 100 percent legal!

Example: Suppose you own a business

with $100,000 in assets. Also suppose that your brother held a valid $100,000 mortgage against these same assets. Finally, assume your business owed $200,000 to general unsecured creditors. Since your brother's mortgage must be satisfied first in bankruptcy or a liquidation, unsecured creditors would be totally wiped out should the business fail. That's precisely the leverage you need if your business runs into serious trouble and you must battle your creditors. Without this friendly mortgage your unsecured creditors have first claim. Although these creditors may not fully recover what they are owed, they nevertheless would control the future of your enterprise because they, not you, control your business assets.

With a friendly mortgage in place you never lose control over your business. No matter what the creditors do, your cooperative mortgagee can always foreclose and resell these same assets to a newly formed corporation. In a few days you're back in the very same business, but without those nagging debts. It's not even necessary for funds to change hands. Your mortgagee can finance the purchase by substituting loans between your old and new corporation. Caution: Avoid a sham mortgage that won't stand up to close scrutiny. You need a legitimate mortgage with documented consideration. Since total honesty is essential, rely on one of several ways to establish that friendly mortgage:

- Whatever you invest to buy or start your business, never invest directly into the business. Your investment would then be subordinate to creditor claims. Indirectly, through a cooperative friend or relative, loan the money to your own business as a secured loan.
- An affiliated corporation you own can perform consulting or other services, and thus be owed substantial funds by this company. The affiliated corporation would then be entitled to a mortgage to secure payment of the amount owed.
- Did you transfer personal assets, other than cash, to your corporation? Why not make the transaction your opportunity to create a friendly mortgage on your business for the value of those assets?
- Do you have a key supplier you want protected should your business fail? Give your supplier a mortgage to secure what may be owed. In turn, demand his cooperation to help defend your business against less-favored creditors should later problems arise.

Remember, it's never safe for you as the owner to loan directly to your business and accept a mortgage as security. Bankruptcy courts void mortgages held by owners against their own business. The mortgage should always be between your business and a third-party, one who is both trusted and as remote as possible from you. Avoid transactions that appear collusive.

Many possible variations on the theme exist since there are many ways to set up a mortgage against your business. If your business is presently unencumbered, or is secured by unfriendly mortgage holders, then at least slip in a friendly mortgage to help protect your business from tax and unsecured claims that would then stand behind the mortgage in priority.

The friendly mortgage strategy particularly works well against the IRS. For maximum protection have your friendly mortgage plus any prior mortgages approximate the liquidation value of the business assets. The IRS and other creditors then have no equity to seize. IRS collection guidelines discourage seizure of assets if there is no equity to cover the IRS costs of seizure. Still, this doesn't guarantee the IRS won't seize a heavily-encumbered business. The IRS may inaccurately appraise the assets and mistakenly believe that liquidation will yield a surplus. Even when the IRS is convinced there's no equity in the business, they often seize with hopes its owner will pay rather than lose the business.

Remember–with a friendly mortgage as a shield, you'll always stay in control. At worst, your friendly mortgagee can foreclose on the business and sell you back your assets free of other creditor claims. You can even by-pass a public auction. The mortgagee can legally conduct a private sale, provided it's for an amount above its appraised liquidation value. The IRS, if they hold a lien, must receive 25 days advance notice of the sale, but as a practical matter there is nothing they, or any other creditor can do to stop the sale unless they bid a higher price.

How To Control The Lease To Protect Your Business

Does your business have a favorable long-term lease for its premises? Is it the type business where a good location is important? If so, your lease may be its most important asset and the one in need of special protection.

The key strategy: Don't have your business the tenant under the lease. Should your business fail, the bankruptcy court can order the lease transferred to a high-bidder. This can even occur against the landlord's consent, and despite provisions in the lease that prevent assignment or sublet of the lease. Under these circumstances, you lose control of the location and with it your business.

Your lease can be your most valuable asset. With your lease in jeopardy you lose negotiating power against your creditors. Creditors, through the bankruptcy court, can sell your business as a going business concern since they control the lease as a business asset. That's why the lease must never be an asset of the business. How can this be accomplished?

- *Best strategy:* Have the lease stand in the name of another corporation that you organize for that purpose. This corporation can then assign or sublet the lease to your operating company on a month-to-month tenancy. Since the operating company has no rights to a longer tenancy, you and not your creditors continue to control the location should your business fail. Because you hold the lease through a separate corporation, you can evict your failing business with only one month's notice and either sublet to a new tenant, or you can set up a new business at the same location under a new sublet agreement.

• *Second best strategy:* Have the lease pledged as collateral security to a friendly mortgagee. At the first sign of business difficulty the loan can go into default and the mortgagee can take over the lease and re-lease to a new business you would organize. The landlord must agree to this arrangement and may as quickly agree to the first strategy.

• *Third best strategy:* At the first sign of business trouble have your landlord cancel your current lease and rent to your business on a month-to-month tenancy. Simultaneously, the landlord can grant you an option to lease the premises through another corporation, should your existing corporation fail. This new lease would be on the same terms as your present lease. Your option to lease could be exercised upon any termination of its tenancy by your troubled corporation. You benefit because you, not your creditors still control the lease. Your landlord benefits because either you, a favored tenant, come back into tenancy, or if you fail to exercise your option, your landlord can seek a new tenant.

Safeguarding a favorable location is vital strategy for restaurants, gas stations, retail businesses and the many other businesses that demand good traffic. These businesses often fail for reasons other than location. Many of these failed businesses could have survived had their owners the foresight to control the location. If location is critical to your business consider these safeguards today!

SECRET #195

Why Never To Bank Where You Borrow

It's true! It's almost always a big mistake to have checking or savings accounts in banks where you borrow. This, of course, is never a problem when relations between you and your banker are strong and cordial. It only becomes dangerous once your business gets shaky and your bank becomes nervous. The bank, without notice, may then set-off and apply the funds in your account against your loans. This common tactic usually comes at the worst possible time–when you are most in need of cash.

Another danger to banking where you borrow: Creditors, particularly tax agencies with the power to levy your bank accounts, assume you deposit in banks that finance you. The lender's identity is easily discovered through a lien check in the public records.

Lenders rightfully insist you bank with them, and that's sensible while banking relationships are strong. But don't allow your banker to grab your funds once relationships cool. That's when your funds should be safely transferred to another bank. Your lender need not know that you're now banking elsewhere. Maintain a small balance and keep your account active with small deposits. With your account active your banker is less likely to notice the absence of large deposits or detect your defection.

How Your Bank Can Protect Your Business From Other Creditors

It pays to have a good relationship with your banker for one often-overlooked reason: Your banker is usually in the best position to run interference against other creditors-particularly the IRS.

For instance, your bank can protect your business from IRS levy on your bank accounts. How? Have your banker agree to apply all funds in your account against your outstanding loan should they receive an IRS levy. With no funds in your account, the bank can truthfully return the IRS levy marked "no funds". The bank can then replenish your account by re-loaning you the same funds. Facing repeated IRS levies? It's safer-and your banker will be less inconvenienced-if you move your account to a new bank unknown to the IRS.

Make your banker your ally if the IRS attempts to seize your business assets. Your banker, for example, may discourage IRS seizure by showing there's no equity for the IRS above the bank mortgage. Your banker can also be a credible voice in confirming to the IRS that there are prospects for the business-buyers or lenders who may provide the necessary cash to pay the overdue taxes. The IRS often listens to a lender working closely with a troubled business-long after the business owner lost credibility.

Banks don't protect troubled businesses for any reason other than it helps protect them as well. Lenders know their best chance for a fully repaid loan is when the business stays in business. An IRS seizure can destroy the bank's chances of that full recovery.

Four Commonly Overlooked Ways To Protect Your Trade Secrets

Protecting tangible assets is only one objective. Your long-term survival and competitive edge also depends on how effectively you protect trade secrets and proprietary information-operating procedures, marketing studies, business plans and customer lists. Without their sound protection you may discover present employees and many others soon will be competing with you, using precisely the confidential information you failed to protect.

There's no way to totally protect your ideas and proprietary information, but you can significantly reduce misappropriation of these valuable assets with four simple steps:

- *Identify your trade secrets.* List the specific information you consider protected trade secrets so both you and your employees recognize exactly what is protected.
- *Require all employees to sign confidentiality and non-disclosure agreements.* This policy should extend to all employees. A court is far more likely to enforce rights to proprietary information when a confidentiality agreement exists. Also consider non-competition agreements. Courts do enforce such agreements against employees–when they are reasonable.
- *Establish and control procedures.* Design your asset protection system by first carefully reviewing how your confidential documents are produced, circulated, handled by others, stored and finally discarded. Control of confidential documents is probably the most critical part of your security system.
- *Expand your trade secrets protection to non-employees who may have access to them*: Vendors, consultants, franchisees and licensees, sales agents, customers, and even potential acquirers. How much access will each be allowed? What restrictive covenants and non-disclosures should each agree to? What additional methods can be used to monitor confidentiality?

Trade secrets law is complex. Before establishing your policy, have your attorney show you how to protect key information by established legal methods. This is essential if you are to develop and manage an effective asset protection program.

SECRET #198

How To Legally Recoup Your Investment From Your Failing Business

When your business turns bad your thoughts naturally turn to recouping your investment in your business. Skimming receipts "off the books" avoids easy detection but it's not your best method. Conversely, to dutifully record all withdrawals may invite claims for repayment from a bankruptcy trustee. So how can you both safely and legally take money out of your failing company?

- If you repay yourself for an earlier loan to the company, then fight to keep the business out of bankruptcy court for at least one year after you're repaid. Since you are an insider, creditors can recover preferential payments made to yourself (or any relative, or officer, director or stockholder of your corporation) within the year preceding the bankruptcy.
- Stagger your repayments as much as possible. Instead of large, easily detected payments to one or two individuals, make many smaller payments to a larger number of individ-

uals. It's considerably safer. These withdrawals are not easily detected and a bankruptcy trustee will be less inclined to start many lawsuits against numerous individuals. This is particularly true when the funds repaid a variety of obligations-from reimbursed expenses to wages to consulting fees.

- Try to earmark withdrawn funds as wages. Grossly excessive wages may be considered a fraudulent transfer and a misappropriation of funds, as may obviously excessive compensation paid to relatives or friends whose services to the troubled company are of questionable value. Still, wage payments are less easily challenged than are withdrawals for other purposes-such as loan repayments.

Caution: Does your company carry loans to you on its books? You can easily forget an old $20,000 loan from your business, but once documented on your books the bankruptcy trustee has little choice but to pursue collection. Can you debit the loan against other obligations the business may now owe you? Did you transfer some personal assets to the business in repayment? You see the point. Have the loan cancelled by your accountant before you turn your books and records over to the bankruptcy trustee. Another strategy: If you personally guaranteed business debts, then transform the loan into payment for serving as a guarantor to the business. It will create taxable income to you, but this tactic can help you avoid a lawsuit to repay the funds to your business creditors.

Information You Must Safeguard From Creditors

If you are in financial trouble, don't inadvertently give creditors information that improves their chances for collection at the expense of your business. What *can* you safely let creditors know and what *must* you conceal when the road is bumpy?

- Admit to creditors your temporary financial difficulties, but *never* openly admit insolvency, and certainly not in writing. Creditors can use your admission of insolvency to petition your business into bankruptcy.
- Never reveal to a creditor the names of your other creditors, or give a creditor your supplier list. Without this information a creditor cannot easily find two other creditors to join in a bankruptcy petition.
- Never disclose to creditors payment arrangements you negotiated with other creditors. If creditors discover other creditors obtained preferential treatment, they will have more cause to force you into bankruptcy.
- Never confide in a creditor your plans for your business. Creditors who do not see your plan as in their own best interests will sabotage those plans.

Conversely, there are a number of steps you can take to encourage creditor support when your business is in trouble.

- *Communicate.* Creditors become most anxious when debtors don't communicate with them. Accept your creditors phone calls. Better: Take the initiative and notify your creditors if you can't meet your obligations and need a moratorium to work things out. Good communication greatly increases your credibility and reduces creditor anxiety.
- *Anticipate concerns.* Assure creditors they are being treated equally. Creditors rightfully become most inpatient when they believe other creditors are gaining an advantage.
- *Be honest.* Creditors rightfully turn against customers who play games. Guaranteed to make creditors angry: Bad checks on COD purchases lead the list. Finding you violated your word and preferred other creditors with payment is another. Suspicions you diverted assets or embezzled funds is the most serious. Creditors usually cooperate with honest debtors and creditor cooperation is essential if your troubled business is to survive.

SECRET #200

Three Advantages Of An Out-Of-Court Creditor Settlement

If your business is in serious financial difficulty don't rush to file Chapter 11. Try first to negotiate an out-of-court workout. Debt restructuring outside of bankruptcy court gives you and your creditors several big advantages:

- An out-of-court workout is far less costly than a Chapter 11 reorganization. It can cost $50,000 or more in professional fees to navigate even a small business through a successful Chapter 11 reorganization. Negotiating the same arrangement with creditors–without Chapter 11–may cut your fees in half.
- Privacy is another advantage. With an out-of-court workout your financial woes are private. This is important if you may lose vital clients who learn of your financial difficulties. Your employees, similarly, may seek more secure employment once your company goes into Chapter 11. An out-of-court workout provides considerably more confidentiality since no one but you and your creditors are involved.
- A third advantage of the out-of-court workout is that you avoid the many rules and restraints of a Chapter 11. You enjoy more flexibility both in how you may design your repayment plan and how you operate your business during the workout.

An out-of-court workout, however, is not always your ideal alternative. One big drawback: Dissenting creditors who do not accept your settlement plan can still sue your business or petition it into bankruptcy. These dissenting creditors often upset a workout plan between a company and its assenting creditors.

Consider as an alternative a pre-packaged Chapter 11: Here your creditors accept your proposed repayment plan, but provide that if it should be necessary to file Chapter 11, creditor assent to the informal workout plan constitutes acceptance to an equivalent plan under Chapter 11. Convince only a majority of your creditors to accept your out-of-court plan and you can automatically force it upon the dissident creditors by filing a Chapter 11. The big benefit: You can quickly be out of Chapter 11 in a month or two instead of the year or two which is more typical when you go into Chapter 11 without a pre-approved plan. This strategy saves time, aggravation and the big fees of a long and drawn-out Chapter 11.

SECRET #201

When Chapter 11 Is Your Right Remedy

Far too many troubled companies file Chapter 11 when less involved procedures, such as out-of-court workouts, could rehabilitate their business more efficiently and economically. But there are four cases when a Chapter 11 is the only solution:

- If the IRS is threatening seizure, or has already seized, and you cannot pay the taxes within the short time the IRS gives you. Under a Chapter 11 you have up to six years from date of assessment to pay the IRS. The same is true of taxes owed state taxing agencies.
- If a secured lender is threatening seizure. The Chapter 11 automatically stays a foreclosure of assets or the repossession of leased equipment. The bankruptcy court may later allow the lender to foreclose, but in the interim your business is safe.
- If your business has been petitioned into bankruptcy by creditors and you cannot defend against the bankruptcy. You can then automatically put your business into Chapter 11 with a simple motion to convert proceedings from a Chapter 7 to Chapter 11.
- If you have so large a number of creditors that it's unlikely you can successfully reach agreement on a repayment plan without an orderly Chapter 11.

Tip: Don't quickly accept your attorney's recommendation to file Chapter 11. While there are many good alternatives, lawyers most often recommend Chapter 11 because it is the traditional remedy and the one taught in law school. Chapter 11's also generate big legal fees which hardly discourages lawyers. Check out other possible solutions in *How to Save Your business From Bankruptcy* (Garrett Publishing), listed in the Appendix. You'll discover many strategies that can bail you out faster and for less money.

How To Structure Successful Workout Plans

Whether your troubled business is in Chapter 11 or is attempting an out-of-court workout, the key to success is a debt repayment plan your creditors accept as *feasible, fair,* and *equitable.*

A plan is *feasible* if your business can afford to repay what is promised, when it is promised. It is *fair* when the repayment is for an amount more than creditors would get under a forced liquidation. Finally, it is *equitable* when all creditors (within each class) receive a proportionately equivalent amount on their claim. Still, within these three parameters there is considerable room for negotiation:

- *How much will you pay?* Obviously, the major objective of creditors is to be repaid as much as possible. A lowest settlement offer must at least equal what creditors would recover if your business were liquidated. You must inevitably offer more as an incentive for creditors to keep you in business. The maximum debt your business can safely carry into the future? The amount you can comfortably pay back from surplus cash flow within two or three years.
- *How much now and how much later?* Creditors also want fast payment. You cannot, however, pay more up-front cash than you have

on hand. Nor can you promise future payments above what the business can afford. Tip: Use conservative cash flow projections and never allow creditors to intimidate you into investing more personal funds so they receive faster or larger payments. Make your business stand on its own.

- *Length of payments?* Creditors will prod for as long a payment period as is necessary to fully repay what you owe. Don't let them mortgage your future for more than two or three years.
- *What about interest?* Creditors bargain for interest and interest at the prime rate is reasonable. Creditors should be reminded they'll wait two to three years to see payments under bankruptcy–and the bankruptcy court doesn't pay interest.
- *Will you personally guarantee the payments?* Whether you agree depends on the total debt, your personal financial situation, the risk, and how important the business is to you. Bargain for a limited guarantee. This limits your exposure while convincing creditors of your commitment to see the business succeed.
- *Will you secure the payments with a mortgage on your business?* Knowledgeable creditors bargain for a mortgage. A mortgage gives them an easy way to enforce their rights if you default. Equally important, it ensures current creditors receive priority of payment over

future creditors should you fail later. This may be a point to concede.

There are many less important points to negotiate. Will you give your creditors some stock in your business? It may be an attractive proposition if it looks like your company will enjoy rapid growth and possibly go public. Will you agree to a bonus payment if your company makes more money than anticipated? Be creative. There are many possible terms to consider when designing a repayment plan with creditors. Being the architect of an attractive settlement plan may be just what it takes to save your business.

One powerful way to coax more creditors into accepting a payment plan: Offer several options. For example, you may offer creditors: 1) 20 percent of their claim payable in four annual installments of five percent each, 2) a lump sum payment of 10 percent of their claim, or 3) five percent now and a share of the profits over the next three years. Each creditor can elect to accept the option considered most attractive.

Why does this technique work so well on creditors? It's largely psychological. When you offer a creditor only one plan, the creditor is forced to decide whether he should accept or not. When you offer alternate plans, the creditor thinks in terms of "which plan should I accept", rather than "should I accept the offered plan". Psychology is all-important when your goal is to tame angry creditors.

Six Reasons Your Business May Not Survive Chapter 11

Nearly nine out of ten companies that file Chapter 11 do not successfully emerge from bankruptcy court. They are instead liquidated under Chapter 7. Many that had their reorganization confirmed fail within three years of their reorganization. This leaves only a handful of companies that go into Chapter 11 alive three years later. Why do so many businesses succumb? What can you do to increase your chances of survival?

- One common reason for failure is that few smaller businesses can successfully finance themselves through a Chapter 11. While a Chapter 11 encourages more lenient credit and innovative borrowing, acute cash shortages can still prove fatal. When contemplating a Chapter 11 for your business, do so with a clear understanding of how you'll stay afloat–particularly if your company still operates with a negative cash flow and you lack strong lender and creditor cooperation.
- Companies also look to Chapter 11 as a safe harbor from foreclosing creditors. The protection is short lived if the bankruptcy court finds the lender is not adequately protected and authorizes foreclosure. And the court will if your company continues to lose money while collateral erodes and interest on the debt continues to mount.

- Creditors may force you to sell your most profitable units to raise quick cash for creditor dividends. While helpful to your creditors, this strategy is counter-productive to the long-term profitability and survivability of your business. This one big mistake accounts for a large number of reorganization failures.
- A surprisingly large number of businesses simply sink into the Chapter 11 quicksand of bureaucratic rules and restrictions, as well as the politics that abound in any Chapter 11. Bureaucratic death is particularly true of small businesses that are taken less seriously by bankruptcy courts.
- Creditors may also be hostile and unreceptive to even the most generous reorganization plan, particularly when creditors feel the owner has had less than honest dealings.
- Finally, is the fact that many companies mistakenly believe they've solved their problems simply by filing Chapter 11. These same firms come out of bankruptcy losing money just as before. The essence of Chapter 11, or any other business reorganization, is to give you another opportunity to put your business back on its feet. That means a business that earns a profit and operates with a positive cash flow.

Would your company survive a Chapter 11? Examine these five characteristics of long-term survivors:

- Survivors go into Chapter 11 with sufficient assets and a viable base of business activity from which to restructure and rebuild. Losers allow their asset base to dwindle until nothing is left to rebuild with.
- Survivors enjoy creditor cooperation and creditor support—particularly in obtaining new credit and financing. Losers have no credibility and earn no creditor cooperation.
- Survivors maintain a positive cash flow throughout the reorganization process. Losers continue to hemorrhage money.
- Survivors address and cure their underlying problems and design a coherent plan for new profitability and growth. Losers see no need to reshape for the future.
- Survivors restructure their debt to conform to the repayment capabilities of the company. Losers either offer too little and lose creditor support, or offer too much—only to default later and be liquidated by impatient creditors.

SECRET #204

How To Find Fast Cash In Your Failing Business

When creditors grow anxious, a key objective should be to turn unencumbered assets into cash as quickly as possible. This can provide you sufficient liquidity to finance your way through a Chapter 11. Cash-under any circumstances-gives you, not your creditors, the greatest flexibility should you have other objectives. Two assets often overlooked in this cash raising exercise: Accounts receivable and capital assets such as equipment, fixtures and motor vehicles.

Accounts receivable are best factored if they qualify for a factoring arrangement. This means your receivables must be owed by business customers with acceptable credit, and that the amount owed you cost-justifies factoring. The upside: Once you factor your receivables you immediately receive cash for about 90 percent of your receivables. More importantly, with receivables factored, your creditors lose access to them.

Factoring is perhaps your only solution short of Chapter 11 when the IRS attempts to levy your receivables. No business with substantial receivables can survive an IRS levy. Even if you should survive the cash flow crunch from an IRS intercept of all incoming checks, its adverse impact on customer relations is bound to destroy your business. As a practical matter you have no alternative but to factor your receivables so they are no longer subject to a threatened IRS levy.

Chart a similar course with capital assets. For example, here you may enter into a sale/leaseback arrangement. The sale/lease-back firm would buy your equipment, vehicles, or real estate, and then lease these assets back to you. Its net effect: You turned your equity into instant cash, which again, is a far more illusive asset for creditors to reach.

For these two cash-raising strategies to work, your receivables and capital assets must be free of liens and encumbrances. But even with liens, there may still be a sizeable equity to be tapped.

Eight Essential Insurances Most Businesses Overlook

Protection of your business must finally include a comprehensive insurance program to shield your business from as many possible claims, sources of liability and opportunity for loss as the business can reasonably afford to pay.

Most businesses carry basic fire and general liability insurance, yet these may not be the most important coverages for your business. Consider these eight often overlooked insurances:

- *Credit insurance:* Covers you for bad debts and should be considered to insure the collectibility of extraordinarily large debts that would sink your company if unpaid.
- *Accounts receivable insurance:* Reimburses you for your inability to collect receivables due to physical casualty to your books of account or receivable records.
- *Profits and commission insurance:* Consider this if you are a commission agent. It reimburses you for lost profits or commissions due you in

the event the company you sell for fails to provide the product to your customer after you made the sale.

- *Business interruption insurance:* Pays your ongoing overhead and lost profits until your business can become operational again following a casualty.
- *Supplemental perils:* Fire insurance covers only fire. This protects you from sprinkler damage or vandalism following a fire.
- *Floater and transit coverage:* This insurance takes several forms. A floater covers goods wherever they are located. A transit policy covers goods only along a specific route.
- *Bonding insurance:* Absolutely essential to protect yourself from embezzlement by employees with access to large sums of money.
- *Extended coverage:* Your standard liability policy covers you for negligent acts within your place of business. To protect yourself for wrongful acts beyond your business premises buy extended coverage.

Review your insurance needs annually. As a business grows and takes on new activities and procedures its insurance needs also change.

SECRET #206

How To Slash Your Insurance Costs

Concerned about the cost for more insurance? A few cost-cutting strategies can more than compensate for the expense of increased protection where it counts:

- Analyze the cost for each type of insurance you now carry. You may find one type coverage had its premiums increase by 300 percent whereas other coverages decreased. Armed with this information you can better decide what coverage is worthwhile and what coverage should be reduced or eliminated.
- Increase deductibles. Absorb the first $1000 to $5000 in losses and you'll reduce premiums substantially.
- Has your property been recently reclassified? Fire insurance, for example, is based on the rating for your building. The rating board considers the neighborhood, tenants and general condition of the property. Perhaps a bakery opened beside you. This, for example, can dramatically increase your rating because of the increased fire hazard. You have the right to check your property rating to contest any changes.
- Invest in sprinklers, fire extinguishers, smoke and fire detectors or a fire wall between you and a high-risk tenant. It pays big dividends. Review these possibilities with your insurance company.
- Take advantage of free programs that reduce insurance costs. For instance, progressive companies obtain reduced vehicle insurance premiums by enrolling their drivers

in drivers' education classes.
- Located in a "red line" or distressed area? You may be eligible for federal insurance or governmentally subsidized coverage. Inquire at the office of your state insurance commissioner.
- Do you belong to a trade association? Many companies report substantial savings by joining a group program sponsored by their associations. If your association doesn't offer such an arrangement, encourage your association to check into it. It can dramatically boost membership as well as insurance savings.
- If you own multiple businesses, investigate a package policy. This can reduce premiums by 25 percent or more.
- Buy only the insurance you need. As equipment depreciates, lower the coverage to conform to those decreasing values. Remember, an insurance company is only obligated to pay fair value for any lost asset. Any insurance beyond that fair value is a wasted payment.
- Shop around. Insurance rates are fixed in only a few states. Decide what coverage you want and have five companies bid. Repeat the process every few years. A company with the lowest rates today may be noncompetitive three years from now.

Key Secrets To Remember

- Your business requires no less financial protection than you do personally. Your business may need even more protection since it has a greater chance of financial problems.
- Incorporating your business is the cornerstone of your asset protection program. Only a corporation will save your personal assets from business debts.
- Divide your business into as many different corporations as practical. This will insulate your winners from your losers.
- Hold important business assets in a non-operating company where they will not be exposed to creditors.
- A friendly mortgage offers the ultimate protection because it guarantees you control over your business assets no matter what happens.
- Guard your lease–if your location is critical to the success of your business.
- The protection of trade secrets and proprietary rights is as important as the protection of tangible assets.
- There are a number of ways to resolve creditor problems. Chapter 11 should be your last–not your first –survival strategy.

16

MORE SECRETS TO SAFEGUARD YOUR WEALTH

There are many asset protection secrets to reveal. Not all fall squarely within one of the previous chapters. But the wealth preservation strategies found in this final chapter are no less important. In fact, they represent issues of great concern and importance in asset protection planning. Read this chapter carefully. You'll undoubtedly find some valuable advice to help you better safeguard your assets.

How To Protect An Inheritance From Creditors

Creditors cannot reach an inheritance until distributed from the estate and delivered to the beneficiary. A spendthrift clause in a trust will prevent creditors of a beneficiary from anticipating the inheritance and seizing either principal or sums due the beneficiary. A spendthrift clause does not safekeep funds already paid to the beneficiary. These should be protected in some other way. Two strategies help safekeep inheritances:

- If the beneficiary has serious creditor problems, then the beneficiary should declare bankruptcy well before the inheritance is received. The bankruptcy should be at least six months before the anticipated receipt of the legacy, because inheritances received within six months of bankruptcy can be claimed by the bankruptcy trustee. Inheritances received later are safe.
- Disclaim the inheritance. If you are a beneficiary, this will allow your inheritance to safely pass to the

next generation. This is an effective strategy when you want your children to have the inheritance, and you have serious financial problems. Your children, in turn, can loan or gift funds back to you.

A disclaimer is a complete and unqualified refusal to accept rights or property. It applies to both gifts and inheritances. You may disclaim an inheritance, for example, when you have creditors-including the IRS-waiting to seize any inheritance you receive. You will particularly want to disclaim property when the alternate beneficiaries are your children, or other individual(s) you prefer to receive the property. For disclaimers to be valid:

• The disclaimer must be in writing.
• The recipient must not have accepted any part of the property or the benefits of ownership.
• The written disclaimer must be received by the transferor no later than nine months after the date on which the transfer creating the interest is made.

If you are the testator bequeathing the property, you must decide how you will transfer your assets free of claims from your own creditors. Most people are sufficiently solvent to fully pay their debts from their estate. But this is not always the case. You may have more debts than assets. How then can you by-pass probate and this last opportunity for creditors to file a claim against your assets?

Several strategies can be used to avoid probate-and creditor claims that can be filed against your estate in probate, they include:

• living trusts
• insurance trusts
• joint tenancies
• gifts during your lifetime

Which method you use to avoid probate will depend on many factors. But it's important to remember that your assets can be as vulnerable to creditor attack while you are alive as when you die.

Transfers Creditors Most Easily Attack

The most vulnerable transfers? Gifts to family members. Unfortunately, these are also the most common transfers, because many debtors mistakenly believe that all they need do to protect themselves is to transfer title to a spouse, or put their property in the name of a child or parent. To the extent such transfers are without consideration and leave the debtor insolvent, creditors in these cases have the least difficulty proving a fraudulent conveyance or recovering the property. Outright gifts to family members should only be considered if you don't have major creditors at the time of the gift-and you don't contemplate bankruptcy anytime soon.

When you do make gifts be certain that the necessary gift tax returns are filed. This prevents creditors from claiming you intended to reclaim the property later.

SECRET #209

How Your Automobile Should Be Owned For Maximum Safety

Automobiles are usually a small part of a debtor's total assets. Still, the automobile is one of the first assets investigated by creditors. An automobile should be titled or leased to the less vulnerable spouse, if only to protect against uninsured accidents.

For asset protection purposes, it is usually sufficient to simply refinance the vehicle so there is little or no equity available for creditors. Refinancing is the easiest and most practical protection strategy–and also the safest.

An asset, such as an auto, boat, airplane or recreational vehicle, will be safe from creditors if it has loans against it for about 75 percent of its value. These assets, at auction, seldom bring more to produce a surplus for creditors.

SECRET #210

Dangers Of Titling Assets With Your Spouse

Worried about creditors? Why not put all your assets in your spouse's name? There are, as you might expect, several problems with having your assets owned by your spouse.

First, you cannot be certain your spouse will always remain creditor-free. Liability frequently strikes the spouse assumed to be relatively free of potential problems.

Second, divorces do occur. Divorce courts can make an equitable distribution of marital assets regardless of how titled, however, a spouse who holds title may sell or conceal the assets before the court can freeze the property.

Third, concentrating all assets on one spouse may create an estate in excess of $600,000 and cause an estate tax that's avoided by distributing assets between spouses.

These same pitfalls also apply to titling your assets in the name of another relative or friend. These individuals may be quite trustworthy and still run into financial problems that jeopardize your assets.

Your best bet: Hold title in a limited partnership, corporation or trust. The finances of another individual won't cause you to lose your assets or your sleep.

SECRET #211

How Savvy Physicians Avoid Lawsuits

Physicians–and other healthcare professionals–justifiably have great concern over liability since they face its threat everyday in the form of a potential malpractice suit.

Why the rapid surge in malpractice cases over the past twenty years? Depersonalization of relationships between physician and patient is one factor. So too is the general increase in lawsuits and the willingness of more lawyers to accept these cases.

Advanced medical technology and increased patient expectations are other often cited reasons.

What is clear is that the quality of medical care-or physician competence-has not decreased. This is of small consolation if you are that physician who must constantly guard against that one patient who can cause you to lose all your personal assets. If you're that physician, what steps can you take? Four strategies recommended for physicians anxious to avoid lawsuits are:

- Know the patient: Some patients are lawsuit prone. Whether they sue for financial reasons alone or because they honestly believe they suffered negligent treatment, is unimportant. What is important is that all physicians must beware of patients who are hostile, argumentative, demanding or threaten litigation. These patients must be treated with legal considerations foremost in mind-if they are to be accepted as patients. There are services that, for a small fee, will furnish a litigation profile on any new patient. You can then discover whether the patient previously sued other physicians.
- Never promise good results: Many malpractice suits arise because the patient did not obtain the outcome promised by the physician. The patient may then conclude that the poor outcome was the result of physician negligence.
- Maintain good records: Good records are a key weapon in the defense of a malpractice case. Ade-quate records often explain an unfavorable result that otherwise may be thought to result from negligence.
- Never admit your mistakes: Don't compound the problem by admitting your errors to the patient. Not only are such admissions evidence that can be used in court, but they may prompt the patient to file a lawsuit that might otherwise have been avoided.

SECRET #212

Why Employer Provided Malpractice Coverage May Not Protect You

Many more physicians are practicing today as employees in HMO's, clinics and other institutional healthcare facilities. One big reason: Physicians are provided malpractice coverage as a fringe benefit.

Unfortunately, this doesn't always guarantee the employed physician the total protection they believe they have. The practical problem of employer coverage: The insurance company may not be obligated to defend on behalf of the employee or pay a judgment against the employee. The latter point is not as serious as it may seem because the employer will ordinarily be liable for the negligent actions of the employee. Therefore, a judgment against the employee will result in the same judgment against the employer. Because the employer's liability will be paid by the insurance company, this payment will likewise satisfy the patient's claim against the employee. Health providers who rely on employer malpractice coverage still run several risks:

- How does the employee pay the cost of defending himself should the employer's insurance company refuse?
- What protection does an employee have if the employer's insurance company takes the position that the employer is not liable for the complained act of the employee?
- What protection remains for the employee if the employer's policy is terminated–without the knowledge of the employee?
- What if the employer carries inadequate insurance leaving the employee exposed against large judgments?

Employee-healthcare providers often ignore these potential pitfalls only to find non-existent or inadequate insurance protection once a lawsuit is filed. Employed healthcare providers must protect themselves with three defensive strategies:

- Review your employer's policy. Satisfy yourself that the insurance underwriter is obligated to defend and protect not only the employer but the employee as well.
- Evaluate the coverage. In an age of astronomical judgments, a jury award of $1 million or more is no longer unusual. Coverage of less than $1 million is plainly inadequate. If you don't have that cover-

age from your employer's policy, then supplement it with added coverage of your own.
- Consider the financial stability of the employer. Many healthcare organizations with financial problems reduce or even cancel their insurance. Your goal: Satisfy yourself that the coverage you are relying upon will remain in force and not be cancelled due to your employer's poor financial condition. A notification requirement can protect you here.

SECRET #213

Does "Going Bare" Without Malpractice Insurance Really Work?

There are two reasons why physicians are increasingly "going bare" without insurance protection.

First, is cost. Malpractice insurance is over $100,000 a year for certain medical specialists, particularly those in California. Even the average malpractice policy, with a $25,000 annual premium, can be prohibitively expensive for some physicians. Many physicians, to avoid these huge premiums, willingly gamble that they won't be sued. Obviously, this gamble makes sense only when the physician is 100 percent judgment proof with little to lose should a claim arise.

Second, is the deterrent factor. The lack of insurance is seen as an important factor in discouraging a lawsuit. A large policy may attract more claims as well as encourage plaintiff demands for a higher settlement. A "going bare" strategy, of course, only works when the physician lets the patient know in advance that he is without insurance and assets. Many physicians cannot bring themselves to this degree of candor. More importantly, many patients don't believe it even when they hear it.

Preliminary statistics suggest that "going bare" does decrease the likelihood of a malpractice claim. Patients may file suit but withdraw it or settle cheaply shortly thereafter once the physician demonstrates he is without resources to satisfy a judgment.

Consider a compromise strategy: Go without malpractice coverage–but do insure yourself a legal defense if suit is filed against you. It can cost $50,000 to $100,000 to defend against a major malpractice claim. Even if you are blameless and without assets to lose–you must defend against a suit or risk a default judgment. Local law firms may agree to an arrangement whereby you would pay them $2000-$3000 a year in exchange for their agreement to defend you–without further charge–should a suit arise. This can be an excellent form of insurance.

SECRET #214

How To Buy A Malpractice Policy

When you buy malpractice insurance you must know what you are buying. Malpractice coverage differs from other types of insurance. Consider three main features that require special attention:

- *Scope of coverage:* Your policy will define the type of errors and negligence that are covered. Most policies are broad enough to cover all types of professional negligence, but may not cover all possible sources of liability. Acts commonly not covered: Assault and battery, defamation, invasion of privacy, false imprisonment, intentional wrong-doing or acts involving violation of law. Liability often arises from one or more of these excluded acts.

- *Term of coverage:* Some policies cover claims when incurred regardless of when the suit is filed. Other policies cover claims made within the policy year, even though the malpractice may have occurred years earlier. This is known as a "claims made" policy. This latter type policy helps the insurance company determine their potential liability at the close of the insurance year, since they are not responsible for claims filed later. Regardless of the type policy, be certain you have continuity of coverage either when you switch from one type policy to the other or when you retire and wish to discontinue coverage. You then want continued coverage for acts that occurred while you were in practice.

- *Deductibles:* The portion per claim payable by the insured physician can vary between policies. Most physicians choose a policy with a large deductible since this significantly reduces the premium without significantly sacrificing protection. The trend in malpractice coverage is for physicians to buy policies with both greater coverage and greater deductibles.

The One Most Important Asset Protection Insurance

Umbrella liability insurance for $1 million or more is essential today for every family or individual. Umbrella coverage provides protection for a wide array of claims not covered by more specific insurance coverage. It also adds coverage above and beyond what other policies–such as homeowners and motor vehicle insurance–protect against.

Many Americans remain unaware of umbrella policies, or the fact that it offers so much additional protection for under several hundred dollars a year. Discuss umbrella liability insurance with your insurance agent. You too may discover that it is a worthwhile investment and an important part of your asset protection program.

Why Professionals Should Never Operate Under A General Partnership

General partners are personally liable for the liabilities brought about by other partners as well as themselves. For that reason, professionals should instead incorporate separately and have their respective corporations affiliate as partners. This will provide much greater protection to each individual professional. Example: If three physicians organize a medical partnership, the negligent acts of any one partner would jeopardize the personal assets of each partner. This arrangement expands liability.

Conversely, if each physician incorporated separately, the three corporations could be the partners. Each corporation would be liable for the liabilities of the general partnership, but the personal assets of the physician-stockholder would now be safe from partnership claims. With few assets in the corporation, there would be little risk.

How To Use Mortgages As Your Most Effective Shield Against Creditors

A mortgage or lien against your personal property is an excellent liability insulator because a mortgage reduces equity in the asset for creditors. Do you owe family members or close friends? Give them as security a mortgage on your home, or a lien on personal property such as a boat or auto. Be prepared to show that the debt is valid. Creditors can challenge and void as fraudulent a mortgage for a sham debt.

Another strategy: Grant a bank or other lender a mortgage on threatened assets for a new loan. The loan proceeds can then be deposited in an offshore account or invested in homesteaded property while the once exposed asset remains protected from creditors by the high mortgage.

Encumbering property is often an easier and more effective a way to protect property than is a transfer. A mortgage also attracts less attention from creditors who are less likely to question it, particularly if you borrow from a recognized lender.

Mortgages can similarly be used in business situations. Obtain the maximum loan possible against your business assets. The proceeds can be used to establish a generous and exempt qualified pension or profit-sharing plan. This produces a highly-leveraged and well-protected business. It gives you, in turn, an exempt qualified pension or profit-sharing plan.

SECRET #218

How Small Businesses Can Offer Employees Creditor-Proof Retirement Plans

Here's a new trend: Small businesses are increasingly grouping together to start multiple employer retirement trusts. Under the program, each employer-member contributes the same amount to the trust as under a single or unitary plan. Separate accounts are established for each business. Severance pay benefits can also be included in the plan.

There are two key advantages to this arrangement. Costs of administration are allocated among the several participating businesses and result in lowered costs of administration for each company. Insurance benefits can be included. Most importantly–creditors cannot pierce a multi-employer trust as they can IRA's and Keogh's. For this reason a multi-employer retirement trust can be an ideal way to protect retirement funds. Investigate this if you are a small business owner.

SECRET #219

How To Set Up Bank Accounts For Maximum Protection

Diversification is the key to bank account protection. Your strategy is to make it as difficult as possible for creditors to attach your account. This means: 1) You must open up as many separate accounts as you reasonably can, 2) That the accounts are titled in as many different names as possible, and 3) That as many accounts as possible are in other states. One or more substantial accounts may even be placed in a safe offshore haven for optimum privacy.

Try to establish accounts in the name of corporations–with their own taxpayer identification number on the account - rather than your social security number. A good rule of thumb: Never have more money in an account than you can afford to lose.

Why You Should Not Overlook Lifetime Giving

Gifts made by you during your lifetime can accomplish two key objectives: 1) Reduce your estate taxes, and 2) Reduce your assets for asset protection purposes.

The tax savings possibilities are two-fold: First, you save income taxes by transferring income producing assets to a recipient in a lower tax bracket. Second, you reduce your taxable estate and the corresponding estate tax. The property you transfer should ideally satisfy both tax objectives as well as making you and your assets less vulnerable to creditors.

The annual gift tax exclusion allows a tax-free transfer of $10,000 per year to each donee provided the gifted asset is immediately available to that donee. If your spouse jointly owns and also gifts the property with you, the exclusion is doubled to $20,000 each. This means $60,000 per year in tax-free giving for a couple with three children is possible. Tax savings are important even if you are divorced or widowed. Example: If you have four married children and six grandchildren, you can gift to your children and their spouses, and also your grandchildren, up to $140,000, tax-free.

You may want to make larger or more rapid gifts to quickly deplete your estate for asset protection purposes. But how can it be accomplished without incurring gift taxes? Here are several strategies to consider:

- Gift a part interest each year to keep the gift below $10,000 per donee per year.
- Transfer property through an installment sale, accepting notes that are payable annually. You can later cancel or forgive the payments. If the installment is for $10,000 or less it will be without taxable consequences. This strategy also makes the transfer supported by consideration and therefore more difficult for creditors to set aside as fraudulent.
- By-pass generation gifts can help you divest yourself of property even more rapidly. Caution: These by-pass generation gifts become subject to a generation skipping transfer tax of 50 percent, in addition to the gift tax. There are some broad exemptions, but this applies only to large gifts.
- Always gift first those assets most vulnerable to creditors. If asset protection is your gift-giving objective, then retain assets that are exempt from creditors.
- Gift-giving to save estate taxes? It's unwise from an income tax viewpoint to gift property that has significantly increased in value. Since the tax basis of this property is not stepped up, the recipient will have a potential income tax liability. This tax is avoided if the asset is retained and distributed later by inheritance.

Similarly, business property should not be gifted when it has been depreciated. The gift will trigger recapture of this depreciation deduction, but would not under an inheritance.

•One method to transfer property to a minor child is through transfer under a minor's trust. Another method is to leave property under the Uniform Transfers to Minors Act. Most states have enacted this law. Under the Uniform Transfers to Minors Act, you bequeath property to a minor either under a will or living trust. You also appoint a custodian to oversee the safe and proper use of the property until the child reaches majority age as defined by state law. You may, however, specify that the child is to receive the money at a later date. A minor's trust can be either revocable or irrevocable. The trust, however, will only be safe from creditors of the grantor if it is irrevocable. Creditors of the beneficiaries cannot gain access to the funds until distributed to the beneficiary.

•A gift that passes the gift tax obligation on to the recipient is a "net gift". There are definite advantages to it from the viewpoint of the donor: The gift tax paid by the donee is based on a value lower than if the donor paid the tax-since the net gift is based on the value of the gift less the tax. See your accountant or tax lawyer on this point. It can save money on any gift you may give-or receive.

How To Use Your Corporation In Estate Planning

Your corporation can be a helpful intermediary for disposing of property. Under this plan you would transfer selected assets to your newly organized corporation in exchange for its shares of stock. You can then bequeath or transfer to your designated beneficiaries the desired amount of shares. These shares may be distributed either all at once, or over a period of years, to take advantage of the annual gift tax exclusions. Consider the advantages:

•Property held in the corporation may be safer from creditors than if owned by the donor or donee.
•Property can be gifted immediately through shares, while it may not be feasible to divide or split the assets.
•The donor gains considerable flexibility in selecting the number of beneficiaries as well as the division of ownership each will receive.

How Property Left To Your Spouse Can Be Protected From Your Creditors

The idea of transferring substantial assets to a surviving spouse troubles many donors. The spouse may be too unsophisticated financially or may attract opportunists who will take advantage of the situation.

One possibility: Give the surviving spouse a life interest with the property to pass to a second generation upon his or her death. This can be efficiently accomplished with a so-called Q-Tip trust. For a Q-Tip trust to be used, the interest must be at least a qualifying life interest in a qualified terminable interest property. The donor or his executor must elect to irrevocably claim the marital deduction for all or a portion of the qualified terminable property. The Q-Tip trust may be created either by a lifetime gift or upon death.

The Q-Tip trust offers a flexible method for minimizing taxes on the estate of both the donor and surviving spouse. Another big advantage: It also protects assets from creditors of both spouses.

SECRET #223

How Your Last Will Can Reveal Assets To Creditors

Your last will and testament is one of the most fundamental ways to insure an orderly transfer of property. A detailed last will, however, can be counterproductive for asset protection purposes as it may needlessly disclose ownership of assets.

Your creditors can examine your will for purposes of discovering attachable assets. Not only can your will be examined, but creditors can also view worksheets and other estate planning documents provided they are not privileged communications between your attorney and yourself. How can you gain greater privacy in your last will?

- Destroy all estate planning worksheets or lists of assets, other than those retained by your attorney in his file.
- Never bequest specific amounts of money in your will. Bequests should be expressed as a percentile of your estate.
- By-pass probate and the need for wills entirely. Use living trusts (preferably irrevocable trusts), or hold property under joint ownership to automatically transmit your assets to your beneficiaries. Another benefit of avoiding probate with an estate: Any number of claimants can file claims. A trust eliminates probate since there is no estate to process. The absence of a pooled estate will help insure the flow of assets to beneficiaries without intervening claimants.
- Never list specific assets in your will. A will usually isn't prepared often enough to list specific assets. You don't want your creditors to see such a list. Tip: Write a letter of instruction that notes your individual assets and their locations, and

file it separately with your attorney. This list will be protected from curious creditors.

SECRET #224

How To Protect Your Wealth When Incapacitated

Whether you're wealthy or have only modest assets, appoint someone responsible to manage your legal and financial affairs when you are disabled and unable to act for yourself.

You accomplish this through a durable power of attorney (or an "evergreen power of attorney"). Unlike ordinary powers of attorney, a durable power of attorney activates and remains in effect only when you are unable to act. By granting someone the legal right to manage your affairs, the durable power of attorney insures someone is authorized to do whatever is necessary to protect you and your assets. Don't assume your spouse automatically has this authority. A spouse has no authority to enter into formal or important contracts on your behalf, commence or defend you against lawsuits, or transfer title to any of your assets unless appointed under a power of attorney. Without a durable power of attorney, your spouse, or any other person, can act for you only if they have been appointed conservator or guardian by a court. But this can take weeks, or even months. The durable power of attorney is essential if you want continuity of protection. You can always revoke a power of attorney.

In terms of asset protection, appoint an agent well-qualified to make the legal and financial decisions necessary to properly protect your assets. This individual may be someone with far different qualifications than an agent appointed to make healthcare or other personal decisions for you.

SECRET #225

How To Shelter Insurance Policies

Many states automatically exempt insurance from creditor claims. In other states an insurance trust can effectively insulate your policies from creditor claims whether against the insured or the beneficiaries.

With an insurance trust your insurance policies are assigned to a fiduciary trustee for the benefit of you, the insured and the beneficiary. Since you no longer own the policies, your creditors also lose access to them.

Another advantage: You as the donor, can transfer income-producing assets into the trust for purposes of funding future premiums. The trust then not only protects the insurance policy but the income-producing property as well.

When a decedent owes taxes to the IRS, the IRS can, and often does, attach the cash surrender value of any life insurance policies. This is true even if the insured gifted or transferred the policies years earlier, provided the insured retained any significant rights of ownership. This includes the right to change beneficiaries, terminate the policy, or control disposition of the cash surrender value.

The best way to protect insurance? Buy only term insurance without cash value. Second best: Put your insurance into an insurance trust.

SECRET #226

When Others Should Own Your Life Insurance

While insurance is income tax free, inheritance tax free and probate free, insurance is nevertheless counted as part of your estate. You'll therefore pay estate taxes on it. But why purchase insurance to pay estate taxes when the insurance itself increases the value of your estate? Your objective should be to keep the insurance outside your estate so it is not a taxable asset.

You can accomplish this goal through third-party ownership. You may, for instance, have your children beneficiaries of the insurance policy. This will give you an incentive to keep the insurance in force. You can also gift to your children the funds to pay the insurance premiums. Caution: Observe the gift tax limitations.

From an asset protection viewpoint, third-party ownership may be either an advantage or disadvantage–depending on whether the insured or the third-party is more likely to incur liability. This requires careful assessment.

SECRET #227

Your Insurance Company Must Protect You On Excess Claims

Insurance underwriters must properly defend the insured, or the insured may very well have a claim against the underwriter for any excess judgment above the amount of coverage. To avoid such a claim, the insurance company must:

- Notify the insured of the excess claim.
- Settle the claim in good faith. This means your insurer cannot refuse a reasonable settlement on the case, if the refusal would jeopardize the insured for excess liability. The insurer may then be liable to the insured for any excess judgment.

Similarly, an insurance company may decline a claim on the grounds the policy does not cover it. If there can be any question, then demand that the insurance company defend and indemnify you as provided under the policy. Once challenged, your insurance company may accept the claim, or at least provide the defense, reserving to itself the later right not to pay on any award and litigate with you whether it is, in fact, liable for coverage under the policy.

SECRET #228

Four Ways An Assignment For The Benefit Of Creditors Beats Bankruptcy

In many states it is possible to avoid business bankruptcy by filing an Assignment for the Benefit of Creditors (ABC). Under an

ABC you transfer your non-exempt assets to an assignee who liquidates the assets and pays assenting creditors their pro-rata shares of the proceeds in full satisfaction of their claim. An ABC offers several advantages over bankruptcy:

- ABC's are simple proceedings. There are no court appearances, or complex or formal documents to be prepared.
- ABC's are less expensive. You usually incur no fees with an ABC, as the assignee takes his fee from the liquidation proceeds of your assets.
- ABC's offer you more protection than bankruptcy. Unlike bankruptcy, you do not have to concern yourself with preferences.
- Assignees are also less likely to pursue fraudulent transfers because they do not have the same broad recovery powers as trustees in bankruptcy.

ABC's are ideal for the liquidation of an insolvent, incorporated business. With a corporate debtor there is no concern whether creditors assent. Because of its advantages, a small or mid-sized corporation should not voluntarily put itself into a Chapter 7 bankruptcy when their state law allows ABC's. There are simply too many advantages of an ABC and too many disadvantages with bankruptcy. An individual engaged in business will not find an ABC an appropriate remedy unless all creditors assent to the discharge of the debtor. This is not necessary with a corporation.

Why Its's Smart To Become Your Own Creditor

Did you ever think about becoming your own creditor? Claims for monies due, accounts receivable, judgments and choses in action (rights to sue) can be bought and sold like any other commodity. Why then shouldn't you buy a creditor's claim against yourself? You may be able to acquire the claim for as little as a few-cents-on-the-dollar.

Suppose you owe a creditor $10,000. You may not be able to settle with the creditor for $1000, yet a friend may successfully buy that same claim for $1000. Why would a creditor sell the claim for $1000, yet not settle with you for the same amount? Psychology. Animosity between yourself and your creditor may prevent a favorable settlement–even when the creditor knows it will be difficult to collect more. A buyer of the claim does not have that obstacle. Moreover, a "straw" buyer can validate to your creditor your poverty and thus the worthlessness of the claim.

Bonus: Once your friend owns the claim, why not give your friend some protection for his claim? Can he sue you for the $10,000 and attach your assets? Maybe you can transfer property to your friend in satisfaction of the claim. A mortgage may be used to secure the debt. You see the point: Your friend with his valid $10,000 claim against you can help protect your assets against creditors in a variety of ways. In sum, you buy and then use one creditor's claim to gain protection against all other creditors.

How Co-Ownership Of Personal Property Can Stall Creditors

Co-ownership of real estate makes it more difficult for creditors to seize. Stocks, automobile, boats, even a business–are all examples of assets that can be shared with others. Why divide ownership? One good reason is that partial interests in property are normally worth disproportionately less. Example: You own a boat worth $20,000. Sell a 50 percent interest to your friend. Your one-half interest is now less than $10,000 because it's more difficult to sell a one-half interest in the boat. Few people would pay much for the right to share a boat with a stranger. Selling a co-ownership interest to a friend or relative can be a smart asset protection strategy when creditors are on the prowl.

Three Legal Ways To Depress The Value Of Your Property To Creditors

It's not always necessary to actually transfer legal title to assets to modify your ownership rights. There are three other equally effective ways to depress the value of your assets to creditors:

- Option the property: Give someone an option to buy the property. As long as the price is reasonable it will withstand creditor challenge. Your creditors may seize the property under option, but they take the property subject to the option. This prevents them from selling the asset while the option is in force. Burdened with a long-term option–and the high costs of maintaining the asset–the property may have little or no value to the creditor.
- Leases: Why not lease the property? Leased property may be far more difficult to sell. The downside: Your creditors will be entitled to collect the rents. Solution: Assign the rents to a friendly creditor who can then "reloan" the rental income to you.
- Restricting sales: Do you own a small corporation or partnership? Enter into an agreement with your partner(s) to restrict or prohibit transfers of ownership interests in the business to third-parties. This impairs the rights of creditors, particularly if the restriction was coupled with an option granting your partner(s) the right to acquire your ownership interest for a low price and with extended payments.

Three Reasons Why Reducing The Value Of Your Property To Creditors Can Backfire

One objective in dealing with creditors is to depress the asset value so it becomes worth less to creditors. This may help you to negotiate the release of the property for a smaller settlement. It may even discourage creditors from pursuing the property. How can you depress the value of your property? One answer is to neglect the property. Your car or boat may be in disrepair. Your home may become shoddy. In this way you reduce resale values. You may also remove enhancements such as an expensive chandelier or carpeting. Even the removal of one key bolt from a piece of machinery may render it near worthless on the auction block. Beware of certain risks when pursuing this strategy:

- Your creditor may easily repair the property and you will have wasted your time and effort.
- You may be hurting yourself. If the asset now brings less at auction it will increase the deficiency you owe the creditor. If this is of concern, your strategy should be to enhance not diminish the value of the asset.
- Willful destruction of assets pledged as collateral can be a criminal violation.

While there is always the temptation to destroy assets under seizure, in most instances you'll come out ahead by being cooperative with your creditors. A voluntary surrender of collateral in good condition will win you your creditors' respect, and possibly even future credit.

How To Protect Your Personal Effects From Creditors

Most states exempt at least a portion of your household goods and personal items from creditor claims. Furthermore, ordinary household items–including furniture–have little or no resale value and generally are of no interest to creditors.

However, there are certain items your creditors may go after as they may be valuable and at the same time unprotected. These assets include:

- antiques
- heirlooms
- art
- expensive carpets
- pianos
- expensive electronics (stereos)
- jewelry (including watches)
- valuable collections (stamps, coins, etc.)
- furs
- silver

These assets are not exempt. If you want to protect these assets your three best strategies are to:

- Sell the assets and dispose of the cash proceeds.
- Gift the assets.
- Transfer the assets out-of-state. Simultaneously declare the assets gifted or sold. In that way you will not commit perjury when you do not declare these assets on your bankruptcy schedule or when questioned by creditors about ownership of these items.

How To Legally And Safely Dispose Of Cash

You may sell assets in advance of creditor attachment–but how do you account for cash? What can you do to legally protect cash from creditors? Here are several possibilities:

- Make cash gifts to family members.
- Reduce debts on exempt assets.
- Buy exempt assets.
- Pay "friendly" creditors.
- Discharge non-dischargeable debts.
- Pre-pay certain expenses.
- Use offshore accounts.

Faced with financial problems many individuals gamble away their money at Las Vegas or other gambling havens. Often they hope to parlay their cash into sufficient winnings to fully pay their creditors. This, of course, seldom happens.

While nobody can prove whether you won or lost money at the casinos, you should at least be able to prove you were there. Keep airline tickets, hotel receipts, etc. Creditors may or may not believe your story, but there's little they can do to recover your lost gambling stake. With a judgment creditor, or the IRS, after your cash, you will need a few more solid strategies to keep it:

- Don't accumulate more money in a bank account than you can afford to lose.
- Don't stay on as a trustee, joint owner or custodian of any accounts with or on behalf of anyone else. This only invites litigation whether you're entitled to the money.
- Don't maintain an account at any bank you owe money to. It's subject to setoff by the bank.
- Don't send checks to the IRS or any other creditor from a bank where you maintain accounts. Use money orders.
- Learn how to use cash. Many debtors do. It is not illegal to trade in actual cash currency, but it is nearly impossible for creditors to find and seize cash. In fact, when cash is your major asset you are in the very best position to protect your wealth.

APPENDIX

GLOSSARY OF USEFUL TERMS

Adequate Protection – The standard of protection granted a creditor by the trustee or debtor-in-possession in order to avoid the court allowing the creditor to foreclose on its property.

Automatic Stay – An injunction, or court order, that takes effect when a bankruptcy petition is filed. An automatic stay prohibits all collection action against a debtor.

Avoidance Powers – The powers used by a trusteed to reverse transfers of the debtor's property.

Balance Sheet – A statement of financial conditions as of a specific date. It is different from a cash flow statement, which summarizes income and expenses.

Bankruptcy Code – The body of a federal statutory law that governs the bankruptcy process.

Bankruptcy Petition – The legal instrument filed with the bankruptcy court that commences a bankruptcy proceeding.

Bar Date – The last date for filing a proof of claim.

Chapter 7 – In a Chapter 7 proceeding, the debtor's business is liquidated and its assets are distributed to creditors with allowed proofs of claims.

Chapter 11 – Normally, a Chapter 11 proceeding is a reorganization proceeding. The debtor continues to operate its business after the bankruptcy is filed. Chapter 11 liquidations are not uncommon and usually are the result of an unsuccessful reorganization attempt.

Chapter 11 Plan – In a Chapter 11 proceeding, the reorganization plan sets forth the rights of all classes of creditors. It may also include various repayment schedules pertaining to the various creditors.

Chapter 13 – May only be filed by an individual debtor with limited debt. In essence, it allows a payment plan for an individual's financial and/or business debts.

Closing – When a bankruptcy case is closed, it is no longer on the court's docket.

Collateral – Property of a debtor in which a creditor has a lien securing its debt.

Complaint – A pleading that is filed to initiate a lawsuit or an adversary proceeding.

Composition – Out of court agreement to pay a percentage of a debt in full settlement.

Consumer Credit Counseling Services – Are non-profit organizations established to help debtors make payment arrangements with creditors.

Conversion – The conversion of a bankruptcy case from one chapter type to another.

Cram-Down – The confirmation of a plan to reorganize over the objection of a creditor or class of creditors by the votes of other creditors.

Creditor – One to whom you owe money.

Debtor – One who owes debts. In bankruptcy, the bankrupt business that is under the control and protection of the bankruptcy court is the debtor.

Debtor-in-Possession (DIP) – The business debtor in a Chapter 11 reorganization. In a Chapter 11, the debtor retaining possession of the assets involved in the bankruptcy.

Discharge – A discharge in bankruptcy relieves the debtor of the dischargeable debts incurred prior to filing. *Discharge* is the legal term for the elimination of debt through bankruptcy.

Dismissal – The dismissal of a bankruptcy case, for all intents and purposes, returns the debtor to the same place it was before bankruptcy was filed.

Examiner – An officer of the court sometimes appointed to investigate the financial affairs of the debtor.

Exemption or Exempt Property – Property of an individual debtor that the law protects from the actions of creditors, such as the debtor's residence or homestead, automobile, and the like.

Foreclosure – A debt-collection procedure whereby property of the debtor is sold on the courthouse steps to satisfy debts. Foreclosure often involves real estate of the debtor.

General, Unsecured Claim – A claim that is neither secured nor granted a priority by the Bankruptcy Code. Most trade debts are general, unsecured claims.

Involuntary Bankruptcy Proceeding – In an involuntary bankruptcy proceeding the debtor is forced into bankruptcy by creditors. Involuntary bankruptcies are relatively rare.

Judicial Lien – A lien created by the order of a Court, such as the lien created by taking a judgment against a debtor.

Jurisdiction – The power and authority of a court to issue binding orders after hearing controversies.

Levy and Execution – A judicial debt-collection procedure in which the court orders the sheriff to seize the debtor's property found in the county to sell in satisfaction of the debtor's debt or debts.

Lien – An interest in property securing the repayment of a debt.

Motion – A request for the court to act. A motion may be filed within a lawsuit, adversary proceeding, or bankruptcy case.

Personal Property – Moveable property. Property that is not permanently attached to land is considered *personalty*.

Petition for Relief – The papers filed initiating a bankruptcy case.

Possessory Security Interest – A security interest or lien on property that requires the creditor to have possession of the property, such as a pawn or pledge.

Preference – A transfer of property of the debtor to a creditor made immediately prior to the debtor's bankruptcy that enables the creditor to receive more than it would have received from the bankruptcy. A preferential transfer must be made while the debtor was insolvent and as payment for a debt that existed prior to the transfer of property.

Priority – Certain categories of claims are designated as priority claims by the Bankruptcy Code, such as claims for lost wages or taxes. Each classification of claims must be paid in order of priority (the claims in one class must be paid in full before the next class receives any payment).

Priority Proof of Claim or Priority Claim – A proof of claim of the type granted priority by the Bankruptcy Code.

Proof of Claim – The document filed in a bankruptcy case that establishes a creditor's claim for payment against the debtor.

Realty or Real Property – Immovable property, such as land and/or buildings attached to land.

Redemption – The right of a debtor in a bankruptcy to purchase certain real or personal property from a secured creditor by paying the current value of the property (regardless of the amount owed on the property).

Secured Creditor – A creditor whose debt is secured by a lien on property of the debtor.

Secured Proof of Claim – A proof of claim for a debt that is secured by a lien, a judgment, or other security interest.

Security Interest – A lien on the property in the possession of the debtor that acts as security for the debt owed to the creditor.

Statutory Lien – A lien created by operation of law, such as a mechanic's lien or a tax lien. A statutory lien does not require the consent of the parties or a court order.

Trustee – An officer of the court appointed to take custody of the assets of a bankruptcy estate.

Unsecured Creditor – A creditor without security for its debt.

FEDERAL EXEMPTIONS

FEDERAL BANKRUPTCY EXEMPTIONS

Bankruptcy Code Section 522(d)

1. The debtor's aggregate interest, not to exceed $7,500 in value, in real property or personal property that the debtor or a dependent of the debtor uses as a residence, in a cooperative that owns property that the debtor or a dependent of the debtor uses as a residence, or in a burial plot for the debtor or a dependent of the debtor.
2. The debtor's interest, not to exceed $1,200 in value, in one motor vehicle. A couple filing can each have a car with $1,200 equity.
3. The debtor's interest, not to exceed $200 in value in any particular item or $4,000 in aggregate value, in household furnishings, household goods, wearing apparel, appliances, books, animals, crops, or musical instruments, that are held primarily for the personal family, or household use of the debtor or a dependent of the debtor.
4. The debtor's aggregate interest, not to exceed $500 in value, in jewelry held primarily for the personal, family, or household use of the debtor or a dependent of the debtor.
5. The debtor's aggregate interest in any property, not to exceed in value $400 plus up to $3,750 of any unused amount of the exemption provided under paragraph (1) of this subsection.
6. The debtor's aggregate interest, not to exceed $750 in value, in any implements, professional books, or tools of the trade of the debtor or the trade of a dependent of the debtor.
7. Any unmatured life insurance contract owned by the debtor, other than a credit life insurance contract.
8. The debtor's aggregate interest, not to exceed in value $4,000 less any amount of property of the estate transferred in the manner specified in section 542(d) of this title, in any accrued dividend or interest under, or loan value of, any unmatured life insurance contract owned by the debtor under which the insured is the debtor or an individual of whom the debtor is a dependent.
9. Professionally prescribe health aids for the debtor or a dependent of the debtor.
10. The debtor's right to receive -
    (a) a social security benefit, unemployment compensation, or a local public assistance benefit;

(b) a veteran's benefit;

(c) a disability, illness, or unemployment benefit;

(d) alimony, support, or separate maintenance, to the extent reasonably necessary for the support of the debtor and any dependent of the debtor;

(e) a payment under a stock bonus, pension, profit sharing, annuity, or similar plan or contract on account of illness, disability, death, age, or length of service, to the extent reasonably necessary for the support of the debtor and any dependent of the debtor, unless -

(i)   such plan or contract was established by or under the auspices of an insider that employed the debtor at the time the debtor's rights under such plan or contract arose;

(ii)   such payment is on account of age or length of service; and

(iii)   such plan or contract does not qualify under section 401(a), 403(a), 403(b), 408, or 409 of the Internal Revenue Code of 1954 [26 U.S.C. 401(a), 403(a), 403(b), 408, 409].

11.   The debtor's right to receive, or property that is traceable to:

(a) an award under a crime victim's reparation law;

(b) a payment on account of the wrongful death of an individual of whom the debtor was a dependent, to the extent reasonably necessary for the support of the debtor and any dependent of the debtor;

(c) a payment under a life insurance contract that insured the life of an individual of whom the debtor was a dependent on the date of such individual's death, to the extent reasonably necessary for the support of the debtor and any dependent of the debtor;

(d) a payment, not to exceed $7,500, on account of personal bodily injury, not including pain and suffering or compensation for actual pecuniary loss, of the debtor or an individual of whom the debtor is a dependent; or

(e) a payment in compensation of loss of future earnings of the debtor or an individual of whom the debtor is or was a dependent, to the extent reasonably necessary for the support of the debtor and any dependent of the debtor.

STATE EXEMPTIONS

ALABAMA

ASSET	EXEMPT
REAL ESTATE	Real property to $5,000; not in excess of 160 acres
PERSONAL PROPERTY/ HOUSEHOLD GOODS	Books Burial place Church pew Clothing Artwork/portraits
INSURANCE AND ANNUITIES	Annuity proceeds to $250 per month Disability proceeds to $250 per month Fraternal society benefits Proceeds from life insurance if beneficiary is insured's spouse or child Proceeds from life insurance if beneficiary is wife of insured Life insured proceeds if cannot be used to pay beneficiary's creditors
PENSIONS AND RETIREMENT PLANS	Law enforcement officers State employees Teachers
PUBLIC BENEFITS AND ENTITLEMENTS	AFDC, Aid to blind, aged, disabled Coal miners' benefits Crime victims' compensation Southeast Asian War POW's benefits Unemployment compensation Workers' compensation
WAGES	Bankruptcy - 75% of earned but unpaid wages Judgment Creditor - greater of 75% of your weekly net earnings or $114 per week
MISCELLANEOUS	Business partnership property
WILD CARD	$3,000 of any personal property

In Bankruptcy you must claim the state not the federal exemptions.

(Alabama Code Title 6 Sec. 10-2; Sec. 10-5; Sec,. 10-6; Sec. 10-7. Alabama Constitution Article X Sec. 204.)

ALASKA

ASSET	EXEMPT
REAL ESTATE	$54,000 in property
PERSONAL PROPERTY/ HOUSEHOLD GOODS	Motor vehicle to $3,000 Books, musical instruments, clothing, household goods to $3,000 Jewelry to $1,000 Building materials Burial place Pets to $1,000 Proceeds for damaged exempt property Wrongful death recoveries Recovery for personal injury
INSURANCE AND ANNUITIES	Disability benefits Benefits from fraternal society Insurance proceeds for personal injury or wrongful death Life insurance or annuity to $10,000 Life insurance proceeds if beneficiary is insured's spouse or dependent Medical benefits
PENSIONS AND RETIREMENT PLANS	ERISA; Public employees; Teachers; Other pensions
PUBLIC BENEFITS AND ENTITLEMENTS	Unemployment compensation Workers' compensation AFDC Adult assistance to elderly, blind, disabled Alaska longevity bonus Crime victims' compensation Federally exempt public benefits paid or due General relief assistance 50% of permanent fund dividends
WAGES	Weekly net earnings to $350; sole wage earner in household $2,200
MISCELLANEOUS	Alimony and child support Liquor licenses Business partnership property Books & tools of trade to $2,800
WILD CARD	None

In Bankruptcy you must claim the state not the federal exemptions.

(Alaska Statutes Sec. 9.38.010; Sec. 9.30.020; Sec. 9.30.15; Sec. 9.38.030.)

ARIZONA

ASSET	EXEMPT
REAL ESTATE	Real estate to $100,000. Sale proceeds exempt 18 months after sale or until new home purchased, whichever occurs first.
PERSONAL PROPERTY/ HOUSEHOLD GOODS	Bible; bicycle; sewing machine; typewriter; burial plot to $500 total; books to $250; clothing to $500 Furniture and furnishings Wedding & engagement rings to $1,000 Watch to $100 Pets, horses, cows & poultry to $500 Musical instruments to $250 Prostheses, including wheelchair Motor vehicle to $1,500-$4,000 if disabled If homestead is not claimed, prepaid rent or security deposit to $1,000 or 1 1/2 times your rent, whichever is less. Bank deposit to $150 in one account Proceeds for sold or damaged exempt property Food, fuel and provisions for 6 months
INSURANCE AND ANNUITIES	Group life insurance policy or proceeds Health, accident or disability benefits Life insurance cash value to $1,000 per dependent ($5,000 total) Life insurance cash value to $2,000 per dependent ($10,000 total) Life insurance proceeds to $20,000 if beneficiary is spouse or child Fraternal society benefits
PENSIONS AND RETIREMENT PLANS	Board of regents members Elected officials ERISA Firefighters and police officers State employees
PUBLIC BENEFITS AND ENTITLEMENTS	Unemployment compensation Workers' compensation Welfare benefits
WAGES	Minimum 75% of earned but unpaid wages, pension payments Judgment creditor - greater of 75% of your weekly net earnings or $114 per week
MISCELLANEOUS	Minor child's earnings Business partnership property Farm machinery, utensils, feed & animals to $2,500 Teacher aids Equipment, instruments & books to $2,500
WILD CARD	None

In Bankruptcy you must claim the state not the federal exemptions.

(Arizona Revised Statutes Sec. 33-1101; Sec. 33-1123; Sec. 33-1124; Sec,. 33-1125; Sec. 33-1126; Sec. 33-1130; Sec. 33-1131.)

ARKANSAS

ASSET	EXEMPT
REAL ESTATE	Choose one or the other: 1. For head of family; real or personal property used as residence, to an unlimited value; property cannot exceed 1/4 acre, or 80 acres rural. No homestead may exceed 1 acre in city, town or village, or 160 acres elsewhere. 2. Real or personal property used as residence, to $800 if single; $1,250 if married
PERSONAL PROPERTY/ HOUSEHOLD GOODS	Burial plot to 5 acres, in lieu of homestead option 2; clothing; motor vehicle to $1,200 Wedding rings with diamonds not exceeding 1/2 carat
INSURANCE AND ANNUITIES	Disability benefits Group life insurance; Life, health, accident or disability cash value or proceeds paid or due, to $500; Life insurance proceeds if cannot be used to pay beneficiary's creditors; Life insurance proceeds if beneficiary isn't the insured; Annuity contract; Fraternal society benefits Mutual assessment life or disability benefits to $1,000
PENSIONS AND RETIREMENT PLANS	Disabled firefighters and police officers Firefighters and police officers IRA deposits to $20,000, if deposited exceed 1 year before attachment by creditor or bankruptcy School employees
PUBLIC BENEFITS AND ENTITLEMENTS	AFDC, Aid to blind, aged, disabled Crime victims' compensation Unemployment compensation Workers' compensation
WAGES	Earned but unpaid wages due for 60 days, but not under $25 per week
MISCELLANEOUS	Business partnership property Tools of trade to $750
WILD CARD	$500 of any personal property if married or head of family; individuals $200

In Bankruptcy you must claim the state not the federal exemptions.

(Arkansas Statutes Sec. 30-207; Sec. 36-211. Arkansas Constitution Art. 9 Sec. 3-5; Sec. 1,2.)

CALIFORNIA - SYSTEM 1

ASSET	EXEMPT
REAL ESTATE	Real property, mobile home, coop, or condo to $50,000 if single & not disabled; $75,000 for families; $100,000 if 65 or older, or disabled; $100,000 if 55 or older, single & earn under $15,000 or married & earn under $20,000. Sale proceeds exempt for 6 months.
PERSONAL PROPERTY/ HOUSEHOLD GOODS	Furnishings, clothing & food Burial place Bank deposits from Social Security Admin. to $500; $750 if 2 or more payees Building materials to $1,000 Jewelry, heirlooms & art to $2,500 total Motor vehicles to $1,200 Personal injury claims or recoveries Wrongful death causes of action or recoveries Proceeds from exempt property
INSURANCE AND ANNUITIES	Disability or health benefits Fidelity bonds Fraternal benefits -life insurance benefits, to $4,000 loan value, and unemployment benefits Homeowners' insurance proceeds for 6 months after received, to homestead amount Life insurance Unmatured life insurance policy to $4,000 loan value
PENSIONS AND RETIREMENT PLANS	Private retirement benefits, IRAs & Keoghs Public employees Public retirement benefits
PUBLIC BENEFITS AND ENTITLEMENTS	Union benefits due to labor dispute Workers' compensation Aid to blind, aged, disabled, AFDC Financial aid to students Relocation benefits Unemployment benefits
WAGES	Public employees vacation credits 75% of wages paid 30 days before being sought by creditor
MISCELLANEOUS	Business or professional licenses, except liquor licenses Inmates' trust funds to $1,000 Business partnership property County employees Tools, materials, uniforms, books, furnishings, equipment, motor vehicle to $2,500 total; to $5,000 total if both spouses use in same occupation. Motor vehicle cannot be claimed under tools of trade exemption if claimed under personal property.
WILD CARD	None

In Bankruptcy you may choose System 1 or System 2, if you choose the state exemptions, or the federal bankruptcy exemptions.

(California Code of Civil Procedure Sec. 703.080; Sec. 704.010; Sec. 704.020; Sec. 704.030; Sec. 704.040; Sec. 704.050; Sec. 704.060; Sec. 704.070; Sec. 704.080; Sec. 704.090; Sec. 704.113; Sec. 704.140; Sec. 704.150; Sec. 704.200; Sec. 704.730; Sec. 706.050.)

CALIFORNIA - SYSTEM 2

ASSET	EXEMPT
REAL ESTATE property	Real property and coops, to $7,500; unused homestead may be applied to other
PERSONAL PROPERTY/ HOUSEHOLD GOODS	Animals, crops, household goods, books, musical instruments & clothing to $200 per item Burial plot to $7,500, if homestead is not claimed Jewelry to $500 Motor vehicle to $1,200 Personal injury recoveries to $7,500 Wrongful death recoveries
INSURANCE AND ANNUITIES	Disability benefits Fidelity bonds Life insurance proceeds Unmatured life insurance policy
PENSIONS AND RETIREMENT PLANS	ERISA
PUBLIC BENEFITS AND ENTITLEMENTS	Unemployment compensation Veterans' benefits Crime victims' compensation Public assistance Social security
WAGES	None
MISCELLANEOUS	Business partnership property Alimony, child support Business or professional licenses, except liquor license Tools of trade to $750
WILD CARD	$400, any property Unused portion of homestead or burial exemption, of any property

In Bankruptcy you may choose System 1 or System 2, if you choose the state exemptions, or the federal bankruptcy exemptions.

(California Code of Civil Procedure Sec. 703.140.)

COLORADO

ASSET	EXEMPT
REAL ESTATE	Real Property or a mobile home up to $20,000
PERSONAL PROPERTY/ HOUSEHOLD GOODS	Pictures & books to $750 Burial place Clothing to $750 Food & fuel to $300 Household goods to $1,500 Jewelry to $500 total Motor vehicles to $1,000 Personal injury recoveries, unless debt related to injury Proceeds for damaged exempt property
INSURANCE AND ANNUITIES	Disability benefits to $200 per month; lump sum exempt Fraternal society benefits Group life insurance Homeowners' insurance proceeds for 1 year after received, to $20,000 Life insurance to $5,000 Life insurance if cannot be used to pay beneficiary's creditors
PENSIONS AND RETIREMENT PLANS	ERISA Firefighters and police Public employees Teachers
PUBLIC BENEFITS AND ENTITLEMENTS	Veterans' benefits Workers' compensation AFDC, Aid to blind, aged, disabled Crime victims; compensation Unemployment compensation
WAGES	Bankruptcy - minimum 75% of earned but unpaid wages, pension payments Judgment creditor - greater of 75% of your weekly net earnings or $114 per week
MISCELLANEOUS	Business partnership property Horses, machinery, harness & tools of farmer to $2,000 total Library of professional to $1,500 or stock in trade, supplies, fixtures, tools, equipment & books to $1,500 total Livestock to $3,000
WILD CARD	None

In Bankruptcy you must claim the state not the federal exemptions.

(Colorado Revised Statutes Sec. 13-54-102; Sec. 13-54-104; Sec. 38-41-201; Sec. 38-41-201.6.)

CONNECTICUT

ASSET	EXEMPT
REAL ESTATE	None
PERSONAL PROPERTY/ HOUSEHOLD GOODS	Security deposits for residence Appliances & furniture Burial place Motor vehicle to $1,500 Wedding & engagement rings Clothing, food and bedding
INSURANCE AND ANNUITIES	Benefits received under no-fault insurance law Disability benefits paid by association for its members Fraternal benefit society benefits Health or disability benefits Life insurance proceeds if cannot be used to pay beneficiary's creditors
PENSIONS AND RETIREMENT PLANS	ERISA State employees Teachers
PUBLIC BENEFITS AND ENTITLEMENTS	Veterans' benefits Workers' compensation AFDC, Aid to blind, aged, disabled Crime victims' compensation Social security Unemployment compensation
WAGES	Bankruptcy - minimum 75% of earned but unpaid wages Judgment creditor - greater of 75% of your weekly net earnings or $114 per week
MISCELLANEOUS	Alimony and child support Business partnership property Tools, books, instruments & farm animals
WILD CARD	None

In Bankruptcy you may claim either state or federal exemptions.

(Connecticut General Statutes Annotated Sec. 52-352b; Sec. 83-581.)

DELAWARE

ASSET	EXEMPT
REAL ESTATE	None. Property held as tenancy by the entirety exempt against debt of only one spouse
PERSONAL PROPERTY/ HOUSEHOLD GOODS	Clothing, jewelry Burial place Church pew Pianos, organs & sewing machines School books and family library
INSURANCE AND ANNUITIES	Annuity contract proceeds to $350 per month Employee life insurance Health or disability benefits Life insurance proceeds if cannot be used to pay beneficiary's creditors Fraternal society benefits
PENSIONS AND RETIREMENT PLANS	Kent County employees Police officers & volunteer firefighters State employees
PUBLIC BENEFITS AND ENTITLEMENTS	Unemployment compensation Workers' compensation Aid to blind Aid to aged, disabled, AFDC General assistance
WAGES	85% of earned but unpaid wages
MISCELLANEOUS	Business partnership property Tools, implements & fixtures to $75 in New Castle & Sussex Counties; to $50 in Kent County
WILD CARD	$500 of any personal property, if head of family

In Bankruptcy you must claim the state not the federal exemptions.

(Delaware Code Annotated Title Sec. 4902; Sec. 4903; Sec. 4913.)

DISTRICT OF COLUMBIA

ASSET	EXEMPT
REAL ESTATE	None. Exception, property held as tenancy by the entirety exempt against debt of only one spouse
PERSONAL PROPERTY/ HOUSEHOLD GOODS	Cooking utensils, stoves, furniture, furnishings, radios, & sewing machines to $300 Books to $400 Clothing to $300 Cooperative association holdings to $50 Residential condominium deposit Food and fuel for 3 months
INSURANCE AND ANNUITIES	Fraternal society benefits Disability benefits Life insurance proceeds cannot be used to pay creditors Group life insurance Life insurance proceeds Other insurance proceeds to $200 per month, maximum 2 months, for head of family; else $60 per month
PENSIONS AND RETIREMENT PLANS	Public school teachers
PUBLIC BENEFITS AND ENTITLEMENTS	Unemployment compensation Workers' compensation Aid to blind, aged, disabled, AFDC Crime victims' compensation General assistance
WAGES	Bankruptcy - minimum 75% of earned but unpaid wages, pension payments Judgment creditor - greater of 75% of your weekly net earnings or $114 per week Non-wage and non-pension earnings for 60 days to $200 per month for head of family; else $60 per month
MISCELLANEOUS	Business partnership property Library, furniture, tools of professional or artist to $300 Mechanic's tools; tools of trade or business to $200 Motor vehicle, cart, wagon & horse to $500 Stock & materials to $200
WILD CARD	None

In Bankruptcy you may claim either state or federal exemptions.

(District of Columbia Code Sec. 15-501; Sec. 15-503; Sec. 35-521 through 35-525.)

FLORIDA

ASSET	EXEMPT
REAL ESTATE	Real property including mobile home to unlimited value; property cannot exceed 1/2 acre in municipality or 160 contiguous acres elsewhere Tenancy by the entirety property exempt against debt of only one spouse
PERSONAL PROPERTY/ HOUSEHOLD GOODS	Personal property to $1,000
INSURANCE AND ANNUITIES	Annuity contract proceeds Death benefits payable to a specific beneficiary, not the deceased's estate Disability or illness benefits Fraternal society benefits Cash surrender value of life insurance
PENSIONS AND RETIREMENT PLANS	County officers, employees ERISA Police officers and firefighters State officers, employees Teachers
PUBLIC BENEFITS AND ENTITLEMENTS	Veterans' benefits Workers' compensation Crime victims' compensation Public assistance Social security Unemployment compensation
WAGES	Earned but unpaid wages, or wages in bank account Federal government employees pension payments needed for support & received 3 months before being attached by creditor or filing for bankruptcy
MISCELLANEOUS	Alimony, child support Business partnership property
WILD CARD	Any personal property to $1,000

In Bankruptcy you must claim the state not the federal exemptions

(Florida Statutes Annotated Sec. 222.05 Sec. 222-11. Florida Constitution Article 10 Sec. 4.)

GEORGIA

ASSET	EXEMPT
REAL ESTATE	Real property, including coop, to $5,000; unused homestead may be applied to any property
PERSONAL PROPERTY/ HOUSEHOLD GOODS	Burial place Jewelry to $500; motor vehicles to $1,000 Personal injury recoveries to $7,500 Wrongful death recoveries Animals, crops, clothing, books, household goods, musical instruments to $200 per item, $3,500 maximum
INSURANCE AND ANNUITIES	Annuity & endowment benefits Disability or health benefits to $250 per month Fraternal society benefits Life insurance proceeds if needed for support Life insurance proceeds if beneficiary not the insured Unmatured life insurance dividends, interest, loan value or cash value to $2,000
PENSIONS AND RETIREMENT PLANS	ERISA Public employees Any pension needed for support
PUBLIC BENEFITS AND ENTITLEMENTS	Veterans' benefits Workers' compensation Aid to blind and disabled Crime victims' compensation Local public assistance Social security Old age assistance Unemployment compensation
WAGES	Bankruptcy - minimum 75% of earned but unpaid wages for private & federal workers Judgment creditor - greater of 75% of your weekly net earnings or $114 per week
MISCELLANEOUS	Alimony, child support Books & tools of trade to $500
WILD CARD	$400, any property Unused portion of homestead exemption

In Bankruptcy you must claim the state not the federal exemptions

(Georgia Code Annotated Sec. 44-13-100.)

HAWAII

ASSET	EXEMPT
REAL ESTATE	Head of family or over 65 to $30,000. Others to $20,000; not to exceed 1 acre.
PERSONAL PROPERTY/ HOUSEHOLD GOODS	Burial place Clothing Jewelry to $1,000 Motor vehicle to $1,000 Furnishings, appliances & books
INSURANCE AND ANNUITIES	Annuity or endowment policy Disability benefits Fraternal society benefits Group life insurance Life or health insurance policy for spouse or child
PENSIONS AND RETIREMENT PLANS	ERISA Police officers and firefighters Public officers & employees
PUBLIC BENEFITS AND ENTITLEMENTS	Workers' compensation Unemployment compensation Unemployment work relief funds to $60 per month Public assistance paid by DSSH
WAGES	Unpaid wages due for services of past 31 days; after 31 days, 95% of 1st $100; 90% of 2nd $100; 80% of balance Prisoner's wages held by DSSH
MISCELLANEOUS	Business partnership property Tools, implements, books, instruments, uniforms, furnishings, motor vehicle & other personal property needed for livelihood
WILD CARD	None

In Bankruptcy you may claim either state or federal exemptions.

(Hawaii Revised Statutes Sec. 651-92; Sec. 651-121.)

IDAHO

ASSET	EXEMPT
REAL ESTATE	$30,000; proceeds from sale exempt for 6 months
PERSONAL PROPERTY/ HOUSEHOLD GOODS	Books, furnishings, clothing, musical instruments, family portraits & heirlooms to $500 per item, $4,000 maximum Building materials Burial place Jewelry to $250; motor vehicle to $500 Personal injury recoveries needed for support Wrongful death recoveries Crops to $1,000
INSURANCE AND ANNUITIES	Annuity contract proceeds to $350 per month Death or disability benefits Fraternal society benefits Homeowners' insurance proceeds to $25,000 Life insurance Medical benefits
PENSIONS AND RETIREMENT PLANS	ERISA Firefighters and police officers Public employees Any pensions needed for support
PUBLIC BENEFITS AND ENTITLEMENTS	Veterans' benefits Workers' compensation Aid to blind, aged, disabled, AFDC Crime victims' compensation unless debt for treatment of injury incurred during the crime Any type of government assistance General assistance; social security Unemployment compensation
WAGES	Bankruptcy - minimum 75% of earned but unpaid wages, pension payments Judgment creditor - greater of 75% of your weekly net earnings or $114 per week
MISCELLANEOUS	Alimony, child support needed for support Liquor licenses Business partnership property Books & tools of trade to $1,000
WILD CARD	None

In Bankruptcy you must claim the state not the federal exemptions

(Idaho Code Sec. 11-207; Sec. 11-603; Sec. 11-604; Sec. 11-605; Sec. 55-1201.)

ILLINOIS

ASSET	EXEMPT
REAL ESTATE	Real property to $7,500 Proceeds from sale exempt for 1 year from date of sale
PERSONAL PROPERTY/ HOUSEHOLD GOODS	Family pictures, books, clothing; vehicles to $1,200; personal injury recoveries to $7,500; exempt property proceeds; wrongful death recoveries needed for support
INSURANCE AND ANNUITIES	Health or disability benefits Homeowners proceeds for destroyed home, to $7,500 Life insurance, annuity proceeds or cash value if beneficiary is insured's child, parent, spouse or other dependent Fraternal society benefits Life insurance proceeds if cannot be used to pay beneficiary's creditors Life insurance proceeds needed for support
PENSIONS AND RETIREMENT PLANS	Civil service employees; county employees Disabled firefighters; widows & children of firefighters ERISA General assembly members Municipal employees Police officers and firefighters State university employees; teachers
PUBLIC BENEFITS AND ENTITLEMENTS	Veterans' benefits Workers' compensation Aid to aged, blind, disabled, AFDC Crime victims' compensation Social security Unemployment compensation
WAGES	Bankruptcy - minimum 85% of earned but unpaid wages Judgment creditor - greater of 75% of your weekly net earnings or $114 per week
MISCELLANEOUS	Alimony, child support Business partnership property Implements, books & tools of trade to $750
WILD CARD	$2,000 - any personal property

In Bankruptcy you must claim the state not the federal exemptions

(Illinois Code of Civil Procedure Sec. 12-803; Sec. 12-901; Sec. 12-1001.)

INDIANA

ASSET	EXEMPT
REAL ESTATE	Real property claimed as residence to $7,500; In addition, homestead plus personal property (except health aids) up to $10,000. Also, property held as tenancy by the entirety is exempt against debt of only one spouse
PERSONAL PROPERTY/ HOUSEHOLD GOODS	$4,000 of tangible personal property; $100, any intangible personal property, except funds due
INSURANCE AND ANNUITIES	Fraternal society benefits Life insurance Accident proceeds
PENSIONS AND RETIREMENT PLANS	Firefighters, police, sheriffs Public employees State teachers
PUBLIC BENEFITS AND ENTITLEMENTS	Unemployment compensation Workers' compensation Crime victims' compensation unless debt for treatment of injury incurred during the crime
WAGES	Bankruptcy - minimum 75% of earned but unpaid wages Judgment creditor - greater of 75% of your weekly net earnings or $114 per week
MISCELLANEOUS	Business partnership property National guard uniforms, arms & equipment State military personnel's uniforms, arms & equipment
WILD CARD	See personal property

In Bankruptcy you must claim the state not the federal exemptions

(Indiana Statutes Annotated Sec. 24-4.5-5-105; Sec. 34-2-28-1.)

IOWA

ASSET	EXEMPT
REAL ESTATE	Real property unlimited value; property cannot exceed 1/2 acre in town or city, 40 acres elsewhere
PERSONAL PROPERTY/ HOUSEHOLD GOODS	Furnishings & household goods to $2,000 Books, pictures & paintings to $1,000 Burial plot to 1 acre Clothing to $1,000 Motor vehicle & musical instruments to $5,000 Wedding or engagement rings
INSURANCE AND ANNUITIES	Accident, disability, health, illness or life proceeds to $15,000 Employee group insurance Benefits from fraternal benefit society Life insurance proceeds to $10,000, paid to spouse, child or other dependent
PENSIONS AND RETIREMENT PLANS	Firefighters, police, public employees Other pensions needed for support
PUBLIC BENEFITS AND ENTITLEMENTS	Veterans' benefits Workers' compensation Adopted child assistance AFDC Social security Unemployment compensation
WAGES	Bankruptcy - minimum 75% of earned but unpaid wages, pension payments
MISCELLANEOUS	Alimony, child support needed for support Liquor licenses Business partnership property Farming equipment; includes livestock, feed to $10,000; non-farming equipment to $10,000
WILD CARD	$100, any personal property

In Bankruptcy you must claim the state not the federal exemptions

(Iowa Code Annotated Sec. 561.2; Sec. 627.6; Sec. 642.21.)

KANSAS

ASSET	EXEMPT
REAL ESTATE	Real property & mobile home under 1 acre in town or city, 160 acres rural
PERSONAL PROPERTY/ HOUSEHOLD GOODS	Burial place, funeral plan prepayments Clothing Food & fuel Furnishings & household equipment Jewelry to $1,000 Motor vehicle to $20,000
INSURANCE AND ANNUITIES	Life insurance
PENSIONS AND RETIREMENT PLANS	Officials in cities with populations between 120,000 & 200,000 ERISA Police officers & firefighters Government employees State school employees
PUBLIC BENEFITS AND ENTITLEMENTS	Unemployment compensation Workers' compensation AFDC Crime victims' compensation Social welfare General assistance
WAGES	Bankruptcy - minimum 75% of earned but unpaid wages Judgment creditor - greater of 75% of your weekly net earnings or $114 per week
MISCELLANEOUS	Liquor licenses Business partnership property Books, documents, furniture, instruments, equipment, to $7,500 total
WILD CARD	None

In Bankruptcy you must claim the state not the federal exemptions

(Kansas Statutes Annotated Sec. 60-2301; Sec. 60-2304.)

KENTUCKY

ASSET	EXEMPT
REAL ESTATE	Real or personal property claimed as residence to $5,000
PERSONAL PROPERTY/ HOUSEHOLD GOODS	Burial plot to $5,000 Clothing, jewelry, & furnishings to $3,000 total Payments for lost earnings needed for support Medical expenses Reparation benefits Motor vehicle to $2,500 Personal injury recoveries to $7,500 (not to include pain & suffering) Wrongful death recoveries
INSURANCE AND ANNUITIES	Health or disability benefits Annuity contract proceeds to $350 per month Life insurance policy of spouse beneficiary Cooperative life or casualty insurance benefits Fraternal society benefits Life insurance proceeds if proceeds cannot be used to pay beneficiary's creditors
PENSIONS AND RETIREMENT PLANS	Firefighters, police, teachers State employees; county government employees; Other pensions needed for support, IRAs
PUBLIC BENEFITS AND ENTITLEMENTS	Unemployment compensation Workers' compensation Aid to blind, aged, disabled, AFDC Crime victims' compensation;
WAGES	Bankruptcy - minimum 75% of earned but unpaid wages Judgment creditor - greater of 75% of your weekly net earnings or $114 per week
MISCELLANEOUS	Alimony, child support Business partnership property Furnishings of minister, attorney, physician, veterinarian or dentist to $1,000 Motor vehicle of mechanic, minister, attorney, physician, veterinarian or dentist to $2,500 Tools, equipment, livestock of farmer to $3,000 Tools of non-farmer to $300
WILD CARD	$1,000 of any property

In Bankruptcy you must claim the state not the federal exemptions

(Kentucky Revised Statutes Sec. 427.010; Sec. 427.030; 427.040; Sec.427.060; Sec. 427.150; Sec. 427.160.)

LOUISIANA

ASSET	EXEMPT
REAL ESTATE	$15,000; property cannot exceed 160 acres
PERSONAL PROPERTY/ HOUSEHOLD GOODS	Furniture, utensils, clothing, family portraits, musical instruments, heating & cooling equipment, pressing irons, sewing machine, refrigerator, freezer, stove, washer & dryer Burial place Engagement & wedding rings to $5,000
INSURANCE AND ANNUITIES	Fraternal society benefits Insurance policies or proceeds Health, accident or disability proceeds
PENSIONS AND RETIREMENT PLANS	ERISA
PUBLIC BENEFITS AND ENTITLEMENTS	Unemployment compensation Workers' compensation Aid to blind, aged, disabled, AFDC Crime victims' compensation
WAGES	Bankruptcy - minimum 75% of earned but unpaid wages Judgment creditor - greater of 75% of your weekly net earnings or $114 per week
MISCELLANEOUS	Minor child's property Tools, instruments, books, truck (maximum tons) & trailer
WILD CARD	None

In Bankruptcy you must claim the state not the federal exemptions

(Louisiana Revised Statutes Sec. 13:3881; Sec. 20:1.)

MAINE

ASSET	EXEMPT
REAL ESTATE	Real or coop to $7,500; if debtor over 60 or physically or mentally disabled, up to $60,000
PERSONAL PROPERTY/ HOUSEHOLD GOODS	Animals, crops, musical instruments, books, to $200 per item. Clothing, furnishings, household goods, tools of trade (above tools of trade exemption) & personal injury recoveries (above personal injury recovery exemption) to $4,500 total; furnaces & stoves Jewelry (not wedding or engagement rings) to $500 Payments for lost earnings needed for support Motor vehicle to $1,200 Personal injury recoveries to $7,500 (not pain & suffering) Farming tools & equipment Wrongful death recoveries
INSURANCE AND ANNUITIES	Life, endowment, annuity or accident policy, proceeds Annuity proceeds to $450 per month Disability or health proceeds, benefits or avails Group health or life policy or proceeds Fraternal society benefits
PENSIONS AND RETIREMENT PLANS	ERISA Legislators State employees
PUBLIC BENEFITS AND ENTITLEMENTS	Veterans' benefits Workers' compensation AFDC Crime victims' compensation Social security Unemployment compensation
WAGES	Judgment creditor - greater of 75% of your weekly net earnings or $114 per week only (no bankruptcy wage exemption)
MISCELLANEOUS	Alimony & child support (50%) Business partnership property Boat used in commercial fishing up to 5 tons Materials & stock to $1,000 1 of each type of farm implement
WILD CARD	$400 of any property

In Bankruptcy you must claim the state not the federal exemptions

(Maine Revised Statutes Annotated Title 14 Sec. 4422.)

MARYLAND

ASSET	EXEMPT
REAL ESTATE	None. Tenancy by the entirety property exempt against debt of one spouse
PERSONAL PROPERTY/ HOUSEHOLD GOODS	Appliances, furnishings, household goods, books, pets & clothing to $500 total Burial place Recovery for lost future earnings
INSURANCE AND ANNUITIES	Medical benefits deducted from wages Disability or health benefits Fraternal society benefits Life insurance
PENSIONS AND RETIREMENT PLANS	ERISA (except IRAs) Deceased Baltimore police officers State employees Teachers
PUBLIC BENEFITS AND ENTITLEMENTS	Unemployment compensation Workers' compensation AFDC Crime victims' compensation General assistance
WAGES	Earned but unpaid wages; Greater of 75% or $145 per week; in Kent, Caroline, & Queen Anne's of Worcester Counties; Greater of 75% of actual wages or $114 per week
MISCELLANEOUS	Business partnership property Clothing, books, tools & appliances to $2,500
WILD CARD	$5,500 of any property

In Bankruptcy you must claim the state not the federal exemptions

(Maryland Annotated Code of Commercial Law Sec. 15-601.1; Maryland Annotated Code of Cts. and Jud. Proc. Sec. 11-504.)

MASSACHUSETTS

ASSET	EXEMPT
REAL ESTATE	$100,000; if over 65 or disabled, $150,000. Tenancy by the entirety property exempt against debt of only one spouse.
PERSONAL PROPERTY/ HOUSEHOLD GOODS	Bank deposits to $125 Clothing Books to $200 total; sewing machine to $200 Cash for fuel, heat, water or light to $75 per month Cash to $200 per month for rent Coop shares to $100 Furniture to $3,000; motor vehicle to $700 Trust company, bank deposits to $500 Burial place & church pew
INSURANCE AND ANNUITIES	Benefits from fraternal benefit society Life or endowment policy, proceeds or cash value Group annuity policy or proceeds Life insurance policy if beneficiary is married woman or cannot be used to pay beneficiary's creditors Disability benefits to $35 per week Group life insurance policy
PENSIONS AND RETIREMENT PLANS	Private retirement benefits, public employees Savings bank employees
PUBLIC BENEFITS AND ENTITLEMENTS	Veterans' benefits Workers' compensation AFDC, aid to aged, disabled Unemployment compensation
WAGES	Earned but unpaid wages to $125 per week Payment (wage or pension) being received to $100 per week
MISCELLANEOUS	Business partnership property Boats, fishing tackle of fisherman to $500 Tools, & fixtures to $500 total
WILD CARD	None

In Bankruptcy you may claim either state or federal bankruptcy exemptions

(Massachusetts General Laws Annotated Chap. 188 Sec. 1; Chap. 235 Sec. 34; Chap. 246 Sec. 28A; Chap. 175.)

MICHIGAN

ASSET	EXEMPT
REAL ESTATE	Real estate to $3,500; property cannot exceed 1 lot, or 40 acres rural. In addition, tenancy by the entirety property exempt against debt of only one spouse
PERSONAL PROPERTY/ HOUSEHOLD GOODS	Building & loan association shares to $1,000 par value, in lieu of homestead Burial place Church pew, clothing; family pictures Appliances, books, household goods to $1,000 total Food & fuel for 6 months
INSURANCE AND ANNUITIES husband	Life, endowment or annuity proceeds if cannot be used to pay beneficiary's creditors Life or endowment proceeds if beneficiary is insured's spouse or child Life insurance proceeds to $300 per year if beneficiary is a married woman or a Benefits from fraternal benefit society Disability, mutual life or health benefits
PENSIONS AND RETIREMENT PLANS	Firefighters, police officers IRAs Legislators, public school employees, state employees
PUBLIC BENEFITS AND ENTITLEMENTS	Veterans' benefits for veterans Workers' compensation AFDC Crime victims' compensation Social welfare benefits Unemployment compensation
WAGES	60% of earned but unpaid wages for head of household; else 40%. Head of household may keep at least $15 per week + $2 per week per non-spouse dependent; others may keep at least $10 per week
MISCELLANEOUS	Business partnership property Tools, materials, stock, motor vehicle, horse & harness to $1,000 total
WILD CARD	None

In Bankruptcy you may claim either state or federal bankruptcy exemptions

(Michigan Compiled Laws Annotated Sec. 600.6023.)

MINNESOTA

ASSET	EXEMPT
REAL ESTATE	Real estate, cannot exceed 1/2 acre in city of 160 acres rural
PERSONAL PROPERTY/ HOUSEHOLD GOODS	Burial place Church pew; motor vehicle to $2,000 Appliances, furniture, radio, phonographs & TV to $4,500 total Clothing, food & utensils Personal injury and wrongful death recoveries Proceeds for damaged exempt property Books & musical instruments
INSURANCE AND ANNUITIES	Accident or disability proceeds Life insurance or endowment, proceeds if beneficiary isn't the insured or cannot be used to pay beneficiary's creditors Life insurance proceeds if beneficiary is spouse or child of insured to $20,000, plus $5,000 per dependent Police, fire benefits Unmatured life insurance contract dividends, interest or loan value to $4,000 Fraternal society benefits
PENSIONS AND RETIREMENT PLANS	ERISA, including IRAs, needed for support, not above $30,000 in present value Private retirement benefits Public employees and state employees
PUBLIC BENEFITS AND ENTITLEMENTS	Veterans' benefits Workers' compensation AFDC, general or supplemental assistance, supplemental security income Crime victims' compensation Unemployment compensation
WAGES	Bankruptcy - minimum 75% of earned but unpaid wages Judgment creditor - greater of 75% of your weekly net earnings or $114 per week Wages deposited into bank accounts for 20 days after depositing Wages of released inmates paid within 6 months of release
MISCELLANEOUS	Minor child's earnings Business partnership property Farm machines, livestock, crops of farmers to $13,000 total School teacher materials Tools, machines, instruments, furniture, stock in trade & library to $5,000 total
WILD CARD	None

In Bankruptcy you may claim either state or the federal bankruptcy exemptions

(Minnesota Statutes Annotated Sec. 550.37.)

MISSISSIPPI

ASSET	EXEMPT
REAL ESTATE	$30,000; property not above 160 acres
PERSONAL PROPERTY/ HOUSEHOLD GOODS	Personal injury judgments to $10,000 Tangible personal property $10,000
INSURANCE AND ANNUITIES	Disability benefits Homeowners' insurance to $30,000 Life insurance to $50,000 Fraternal society benefits Life insurance proceeds if cannot be used to pay beneficiary's creditors
PENSIONS AND RETIREMENT PLAN	ERISA benefits deposited over 1 year before creditor attachment or filing bankruptcy, IRAs and Keoghs Private retirement benefits Police officers, firefighters State employees Teachers
PUBLIC BENEFITS AND ENTITLEMENTS	Unemployment compensation Workers' compensation Aid to aged, blind and disabled Social security
WAGES	Bankruptcy - earned but unpaid wages owed for 30 days Judgment creditor - 100% first 30 days; after 30 days - greater of 75% of your weekly net earnings or $114 per week
MISCELLANEOUS	Business partnership property
WILD CARD	See personal property

In Bankruptcy you must claim the state not the federal exemptions

(Mississippi Code Sec. 85-3-1; Sec. 85-3-4; Sec. 85-3-17; Sec. 85-3-21.)

MISSOURI

ASSET	EXEMPT
REAL ESTATE	Real property to $8,000, mobile home to $1,000
PERSONAL PROPERTY/ HOUSEHOLD GOODS	Appliances, household goods, clothing, books, crops, animals & musical instruments to $1,000; Jewelry to $500; Motor vehicle to $500; Wrongful death recoveries for person you depended on Burial plot to $100;
INSURANCE AND ANNUITIES	Insurance premium proceeds Death, disability or illness benefits Life insurance dividends, loan value or interest to $5,000 Life insurance Fraternal society benefits to $5,000
PENSIONS AND RETIREMENT PLANS	Employees of cities w/100,000+ people ERISA Public officers & employees, police, highway & transportation, firefighters State employees Teachers
PUBLIC BENEFITS AND ENTITLEMENTS	Veterans' benefits Workers' compensation AFDC; Social security Unemployment compensation
WAGES	Bankruptcy - minimum 75% of earned but unpaid wages (90% for head of family) Judgment creditor - greater of 75% of your weekly net earnings or $114 per week Wages of servant or common laborer to $90
MISCELLANEOUS	Alimony, child support to $500 per month Business partnership property Books & tools of trade to $2,000
WILD CARD	$1,250 of any property if head of family; else $400. Head of family may claim additional $250 per child

In Bankruptcy you must claim the state not the federal exemptions

(Annotated Missouri Statutes Sec. 513-430; Sec. 513.440; Sec. 513.475; Sec. 525.030.)

MONTANA

ASSET	EXEMPT
REAL ESTATE	Real estate; mobile home to $40,000
PERSONAL PROPERTY/ HOUSEHOLD GOODS	Appliances, household furnishings, animals, crops, musical instruments, books, firearms, clothing & jewelry to $600 each, $4,500 total Cooperative association shares to $500 value Motor vehicle to $1,200 Proceeds for damaged or lost exempt property for 6 months after received Burial place Food and provisions for 3 months
INSURANCE AND ANNUITIES	Annuity to $350 per month Disability or illness benefits; medical, surgical or hospital benefits Group life insurance Life insurance proceeds if cannot be used to pay beneficiary's creditors Life insurance proceeds if annual premiums do not exceed $500 Unmatured life insurance contracts to $4,000 Fraternal society benefits
PENSIONS AND RETIREMENT PLAN	ERISA benefits deposited over 1 year before creditor attachment or bankruptcy (in excess of 15% of yearly income) Public employees
PUBLIC BENEFITS AND ENTITLEMENTS	Workers' compensation Veterans' benefits Aid to aged, disabled, AFDC Crime victims' compensation Social security Unemployment compensation Vocational rehabilitation to the blind
WAGES	Bankruptcy - minimum 75% of earned but unpaid wages Judgment creditor - greater of 75% of your weekly net earnings or $114 per week
MISCELLANEOUS	Alimony, child support Business partnership property Books & tools of trade to $3,000
WILD CARD	None

In Bankruptcy you must claim the state not the federal exemptions

(Montana Code Annotated Sec. 25-13-611; Sec. 25-13-612; Sec. 25.13-613; Sec. 25-13-614; Sec. 25-13-617; Sec. 70-32-104.)

NEBRASKA

ASSET	EXEMPT
REAL ESTATE	$10,000; (no more than 2 lots in city, 160 acres elsewhere.) Sale proceeds exempt for 6 months
PERSONAL PROPERTY/ HOUSEHOLD GOODS	Burial place Clothing Furniture & kitchen utensils to $1,500 Perpetual care funds Recovery for personal injury
INSURANCE AND ANNUITIES	Disability benefits to $200 per month Fraternal benefit society benefits to loan value of $10,000
PENSIONS AND RETIREMENT PLANS	County employees, state and school employees ERISA Military disability benefits to $2,000
PUBLIC BENEFITS AND ENTITLEMENTS	Unemployment compensation Workers' compensation Aid to disabled, blind, aged, AFDC
WAGES	Bankruptcy - minimum 85% of earned but unpaid wages or pension payments for head of family; 75% for all others Judgment creditor - greater of 85% (for head of family; all others 75%) of weekly net earnings or $114 per week
MISCELLANEOUS	Business partnership property Equipment or tools to $1,500
WILD CARD	$2,500 of any personal property, if homestead is not claimed; cannot claim wages

In bankruptcy you must claim the state not the federal exemptions

(Revised Statutes of Nebraska Sec. 12-517; Sec. 25-1552; Sec. 25-1556; Sec. 25-1558; Sec. 40-101.)

NEVADA

ASSET	EXEMPT
REAL ESTATE	Real property or trailer to $95,000
PERSONAL PROPERTY/ HOUSEHOLD GOODS	Appliances, household goods, furniture, home & yard equipment to $3,000 total Books to $1,500 Burial place Funeral service contract Motor vehicle to $1,000 Heirlooms
INSURANCE AND ANNUITIES	Group life or health policy or proceeds Benefits from fraternal society Annuity to $350 per month Health proceeds Life insurance proceeds if you're not the insured Life insurance policy or proceeds if annual premiums not over $1,000
PENSIONS AND RETIREMENT PLANS	Public employees
PUBLIC BENEFITS AND ENTITLEMENTS	Vocational rehabilitation benefits Unemployment compensation Aid to blind, aged, disabled, AFDC
WAGES	Bankruptcy - minimum 75% of earned but unpaid wages Judgment creditor - greater of 75% of weekly net earnings or $114 per week
MISCELLANEOUS	Business partnership property Dwelling of miner or prospector; cars, equipment for mining & mining claim you work to $4,500 total Farm trucks, stock, equipment & seed to $4,500 Library, equipment, supplies, tools & materials to $4,500 Uniforms, arms & equipment
WILD CARD	None

In bankruptcy you must claim the state not the federal exemptions

(Nevada Revised Statutes Sec. 21.090; Sec.115.010.)

NEW HAMPSHIRE

ASSET	EXEMPT
REAL ESTATE	Real property or portable housing (must own the land it's on) to $5,000
PERSONAL PROPERTY/ HOUSEHOLD GOODS	Beds, bedsteads, bedding, furniture to $2,000, sewing machine, cooking utensils needed, cooking & heating stoves, refrigerator Automobile to $1,000 Bibles & books to $800 Burial place Jewelry to $500 Proceeds for lost or destroyed exempt property Clothing Cow, 6 sheep or fleece; 4 tons of hay Food & fuel to $400
INSURANCE AND ANNUITIES	Homeowners' insurance proceeds to $5,000 Fraternal benefits Firefighters' aid insurance Life insurance if you're not the insured Life insurance or endowment proceeds if beneficiary is a married woman
PENSIONS AND RETIREMENT PLANS	Police officers, firefighters Public employees Federal pension
PUBLIC BENEFITS AND ENTITLEMENTS	Workers' compensation Unemployment compensation Aid to blind, aged, disabled, AFDC
WAGES	Court decides amount exempt
MISCELLANEOUS	Child support Business partnership property Minor child's wages Tools of your occupation to $1,200 Military member's uniforms, arms & equipment
WILD CARD	None

In bankruptcy you must claim the state not the federal exemptions

(New Hampshire Revised Statutes Annotated Sec. 480:1; Sec. 511:2; Sec. 512:21.)

NEW JERSEY

ASSET	EXEMPT
REAL ESTATE	None
PERSONAL PROPERTY/ HOUSEHOLD GOODS	Personal property & corporation shares to $1,000 total Burial place Clothing Furniture & household goods to $1,000
INSURANCE AND ANNUITIES	Annuity to $500 per month Military disability or death benefits Disability, death, medical or hospital benefits for civil defense workers Life insurance proceeds if cannot be used to pay beneficiary's creditors Life insurance proceeds if another insured Fraternal society benefits Health or disability benefits
PENSIONS AND RETIREMENT PLANS	Alcohol beverage control officers City boards of health employees County employees ERISA Public employees
PUBLIC BENEFITS AND ENTITLEMENTS	Workers' compensation Unemployment compensation Crime victims' compensation Old-age, permanent disability assistance
WAGES	90% of earned but unpaid wages if income under $7,500; if income over $7,500, court decides amount. Wages or allowances of military personnel
MISCELLANEOUS	Business partnership property
WILD CARD	None

In bankruptcy you may claim either state or the federal bankruptcy exemptions

(New Jersey Statutes Annotated Sec. 2A:17-19; Sec. 2A:17-56; Sec. 2A:26-4.)

NEW MEXICO

ASSET	EXEMPT
REAL ESTATE	Up to $20,000 if married, widowed or supporting another
PERSONAL PROPERTY/ HOUSEHOLD GOODS	Books, health equipment & furniture Building supplies Jewelry to $2,500 Materials, tools & machinery (fuel resource related) Motor vehicle to $4,000 Clothing Cooperative shares
INSURANCE AND ANNUITIES	Benevolent association benefits to $5,000 Fraternal society benefits Life, accident, health or annuity benefits, or proceeds
PENSIONS AND RETIREMENT PLANS	Pension or retirement benefits Public school employees
PUBLIC BENEFITS AND ENTITLEMENTS	Workers' compensation Unemployment compensation AFDC Crime victims' compensation General assistance Occupational disease disablement benefits
WAGES	Bankruptcy - minimum 75% of earned but unpaid wages Judgment creditor - greater of 75% of your weekly net earnings or $114 per week
MISCELLANEOUS	Ownership in unincorporated association Business partnership property $1,500 in tools of the trade
WILD CARD	$500 of any personal property $2,000 of any property, if homestead not claimed

In bankruptcy you may claim either state or the federal bankruptcy exemptions

(New Mexico Statutes Annotated Sec. 42-10-1; Sec. 42-10-2; Sec. 42-10-9; Sec. 42-10-10.)

NEW YORK

ASSET	EXEMPT
REAL ESTATE	Real estate condo, coop or mobile home, to $10,000
PERSONAL PROPERTY/ HOUSEHOLD GOODS	Schoolbooks; books to $50; pictures; clothing; church pew; stoves; sewing machine; furniture; refrigerator; TV; radio; wedding ring; to $5,000 total Burial place $2,500 cash or that with annuity totals $5,000; instead of homestead Recovery for lost earnings needed for support Personal injury recoveries to $7,500 (not to include pain & suffering) Security deposits Trust fund principal, 90% of income Wrongful death recoveries for person you depended on needed for support Motor vehicle to $2,400 Food for 60 days
INSURANCE AND ANNUITIES	Annuity benefits; purchased within 6 months of bankruptcy to $5,000 Disability or illness benefits to $400 per month Fraternal society benefits Insurance proceeds for damaged exempt property Life insurance proceeds that cannot pay beneficiary's creditors or if beneficiary is not the insured
PENSIONS AND RETIREMENT PLANS	ERISA, Keoghs and IRAs, needed for support
PUBLIC BENEFITS AND ENTITLEMENTS	Workers' compensation Veterans' benefits Crime victims' compensation Aid to blind, aged, disabled, AFDC Home relief Social security Unemployment compensation
WAGES	90% of earned but unpaid wages received 60 days before creditor attachment or filing for bankruptcy
MISCELLANEOUS	Alimony, child support Business partnership property Farm machinery, team, professional furniture, books & instruments to $600 total Uniforms, arms of military
WILD CARD	None

In Bankruptcy you must claim the state not the federal exemptions.

(New York Civil Practice Law and Rules Sec. 5205; Sec. 5206. New York Debtor and Creditor Law Sec. 282-284.)

NORTH CAROLINA

ASSET	EXEMPT
REAL ESTATE	Real or personal property, claimed as residence to $7,500. Tenancy by the entirety property exempt against debt of one spouse. $2,500 of unused homestead may be applied to other property
PERSONAL PROPERTY/ HOUSEHOLD GOODS	Crops, musical instruments, books, clothing, household goods to $2,500 total, plus $500 per dependent (up to $2,000) Burial plot to $7,500, in lieu of homestead Motor vehicle to $1,000 Wrongful death or injury recoveries for person you depended on
INSURANCE AND ANNUITIES	Benefits from fraternal society Life insurance
PENSIONS AND RETIREMENT PLANS	Legislators Municipal, city & county employees
PUBLIC BENEFITS AND ENTITLEMENTS	Unemployment compensation Workers' compensation AFDC Aid to blind Crime victims' compensation Special adult assistance
WAGES	Earned but unpaid wages received 60 days before filing for bankruptcy
MISCELLANEOUS	Business partnership property Books & tools of trade to $500
WILD CARD	$2,500 less any amount claimed for homestead or burial exemption, of any property

In bankruptcy you must claim the state not the federal exemptions

(North Carolina Constitution Article X, Sec. 1 & 2. General Statutes of North Carolina Sec. 1-362.)

NORTH DAKOTA

ASSET	EXEMPT
REAL ESTATE	Real estate or trailer to $80,000
PERSONAL PROPERTY/ HOUSEHOLD GOODS	Books to $100 & pictures; clothing Burial plots, church pew Cash to $7,500, in lieu of homestead Crops raised (to 160 acres) Motor vehicle to $1,200 Personal injury recoveries to $7,500 (not pain & suffering) Wrongful death recoveries to $7,500 Head of household not claiming crops may claim $5,000 of any personal property or any of the following: Library & tools of professional to $1,000 Livestock & farm implements to $4,500 Tools & stock in trade to $1,000 Furniture to $1,000 Books & musical instruments to $1,500 Non-head of household not claiming crops, may claim $2,500 of any personal property
INSURANCE AND ANNUITIES	Benefits from fraternal society Life insurance
PENSIONS AND RETIREMENT PLANS	Annuities, pensions, IRAs, Keoghs, & ERISA to $100,000 per plan, total cannot exceed $200,000 Disabled veterans' benefits (not military retirement pay) Public employees
PUBLIC BENEFITS AND ENTITLEMENTS	Unemployment compensation Workers' compensation AFDC Crime victims' compensation Social security Vietnam veterans' adjustment compensation
WAGES	Bankruptcy - minimum 75% of earned but unpaid wages Judgment creditor - greater of 75% of your weekly net earnings or $114 per week
MISCELLANEOUS	Business partnership property
WILD CARD	See personal property

In bankruptcy you must claim the state not the federal exemptions

(North Dakota Century Code Sec. 28-22-02; Sec. 28-22-03.1; Sec. 28-22-04; Sec. 28-22-05; Sec. 32-09.1-.03; Sec. 47-18-01.)

OHIO

ASSET	EXEMPT
REAL ESTATE	Real or personal property claimed as residence to $5,000; tenancy by the entirety property exempt against debt of only one spouse
PERSONAL PROPERTY/ HOUSEHOLD GOODS	Animals, crops, books, musical instruments, jewelry to $400, appliances, household goods, furnishings, sporting equipment & firearms to $200 per item, $1,500 total ($2,000 if no homestead claimed) Clothing to $200 per item Cash, money due within 90 days, bank & security deposits & tax refund to $400 total Personal injury recoveries to $5,000 (not pain & suffering) Motor vehicle to $1,000 Wrongful death recoveries Stove & refrigerator to $300 each Burial place
INSURANCE AND ANNUITIES	Benevolent society benefits to $5,000 Disability benefits to $600 per month Benefits from fraternal benefit society Group life insurance policy or proceeds Life, endowment or annuity contract for spouse, child or dependent Life insurance proceeds for a spouse Life insurance proceeds if proceeds cannot be used to pay beneficiary's creditors
PENSIONS AND RETIREMENT PLANS	ERISA, IRAs, Keoghs Firefighters', police officers' death benefits and pensions Public employees State highway patrol employees Volunteer firefighters' dependents
PUBLIC BENEFITS AND ENTITLEMENTS	Unemployment compensation Workers' compensation AFDC Crime victim's compensation Vocational rehabilitation benefits
WAGES	Bankruptcy - minimum 75% of earned but unpaid wages due for 30 days Judgment creditor - greater or 75% of your weekly net earnings or $114 per week
MISCELLANEOUS	Alimony, child support needed for support Property of business partnership Tools of trade to $750
WILD CARD	$400 of any property

In bankruptcy you must claim the state not the federal exemptions

(Ohio Revised Code Sec. 2329.66.)

OKLAHOMA

ASSET	EXEMPT
REAL ESTATE	Real property to unlimited value; property cannot exceed 1/4 acre. If property in excess of 1/4 acre, may claim $5,000 on 1 acre in city, town or village, or 160 acres rural
PERSONAL PROPERTY/ HOUSEHOLD GOODS	Books, portraits, pictures Burial plots Clothing to $4,000 Furniture Motor vehicle to $3,000 Personal injury, wrongful death & workers' compensation recoveries to $50,000 total
INSURANCE AND ANNUITIES	Funeral benefits Life insurance policy or proceeds if another insured Limited stock insurance benefits Fraternal society benefits
PENSIONS AND RETIREMENT PLANS	County employees Disabled veterans ERISA Law enforcement employees, police and firefighters Public employees and teachers Tax exempt benefits
PUBLIC BENEFITS AND ENTITLEMENTS	Unemployment compensation Workers' compensation AFDC Crime victims' compensation Social security
WAGES	75% of wages earned 90 days before creditor attachment or filing for bankruptcy
MISCELLANEOUS	Alimony, child support Business partnership property Farm tools to $5,000 total
WILD CARD	None

In bankruptcy you must claim the state not the federal exemptions

(Oklahoma Statutes Annotated Title 31 Sec. 1 & 2.)

OREGON

ASSET	EXEMPT
REAL ESTATE	Residence to $15,000 ($20,000 for joint owners); if you don't own land then mobile home to $13,000 ($18,000 for joint owners). Sale proceeds exempt 1 year from sale, if you purchase another home
PERSONAL PROPERTY/ HOUSEHOLD GOODS	Bank deposits to $7,500 Books, pictures & musical instruments to $300 total Burial place Clothing, jewelry & other personal items to $900 total Domestic animals, poultry with food to last 60 days to $1,000 Furniture, household items, utensils, radios & TVs to $1,400 total Payments for lost earnings Personal injury recoveries to $7,500, not to include pain & suffering Motor vehicle to $1,200
INSURANCE AND ANNUITIES	Annuity contract benefits to $250 per month Fraternal society benefits Health or disability proceeds Life insurance
PENSIONS AND RETIREMENT PLANS	ERISA benefits, if deposited at least 1 year before creditor attachment or filing for bankruptcy, including IRAs, (but not Keoghs) Government employees
PUBLIC BENEFITS AND ENTITLEMENTS	Unemployment compensation Workers' compensation AFDC Aid to disabled, blind, old age Crime victims' compensation General assistance Medical assistance Vocational rehabilitation
WAGES	Bankruptcy - minimum of 75% of earned but unpaid wages Judgment creditor - greater of 75% of your weekly net earnings or $114 per week Wages withheld in an employees bond savings account
MISCELLANEOUS	Alimony, child support Liquor licenses Business partnership property Tools, library to $750
WILD CARD	$400, any property

In bankruptcy you must claim the state not the federal exemptions

(Oregon Revised Statutes Sec. 23.160; Sec. 23,.164; Sec. 23.185; Sec. 23.200; Sec. 23.240.)

PENNSYLVANIA

ASSET	EXEMPT
REAL ESTATE	None. Tenancy by the entirety property exempt against debt of one spouse
PERSONAL PROPERTY/ HOUSEHOLD GOODS	School books & sewing machines Clothing
INSURANCE AND ANNUITIES Fraternal society benefits	Group life policy or proceeds Life insurance annuity contract payments, cash value or proceeds to $100 per month Life insurance annuity policy, cash value or proceeds Life insurance proceeds if proceeds cannot be used to pay beneficiary's creditors No fault automobile insurance proceeds Accident or disability benefits
PENSIONS AND RETIREMENT PLANS	County, municipal, and state employees Private retirement benefits (if proceeds cannot be used to pay beneficiary's creditors) Self-employment benefits
PUBLIC BENEFITS AND ENTITLEMENTS	Unemployment compensation Workers' compensation Crime victims' compensation Veterans' benefits
WAGES	Earned but unpaid wages
MISCELLANEOUS	Business partnership property
WILD CARD	$300 of any property

In Bankruptcy you may claim either state or the federal bankruptcy exemptions

(Pennsylvania Consolidated Statutes Annotated Title 42 Sec. 8123, 8124 & 8127.)

RHODE ISLAND

ASSET	EXEMPT
REAL ESTATE	None
PERSONAL PROPERTY/ HOUSEHOLD GOODS	Furniture to $1,000 total Books to $300 Burial place Clothing Debts due Certain animals
INSURANCE AND ANNUITIES	Accident or sickness proceeds or benefits Fraternal society benefits Life insurance proceeds if beneficiary is not the insured Temporary disability insurance
PENSIONS AND RETIREMENT PLANS	Private employees State & municipal employees
PUBLIC BENEFITS AND ENTITLEMENTS	Unemployment compensation Workers' compensation Aid to blind, aged, disabled AFDC General assistance State disability benefits Veterans' disability or survivors' death benefits
WAGES	Wages to $50 Wages due military member or survivor on active duty Wages of spouse
MISCELLANEOUS	A minor child's earnings Business partnership property Library Tools of trade to $500
WILD CARD	None

In Bankruptcy you may claim either state or the federal bankruptcy exemptions

(General Laws of Rhode Island Sec. 9-26-4.)

SOUTH CAROLINA

ASSET	EXEMPT
REAL ESTATE	Real property to $5,000
PERSONAL PROPERTY/ HOUSEHOLD GOODS	Animals, crops, books, clothing, furnishings, musical instruments to $2,500 total Burial place to $5,000, if homestead is not claimed Cash to $1,000, in lieu of burial or homestead exemption Jewelry to $500 Motor vehicle to $1,200 Personal injury and wrongful death recoveries
INSURANCE AND ANNUITIES	Life insurance from person you depended on to $4,000 Life insurance proceeds for spouse or child to $25,000 Life insurance proceeds if proceeds cannot be used to pay beneficiary's creditors Fraternal society benefits Disability or illness benefits
PENSIONS AND RETIREMENT PLANS	ERISA Firefighters and police officers Public employees
PUBLIC BENEFITS AND ENTITLEMENTS	Unemployment compensation Workers' compensation AFDC Crime victims' compensation Aid to aged, blind, disabled Social security Veterans' benefits
WAGES	None
MISCELLANEOUS	Alimony, child support Business partnership property Implements & tools of trade to $750
WILD CARD	None

In bankruptcy you must claim the state not the federal exemptions

(Code of Laws of South Carolina Sec. 15-41-200.)

SOUTH DAKOTA

ASSET	EXEMPT
REAL ESTATE	Real property under 1 acre in town or 160 acres elsewhere. Sale proceeds to $30,000 (unlimited if over age 70 or an unmarried widow or widower) exempt for 1 year after sale
PERSONAL PROPERTY/ HOUSEHOLD GOODS	Books to $200, pictures, burial plots, church pew, food, fuel & clothing Head of family may claim $4,000 of any personal property Farming machinery to $1,250 total Furniture to $200 Professional library & tools to $300 Tools of mechanic & stock in trade to $200 None-head of family may claim $2,000 of any personal property
INSURANCE AND ANNUITIES	Endowment, life insurance policy, proceeds or cash value to $20,000 Health benefits to $20,000 Fraternal society benefits Life insurance proceeds if proceeds cannot pay beneficiary's creditors Life insurance proceeds to $10,000, if beneficiary is surviving spouse or child Annuity to $250 per month
PENSIONS AND RETIREMENT PLANS	Public employees
PUBLIC BENEFITS AND ENTITLEMENTS	Unemployment compensation Workers' compensation AFDC
WAGES	Earned wages owed 60 days before being sought by creditor or filing for bankruptcy, needed for support of family
MISCELLANEOUS	Business partnership property
WILD CARD	See personal property

In bankruptcy you must claim the state not the federal exemptions

(South Dakota Codified Laws Sec. 15-20-12; Sec. 43-31-4; Sec. 43-45-2; Sec. 43-45-4.)

TENNESSEE

ASSET	EXEMPT
REAL ESTATE	$5,000; $7,500 for joint owners. Tenancy by the entirety property exempt against debt of one spouse
PERSONAL PROPERTY/ HOUSEHOLD GOODS	School books, portraits Burial place Clothing Payments for lost earnings Personal injury recoveries to $7,500 (not pain & suffering) Wrongful death recoveries to $10,000
INSURANCE AND ANNUITIES	Fraternal society benefits Homeowners' insurance proceeds to $5,000 Life insurance Accident, health or disability benefits
PENSIONS AND RETIREMENT PLANS	ERISA Public employees State & local government employees Teachers
PUBLIC BENEFITS AND ENTITLEMENTS	Unemployment compensation Workers' compensation AFDC Aid to blind, disabled, old age Crime victims' compensation to $5,000 General assistance Social security Veterans' benefits
WAGES	Bankruptcy - minimum 75% of earned but unpaid wages Judgment creditor - greater of 75% of your weekly net earnings or $114 per week (plus $2.50 per week per child)
MISCELLANEOUS	Alimony owed for 30 days prior Business partnership property Tools of trade to $750
WILD CARD	$4,000, any personal property

In bankruptcy you must claim the state not the federal exemptions

(Tennessee Code Annotated Sec. 26-2-102; Sec. 26-2-103; Sec. 26-2-106; Sec. 26-2-111; Sec. 26-2-301; Sec. 26-2-305.)

TEXAS

ASSET	EXEMPT
REAL ESTATE	Unlimited; to 1 acre in town, village, city or 100 acres (200 for families) elsewhere
PERSONAL PROPERTY/ HOUSEHOLD GOODS	Sporting equipment; (includes jewelry); heirlooms; furnishings; food; cars, light trucks not for work, or any 2 of the following: auto, camper, truck, cab or trailer; bicycle or motorcycle to $15,000 total ($30,000 for head of family). Total includes tools of trade, wages and life insurance cash value.
INSURANCE AND ANNUITIES	Life, health, accident or annuity benefits & cash value Retired public school employees group insurance State employee uniform group insurance State college or university employee benefits Benefits from fraternal society
PENSIONS AND RETIREMENT PLANS	County & district employees ERISA government or church benefits, Keoghs and IRAs Firefighters, police, and teachers Law enforcement officers' survivors Municipal employees State employees
PUBLIC BENEFITS AND ENTITLEMENTS	Unemployment compensation Workers' compensation Aid for dependent children Crime victims' compensation Medical assistance
WAGES	Earned but unpaid wages
MISCELLANEOUS	Business partnership property Implements of farming or ranching needed to work; Tools, equipment & books
WILD CARD	None

In Bankruptcy you may claim either state or federal bankruptcy exemptions

(Texas Property Code Annotated Sec. 41.001; Sec. 42.002.)

UTAH

ASSET	EXEMPT
REAL ESTATE	Real property or trailer to $8,000; plus $2,000 for spouse & $500 per dependent
PERSONAL PROPERTY/ HOUSEHOLD GOODS	Animals, books & musical instruments to $500 total Burial place Bed, bedding, carpets, washer & dryer Clothing (not furs) Furnishings & appliances to $500 Heirloom to $500 Proceeds for damaged exempt property Refrigerator, freezer, stove & sewing machine Personal injury recoveries Wrongful death recoveries
INSURANCE AND ANNUITIES	Fraternal society benefits Life insurance policy cash surrender value to $1,500 Life insurance proceeds if beneficiary is insured's spouse or dependent Disability, illness, medical or hospital benefits
PENSIONS AND RETIREMENT PLANS	ERISA Public employees Any pensions needed for support
PUBLIC BENEFITS AND ENTITLEMENTS	Unemployment compensation Workers' compensation AFDC Crime victims' compensation; General assistance Occupational disease disability benefits Veterans' benefits
WAGES	Bankruptcy - minimum 75% of earned but unpaid wages Judgment creditor - greater of 75% of your weekly net earnings or $114 per week
MISCELLANEOUS	Alimony needed for support; Child support; Property of business partnership Books & tools of trade to $1,500 Military property Motor vehicle to $1,500
WILD CARD	None

In bankruptcy you must claim the state not the federal exemptions

(Utah Code Sec. 78-23-3; Sec. 78-23-5; Sec. 78-23-8.)

VERMONT

ASSET	EXEMPT
REAL ESTATE	Real property or mobile home to $30,000; tenancy by the entirety property against debt of only one spouse
PERSONAL PROPERTY/ HOUSEHOLD GOODS	Furnishings, clothing, books, crops, animals, musical instruments to $2,500 total Jewelry to $500; wedding ring unlimited Motor vehicles to $2,500; bank deposits to $700 Stove, refrigerator, water heater & sewing machines Wrongful death recoveries for person you depended on Sidearms Personal injury recoveries
INSURANCE AND ANNUITIES	Group life or health benefits Fraternal society benefits Life insurance proceeds if beneficiary is not the insured Life insurance proceeds if proceeds cannot be used to pay beneficiary's creditors Annuity benefits to $350 per month
PENSIONS AND RETIREMENT PLANS	Municipal employees IRA's, Keoghs to $10,000 State employees & teachers Any pensions
PUBLIC BENEFITS AND ENTITLEMENTS	Unemployment compensation Workers' compensation Aid to blind, aged, disabled, AFDC Crime victims' compensation General assistance Social security Veterans' benefits
WAGES	Bankruptcy - minimum 75% of earned but unpaid wages Judgment creditor - greater of 75% of your weekly net earnings or $114 per week
MISCELLANEOUS	Alimony, child support Business partnership property Books & tools of trade to $5,000
WILD CARD	$7,000 less any amount of appliances, i.e., growing crops, jewelry, motor vehicle & tools of trade claimed, of any property; $400 of any property,

In Bankruptcy you may claim either state or federal exemptions

(Vermont Statutes Annotated Title 12 Sec. 2740; Title 27 Sec. 101.)

VIRGINIA

ASSET	EXEMPT
REAL ESTATE	$5,000; tenancy by the entirety property exempt against debt of one spouse
PERSONAL PROPERTY/ HOUSEHOLD GOODS	Furniture, furnishings & utensils Burial place Wedding, engagements rings
INSURANCE AND ANNUITIES	Cooperative life insurance benefits Benefits from fraternal benefit society Group life insurance policy or proceeds Industrial sick benefits Life insurance cash values to $10,000 Life insurance proceeds if beneficiary is not the insured Burial benefits Accident or disability benefits
PENSIONS AND RETIREMENT PLANS	County & state employees
PUBLIC BENEFITS AND ENTITLEMENTS	Unemployment compensation Workers' compensation Aid to blind, aged, disabled AFDC Crime victims' compensation General assistance
WAGES	Bankruptcy - minimum 75% of earned but unpaid wages, pension payments Judgment creditor - greater of 75% of your weekly net earnings or $114 per week
MISCELLANEOUS	Business partnership property Boat to $1,500 Tools of mechanic and farmer to $1,000 Uniforms, equipment of military
WILD CARD	$5,000 of personal property, if homestead is not claimed $2,000, any property of disabled veterans

In bankruptcy you must claim the state not the federal exemptions

(Code of Virginia Sec. 34-4; Sec. 34-4.1 Sec. 34-6; Sec. 34-26; Sec. 34-27; Sec. 34-29.)

WASHINGTON

ASSET	EXEMPT
REAL ESTATE	Real property to $30,000
PERSONAL PROPERTY/ HOUSEHOLD GOODS	Furniture, household goods to $1,500 total Clothing (only $750 in furs & jewelry) Food & fuel Books to $1,000 Burial place Motor vehicle to $1,200
INSURANCE AND ANNUITIES	Fire insurance proceeds for destroyed exemption Benefits from fraternal benefit society Life insurance proceeds if beneficiary is not the insured Disability proceeds or benefits Annuity to $250 per month
PENSIONS AND RETIREMENT PLANS	Public employees ERISA, IRA's State patrol officers Volunteer firefighters
PUBLIC BENEFITS AND ENTITLEMENTS	Unemployment compensation Workers' compensation Child welfare (AFDC) Crime victims' compensation General assistance Old-age assistance
WAGES	Bankruptcy - minimum 75% of earned but unpaid wages Judgment creditor - greater of 75% of your weekly net earnings or $114 per week
MISCELLANEOUS	Business partnership property Farm trucks, stock, equipment of farmer to $3,000 total Library, office furniture, equipment & supplies of professionals to $3,000 total Tools & materials used in trade to $3,000
WILD CARD	$500 of any personal property (no more than $100 in cash, bank deposits, bonds, stocks & securities)

In Bankruptcy you may claim either state or federal bankruptcy exemptions

(Revised Code of Washington Annotated Sec. 6.12.050; Sec. 6.16.020; Sec. 7.33.280.)

WEST VIRGINIA

ASSET	EXEMPT
REAL ESTATE	Real or personal property claimed as residence to $7,500; unused homestead may be applied to other property
PERSONAL PROPERTY/ HOUSEHOLD GOODS	Crops, clothing, appliances, books, furnishings, musical instruments to $200 per item, $1,000 total Burial plot to $7,500, if homestead is not claimed Payment for lost earnings Motor vehicle to $1,200 Jewelry to $500 Personal injury recoveries to $7,500 (not pain & suffering) Wrongful death recoveries needed for support
INSURANCE AND ANNUITIES	Benefits from fraternal society Group life insurance policy or proceeds Health or disability benefits Life insurance to $4,000, from person you depended on Life insurance proceeds unless you are both policy owner and beneficiary Life insurance proceeds or cash value if beneficiary is married woman
PENSIONS AND RETIREMENT PLANS	ERISA Public employees
PUBLIC BENEFITS AND ENTITLEMENTS	Unemployment compensation Workers' compensation Aid to blind, aged, disabled AFDC Crime victims' compensation General assistance Social security Veterans' benefits
WAGES	Bankruptcy - 80% of earned but unpaid wages Judgment creditor - greater of 80% of your weekly net earnings or $114 per week
MISCELLANEOUS	Alimony, child support Business partnership property Tools of trade to $750
WILD CARD	$400 of any property Unused portion of homestead or burial exemption

In bankruptcy you must claim the state not the federal exemptions

(West Virginia Code Sec. 38-10-4.)

WISCONSIN

ASSET	EXEMPT
REAL ESTATE	$40,000; Proceeds exempt for 2 years
PERSONAL PROPERTY/ HOUSEHOLD GOODS	Automobile to $1,000; food & fuel Bank deposits to $1,000 is homestead is not claimed U.S. savings bonds to $200 Beds & clothing Books, pictures, radio & TV Burial place, church pew, patents Cooking utensils & furniture to $200 Jewelry to $400
INSURANCE AND ANNUITIES	Federal disability insurance Fire proceeds of destroyed exempt property Health, accident or disability benefits to $150/month Life insurance policy or proceeds to $5,000, if beneficiary is a married woman Life insurance proceeds not used to pay beneficiary's creditors Life insurance proceeds if beneficiary is not the insured Benefits from fraternal society
PENSIONS AND RETIREMENT PLANS	Public employees Firefighters, police officers Military pensions Private retirement benefits
PUBLIC BENEFITS AND ENTITLEMENTS	Workers' compensation Veterans' benefits AFDC, other social services payments Unemployment compensation
WAGES	Wages for 30 days; if you have dependents, $120 plus $20 per dependent, not to exceed 75% of your wages. No dependents, no less than $75 nor more than $100
MISCELLANEOUS	Business partnership property Farm utensils, small tools & implements to $300, tractor to $1,500 Printing materials of printer or publisher to $1,500; $400 for wages due workers Tools, implements, stock in trade of mechanic, miner, merchant or trader to $200 Uniform, equipment of national guardsman Books
WILD CARD	None

In Bankruptcy you may claim either state or federal bankruptcy exemptions.

(Wisconsin Statutes Annotated Sec. 815.18; Sec. 815.20.)

WYOMING

ASSET	EXEMPT
REAL ESTATE	Real property to $10,000 (mobile trailer to $6,000). Tenancy by the entirety property exempt against debt of one spouse
PERSONAL PROPERTY/ HOUSEHOLD GOODS	Furniture, household articles & food to $2,000 per person in the home Books Burial place, funeral contracts Clothing & wedding rings up to $1,000
INSURANCE AND ANNUITIES	Benefits from fraternal society Group life or disability policy or proceeds Life insurance proceeds (if beneficiary is not the insured) Life insurance proceeds not used to pay beneficiary's creditors Disability benefits Annuity to $350 per month
PENSIONS AND RETIREMENT PLANS	Firefighters, police officers Public employees
PUBLIC BENEFITS AND ENTITLEMENTS	Unemployment compensation Workers' compensation AFDC Crime victims' compensation General assistance
WAGES	Bankruptcy - minimum 75% of earned but unpaid wages Judgment creditor - greater of 75% of your weekly net earnings or $114 per week Wages of work release prisoners Earnings of national guard members
MISCELLANEOUS	Liquor licenses Business partnership property Library & equipment of professional to $2,000 or, tools, motor vehicle, implements, team & stock in trade to $2,000
WILD CARD	None

In bankruptcy you must claim the state not the federal exemptions

(Wyoming Statutes Annotated Sec. 1-17-411; Sec. 1-20-101; Sec. 1-20-105; Sec. 1-20-106.)

USEFUL REFERENCES

American Academy of Matrimonial Lawyers
150 No. Michigan Avenue, Suite 2040
Chicago, IL 60601
312-263-6477

American Association for Marriage and Family
Therapy
1100 17th Street, N.W., 10th Floor
Washington, DC 20036
202-452-0109

American Society of Appraisers
2777 So. Colorado Blvd., Suite 200
Denver, CO 80222
303-758-6148

Appraisal Institute
875 No. Michigan Avenue, Suite 2400
Chicago, IL 60611
312-335-4100

Center for Dispute Settlement
1666 Connecticut Avenue, N.W., Suite 501
Washington, DC 20009
202-265-9572

E-Z Legal Forms
312 So. Military Trail
Deerfield Beach, FL 33442
305-480-8933

The Garrett Group
366 S.E. 5th Avenue
Delray Beach, FL 33483
407-243-3701

Institute of Business Appraisers
P.O. Box 1447
Boynton Beach, FL 33425
407-732-3202

Internal Revenue Service (IRS)
to obtain tax forms
800-829-1040

International Association of Financial Planning
2 Concourse Parkway, Suite 800
Atlanta, GA 30328
404-395-1605

Jerome Schneider
WFI Corporation
357 S. Robertson Blvd.
Beverly Hills, CA 90211
213-855-1000

Laughlin Associates
2533 No. Carson Street
Carson City, NV 89706
800-648-0966

National Association of Enrolled Agents
6000 Executive Blvd., Suite 205
Rockville, MD 20852
800-424-4339
301-984-6232

National Child Support Enforcement Association
Hall of the States
444 No. Capitol Street, N.W., Suite 613
Washington, DC 20001
202-624-8180

National Foundation for Consumer Credit
8611 2nd Avenue, Suite 100
Silver Springs, MD 20910
800-388-2227

National Institute of Child Support Enforcement
370 L'Enfant Promenade, S.W.
Washington, DC 20447
202-401-5439
202-401-9381

Social Security Administration
800-234-5772

Taxpayers Assistance Corp.
202 So. State Street
Chicago, IL 60
800-IRS-HELP

U.S. Department of Health and Human
Services
Office of Child Support Enforcement
6110 Executive Blvd.
Rockville, MD 20852

INDEX

Index

Professional licenses, as marital
assets, 208
Professionals, and avoidance of
general partnership, 243
Profit-sharing plans, dividing, in
divorce, 207-208
Property. See also Personal property
depressing value of, to
creditors, 251
gifting of, before
bankruptcy, 135
holding title to, in own
name, 65
protecting, after divorce,
211-213
protecting proceeds of
exempt, 52
reasons why reducing value
of, can backfire, 252
setting for no cash down,
170-171
Property agreements, for the already
married, 202-203
Property liens, for child support, 213
Property settlement, without pre-
marriage agreement, 197-198
Property transfer, steps in, 18-19
Proraters, 27
Publicly listed securities, sell of, 14

Q
Q-Tip trust, 247

R
Real estate, business ownership of,
222
Redemption, of seized property, 152-
153
Refinancing of property, 168-169
Repossession
getting car back after, 176
using bankruptcy to stop,
176-177
Request for production of
documents, 34
Residence, owning and qualifying for
Medicaid, 181
Retirement plans, small business
offering employees creditor-
proof, 244
Revised Uniform Limited Partnership
Act, 90, 91
Revocable trust, 99
living trust as, 102, 108
as offering no protection,
101
in protecting assets from
nursing home costs,
186

S
Safe deposit box, safeguarding from
IRS, 154-155
Schneider, Jerome, 119
"S" corporation, 70, 120. See also
Corporation
Scotland, as tax haven, 123
Secret investments, moving funds
into, 115-116
Securities violations, and corporate
liability, 80
Self-defense, asset protection as form
of, 3
Shareholder, invisible, 74-75
Sheriff's sale, 38, 43
Singapore, as tax haven, 123
Small business, offering employees
creditor-proof retirement plans,
244
Social security benefits, in divorce,
207
Social security funds, protection of,
from garnishment, 47
Social security number, disclosure of,
116
Soldiers and Sailors Relief Act, 167-168
Sole proprietor, 220
incorporating, to gain
corporate protection,
68
South Dakota, jointly held property
in, 58
Spendthrift clause, 49
Spendthrift trust, 110, 111
Spousal property, protecting from
creditors, 246-247
Spousal resource allowance, 182-183
Spouse
dangers to titling assets
with, 239
filing for bankruptcy
separately, 131-132
involvement of, in asset
protection, 4
Sprinkling trusts, sheltering assets
with, 109
Stamps, as investment, 114
Standby trust, for business owners,
109
Stock option, dividing in divorce, 207
Subpoena duces tecum, 34-35
Swiss bank accounts, myths and
realities of, 121-122
Switzerland, as tax haven, 123

T
Tax benefits. See also Internal
Revenue Service (IRS)
with bankruptcy, 137
and corporate liability, 79
and lifetime giving, 245-246

of limited partnership, 97
Tax lien
coping with, 147-148
key move in conveying
assets prior to, 146-147
Tax obligations, effects of bankruptcy
on, 158-160
Taxpayer Assistance order, 150
Taxpayer's Assistance Corporation,
160
Taxpayer's Bill of Rights, 160
Tax Reform Act (1986), 103
Tax refunds, 39
Tax returns
filing joint, after divorce,
212
keeping secret, 30-31
Tenancy-by-partnership, 56
Tenancy-by-the-entirety, protection
offered by, 59-62
Tenancy-in-common, hazards in, 56-
57
Term life insurance, owning, and
qualifying for Medicaid, 181
Testamentary trusts, 99
Texas, homestead protection in, 44,
47
Title, holding, in own name, 65
Title state, and division of marital
property, 198
Trademark infringement, 36
Trade secrets, protecting, 226-227
Trust(s)
adding preamble to, 110
business, 102-103
charitable remainder, 107-
108
Clifford, 103
convertible, in protecting
assets from nursing
home costs, 188
creating creditor-proof, 100
discretionary, 186, 187-188
establishing out-of-state, 110
foreign-based, 105-106
insurance, 248
irrevocable, 99, 100, 108,
186-188
IRS perils for, 155-157
land, 105
life insurance, 48, 104-105
living, 99, 102, 108, 186
Medicaid, 106-107, 185-189
minor's, 103
multiple employer
retirement, 244
Q-Tip, 247
revocable, 99, 101-102, 108,
186
spendthrift, 110, 111
sprinkling, 109

Garrett...

GIVES YOU ALL THE TOOLS YOU NEED TO BUILD YOUR FINANCIAL FORTRESS!

Save legal fees! Protect yourself and your financial security in moments with our lawyer prepared do-it-yourself legal kits and books.

Please look through the following pages, then mail, fax or call in your order toll-free.

Telephone: 1-305-480-8543
or fax 1-305-698-0057

Order today!

ORDER FORM

30-Day Money-Back Guarantee!

Photocopy and return to: Garrett Publishing, Inc.
312 S. Military Trail
Deerfield Bch., FL 33442

List the item number(s) of what you order here. Each item number includes both a letter and a number. Please make sure to state both!

_____, _____, _____, _____, _____, _____, _____, _____, _____, _____, _____, _____, _____, _____, _____, _____,

☐   ☐

Total your order here $_____. Are you a Florida resident?   Yes   No

If so, add 6% sales tax here $_____. Total enclosed $_____.

Shipping: Books and reports are sent to your by fourth class/book rate shipping. If you want them faster add $2.00 per item for UPS or first-class postage. Add $1.00 per item for Canada orders.

Payment & Billing: If you are a government agency, college, library or other official public organization, include your Purchase Order # here _____, for all others COMPLETE PAYMENT MUST ACCOMPANY YOUR ORDER. We cannot invoice individuals and private businesses. If paying by check, make it payable to Garrett Publishing, Inc.

If paying by credit card:

☐ MasterCard   ☐ Visa #_____

Expiration date:_____   Signature:_____

For faster service, place your order by telephone at 1-305-480-8543
or fax your order to us at 1-305-698-0057.

Send this order to:

Name: _____
Company or
Organization: _____

Street Address: _____

City: _____ State: _____ Zip: _____

Telephone: (   ) _____

HOW TO GET YOUR ORGANIZATION
A TOP SPEAKER ON A HOT TOPIC
...and yourself a check for up to $2000...or more!

Dr. Arnold S. Goldstein is one of America's top speakers on asset protection strategies...one of the hottest topics today. He has provided interesting, informative and entertaining talks on this and related financial topics before groups of every size and type throughout America.

Yes, you too can now learn about the many asset protection strategies that have endeared Dr. Goldstein to the countless people with assets under financial attack. You'll quickly discover why so many groups and organizations have invited him to their lectures, seminars, workshops and conferences.

Why not invite Dr. Goldstein to speak before a group or organization that you belong to? They'll thank you for the idea because once he takes the podium you're guaranteed fresh, innovative ideas, provocative wealth-preserving concepts, hard-hitting "nuts and bolts" advice and the humorous touch that is the trademark of a Goldstein presentation.

Now here's the best part. Every time you arrange for Dr. Goldstein to speak you get 10% of his speaking fee **plus** 10% of any other revenues he earns from the group. This includes the sale of any of Dr. Goldstein's asset protection publications **and** consultation fees from members of the organization or group.

This can add up to big money for you for very little effort. You may find yourself with a check for $2000-$3000 ... for just a few minutes work!

What makes Dr. Goldstein so easy to sell?

- He can talk on a wide range of asset protection related subjects - and can tailor a presentation precisely to the needs and interests of your group.

- He's a proven performer. Dr. Goldstein comes complete with a stack of recommendations and testimonials. But you can see for yourself how clearly and interestingly he presents material simply by reviewing this book. For your review, request an audio cassette of one of his presentations.

Now think of all the organizations you belong to. What professional or business associations are you affiliated with? Do you work for a large company with employee groups interested in this topic? What alumni, fraternal, or sorority groups do you belong to? Do you know any meeting planners? Do friends or relatives belong to organizations that would benefit from what Dr. Goldstein has to say?

Tell us immediately if your organization is interested. We'll quickly follow-up and make all further arrangements directly with the meeting planner. All you have to do is sit back and await your referral fee.

Do you need more details? We will give you a long list of possible program topics as well as further biographical details and referrals from other organizations. Simply call us at 305-480-8543 and we will be pleased to send you the requested information.

Garrett Publishing, Inc.

...It Only Takes a Phone Call to Put My Asset Protection Expertise to Work For You

Are you ready for your very own Total Financial Protection Plan? Give me a call and let's arrange a personal consultation at your office or at my office in Boca Raton, Florida.

I'll work closely with you and your personal attorney, accountant and/or financial planner to put together an asset protection plan that will best serve your financial and investment objectives, and at the same time give you the best protection possible against any financial or legal problem.

You'll benefit quickly because I can give you the insight and experience based on the successful asset protection strategies that have helped hundreds of other clients throughout the country. Whether you have few assets or enjoy considerable wealth ... you'll have the confidence that what you own is more safe and secure once we meet and begin to safeguard your future.

It's easy to arrange:

Decide where a meeting would be most beneficial, check your schedule and call my office. We'll handle all the details - and if necessary arrange a fast meeting on time-sensitive cases.

Perhaps you don't need a face-to-face consultation but only some quick answers to specific questions. That too can be arranged with a phone call consultation. You can even fax or write me with any issues of concern. As always, I stand ready to help you in any way possible.

There's never an obligation when you call, and, of course, upon your request we will send you a brochure describing my services.

Telephone: 305-480-8543
or
Fax: 305-698-0057

TESTIMONIAL STATEMENT
about *Asset Protection Secrets*

FROM: (Please print or type)

Name _____ Occupation _____

Address _____

City _____ State _____ Zip _____

Daytime Phone _____ Evening Phone _____

STATEMENT:

" _____

_____

_____

_____

_____

_____

_____ "

PERMISSION:

I hereby grant permission to the author and publisher of *Asset Protection Secrets* to use this statement along with my name, occupational title and city for the purpose of promoting this book, seminars, and related publications. This is without restrictions and without further permission, or compensation.

OPTIONAL—Check here if preferred:_____ Please use my initials instead of my full name.

SIGNATURE:_____ DATE: _____

Thank You!

Garrett Publishing, Inc. • 312 S. Military Trail • Deerfield Beach, FL 33442 • (305) 480-8543